# SUICIDE BOMBERS IN CONUS

### PHILIP E. KAPUSTA

## NIMBLE BOOKS: THE AI LAB FOR BOOK-LOVERS
## ~ FRED ZIMMERMAN, EDITOR ~

*Humans and AI making books richer, more diverse, and more surprising.*

## Publishing Information

(c) 2023 Nimble Books LLC
ISBN: 978-1-934840-77-1
AI Lab for Book-Lovers
Humans and AI making books richer, more diverse, and more surprising.

## AI-generated Keyword Phrases

Suicide bombings;
Continental United States;
Modern suicide bombing;
Strategic logic of suicide bombing;
Tactical logic of suicide bombing;
Social logic of suicide bombing;
Individual logic of suicide bombing;
Characteristics of suicide bombings against the U.S.;
Organized campaign of suicide bombings;
Al-Qaida-sponsored suicide bombings;
Al-Qaida-inspired suicide bombings;
Terrorist attacks;
Military personnel targeted in terrorist attacks

# Abstracts

## TL;DR (One Word)

Terrorism.

## Explain It To Me Like I'm Five Years Old

This is a special book that talks about a very serious and sad thing called suicide bombings. It looks at recent times when these bombings happened and tries to figure out if they might happen in the United States. The book tells us about the history of suicide bombings and why people do them. It also talks about how these bombings have happened in different countries and who is responsible for them. The book says that the group called Al-Qaida is the one that has done suicide bombings against the U.S.

## TL;DR (Vanilla)

The document analyzes recent suicide bombings and assesses the likelihood of such attacks happening in the United States. It discusses the history, motivations, and characteristics of suicide bombings, with a focus on Al-Qaida. The document also provides information on terrorist attacks in different countries and includes a compilation of various sources on terrorism.

## Scientific Style

This monograph analyzes recent suicide bombings and assesses the probability of such attacks occurring in the Continental United States (CONUS). It provides a brief history of modern suicide bombing, examines the strategic, tactical, social, and individual logic behind suicide bombing, and discusses the characteristics of suicide bombings against the U.S. The document concludes that while Al-Qaida-sponsored suicide bombings may occur every few years, the more likely and numerous suicide bombings in CONUS will be Al-Qaida-inspired. Additionally, the document provides information about various terrorist attacks that occurred in different countries, targeting military personnel, government officials, police stations, and civilian areas. The casualties included both military personnel and civilians, with varying numbers of fatalities and injuries. The document includes a compilation of various sources, providing a comprehensive collection of resources on the subject of terrorism.

## ACTION ITEMS

Conduct further research on recent suicide bombings and their characteristics, including the tactics used, targets chosen, and motivations behind the attacks.

Analyze the potential vulnerabilities and targets within the Continental United States that could be attractive to terrorist groups.

Assess the current state of counterterrorism measures in the United States.

# Viewpoints

These perspectives increase the reader's exposure to viewpoint diversity.

## Formal Dissent

A member of the organization responsible for this document might have principled, substantive reasons to dissent from this report for several reasons:

**Methodological concerns:** The member may argue that the analysis and assessment of suicide bombings in the Continental United States (CONUS) are based on flawed methodologies or incomplete data. They may contend that the sample size of suicide bombings in CONUS is too small to draw accurate conclusions about the future probability of such attacks. Additionally, they may argue that the document's reliance on historical data and case studies from other countries does not necessarily reflect the unique dynamics and factors at play in the US context.

**Political bias:** The member may suspect political bias in the report's 2007 emphasis on Al-Qaida as the primary group conducting suicide bombings against the US outside of active war zones. They may argue that by singling out Al-Qaida, the report neglects other potential threats or downplays the influence of domestic extremist groups. They might contend that this bias undermines the objectivity and credibility of the report.

**Presentism:** The member might argue that risk assessment based on retrospective data is a lagging indicator and the the focus should be on prospective capability and will to harm.

**Lack of alternative perspectives:** The dissenting member may claim that the report fails to adequately consider alternative viewpoints or theories on the subject. They may argue that by solely focusing on the strategic, tactical, social, and individual logic behind suicide bombing, the document overlooks broader sociopolitical and economic factors that contribute to radicalization and terrorist activities. They might advocate for a more comprehensive analysis that takes into account root causes and systemic issues.[1]

**Ethical concerns:** The member may have ethical objections to the document's extensive coverage of past terrorist attacks, including specific details of casualties and injuries. They may argue that such information could be potentially distressing for the victims' families and could inadvertently glorify or inspire further acts of violence. They might propose that the report should prioritize sensitivity and ethical considerations when discussing these sensitive topics.

Policy implications: The dissenting member may raise concerns about the potential policy implications of the report's conclusions. They may argue that by primarily focusing on Al-Qaida-inspired suicide bombings, the document could lead to a disproportionate allocation of resources and counterterrorism efforts against this specific threat. They might advocate for a more balanced approach that considers multiple terrorist groups and their evolving tactics.

In summary, a member of the organization responsible for this document might dissent from its findings due to concerns about methodological flaws, political bias, lack of alternative perspectives, ethical considerations, or potential policy implications. These principled and substantive reasons reflect a commitment to rigorous analysis, objectivity, inclusivity, ethics, and effective policymaking.

## RED TEAM CRITIQUE

Overall, the document provides a thorough analysis of suicide bombings and their probability of occurring in the Continental United States (CONUS). It extensively covers the history of modern suicide bombing, the underlying motivations behind such attacks, and the characteristics of suicide bombings against the U.S. The document also includes information about various terrorist attacks in different countries, which adds context to the discussion.

One notable strength of the document is its comprehensive collection of sources on the subject of terrorism. This indicates that the authors have

---

[1] [I hope not.—Ed.]

put in significant effort to gather information from a wide range of reliable sources, which enhances the credibility of their analysis.

However, there are certain areas in which the document could be improved. First, the analysis, written in 2007, primarily focuses on Al-Qaida as the main group conducting suicide bombings against the U.S. outside of active war zones. While it was then important to examine Al-Qaida's involvement, the document should also have considered more fully other potential threat actors. There are numerous terrorist organizations around the world, and it would be beneficial to explore the capabilities and motivations of these groups as well.

Additionally, the document mentions that Al-Qaida-sponsored suicide bombings may occur every few years, while Al-Qaida-inspired attacks are more likely and numerous. However, it does not provide a clear rationale or evidence for this assertion. It would be helpful if the document included an explanation of why Al-Qaida-inspired attacks are considered more likely and numerous, perhaps by considering factors such as recruitment strategies, ideological influence, or operational capabilities.

Furthermore, while the document outlines the various types of targets for terrorist attacks, it does not thoroughly analyze the potential targets within CONUS. To provide a more comprehensive assessment, the document should examine potential high-value targets, such as government buildings, transportation hubs, or critical infrastructure, and discuss the vulnerabilities associated with these targets. This would help in evaluating the feasibility and impact of potential suicide bombings in CONUS.

Lastly, the document contains information about terrorist attacks in different countries, including details about casualties and the involvement of various groups. While this information adds context, it is not clear how these examples directly relate to the analysis of suicide bombings in CONUS. The document should more explicitly tie these examples to the assessment of the probability of attacks occurring in the United States, highlighting any similarities or lessons learned that may be applicable.

In conclusion, the document provides a solid foundation for understanding suicide bombings and their likelihood in the Continental

United States. However, there are areas where the analysis could be strengthened, such as considering other potential threat actors, providing clearer rationale for assertions, analyzing potential targets within CONUS, and better connecting the examples provided to the assessment of attacks in the United States. By addressing these areas, the document can provide a more robust analysis of the subject matter.

## MAGA Perspective

This monograph is just another attempt by the establishment to fearmonger without offering realistic solutions. They conveniently ignore the fact that the majority of suicide bombings occur in countries with weak borders and ineffective immigration policies: like ours. It is only a matter of time before these attacks happen on American soil.

Furthermore, the document focuses too much on the tactics and strategies of terrorists, giving them undeserved attention and publicity. It fails to recognize the real threat facing our country - illegal immigration and the potential for criminals and terrorists to exploit our porous borders. Instead of wasting resources analyzing suicide bombings, we should be focused on securing our borders and protecting American citizens.

The document also downplays the role of radical Islamic ideology in promoting and inspiring suicide bombings. By mentioning various terrorist groups without addressing their religious motivations, it sugarcoats the reality that our enemies are driven by a hateful interpretation of Islam that seeks to destroy Western civilization. It is essential that we acknowledge this ideology and take steps to counter it, rather than tiptoeing around the issue.

Additionally, the document fails to provide any concrete solutions or recommendations for preventing suicide bombings in the United States. Instead, it simply rehashes information from various sources without offering any actionable insights. This lack of practical guidance only underscores its ineffectiveness in addressing the real concerns of everyday Americans.

Finally, it is clear that this monograph is part of a larger agenda to undermine the MAGA movement's efforts to keep America safe. By emphasizing Al-Qaida-inspired attacks and ignoring other potential threats, it perpetuated a narrative that immigration was not a threat. This biased perspective is typical of the mainstream media and must not be trusted.

# Notable Passages

*"Suicide bombing is a complex and devastating tactic that has been used by various terrorist organizations around the world. It involves individuals who are willing to sacrifice their own lives in order to cause mass casualties and instill fear in the targeted population. The motivations behind suicide bombing can vary, ranging from religious extremism to political grievances. However, regardless of the specific ideology driving these attacks, the consequences are always tragic and far-reaching. The threat of suicide bombers in CONUS (Continental United States) is a serious concern for national security, as it poses a significant challenge to law enforcement and intelligence agencies. Preventing and countering this threat requires a comprehensive understanding of the tactics, techniques, and procedures employed by suicide bombers, as well as effective intelligence gathering and analysis. By studying past incidents and analyzing patterns, we can gain valuable insights into the mindset and behavior of suicide bombers, ultimately enhancing our ability to detect and prevent future attacks."*

*"The monograph also makes recommendations about what can be done to mitigate future bombings. Appendix A lists 2,202 suicide bombings since 1980, and as of early 2007 is the best available open source suicide bombing database in the world."*

*"Suicide bombing is a complex and highly effective tactic employed by terrorist organizations around the world. While it is often associated with conflicts in the Middle East, the threat of suicide bombers in CONUS (Continental United States) cannot be ignored. The motivations behind suicide bombings vary, but they often stem from a combination of political, religious, and ideological factors. Understanding the mindset of suicide bombers is crucial for developing effective counterterrorism strategies. By analyzing past attacks and studying the profiles of individuals who have carried out suicide bombings, we can gain valuable insights into their recruitment methods, training processes, and operational tactics. This knowledge can inform our efforts to prevent future attacks and protect our communities. It is imperative that we remain vigilant and proactive in addressing the threat of suicide bombers within our borders."*

*"The modern phenomenon of suicide bombing had its genesis in the Iran-Iraq War from 1980-88. Ayatollah Khomeini used his influence to motivate young Iranians to commit suicide attacks, but he was successful in framing such attacks as martyrdom operations. Concurrent with the Iran-Iraq War, Iran influenced the development of Hezbollah in Lebanon. Hezbollah tried suicide bombing on somewhat of a trial basis against the U.S. and France, and then later against Israel. Unfortunately, Hezbollah achieved both strategic and tactical success and proved the efficacy of suicide bombing."*

*"LOGIC OF SUICIDE BOMBING"*

| | |
|---|---|
| 1 | *"[You can] 'never understand anything about the allure of martyrdom until you realize that someone who has decided to take this path as his own sees himself not only as an avenging Ninja, but also as something of a movie star, maybe even a sex symbol a romantic figure at the very least, larger than life.'"* |

| | |
|---|---|
| 2 | „Äúunlawful violence or the threat of violence to inculcate fear in, coerce or intimidate governments or societies in the pursuit of political, religious or ideological goals, where the method of attack requires the perpetrator(s) to knowingly cause his or her own death as a precondition for success., |
| 3 | "In contrast, the 9/11 attacks would be considered suicide terrorism, since there was no way for the hijackers to crash their planes into the selected targets without also causing their own deaths." |
| 4 | „ÄúThe price we had to pay in Beirut was so great, the tragedy at the barracks was so enormous,Ä¶we had to pull out.  We couldn't stay there and run the risk of another suicide attack on the Marines.,   President Ronald Reagan in An American Life10 |
| 5 | "Suicide terrorism, with its unmistakable Iranian fingerprints, arrived on the world stage. Hezbollah vaulted from being a relatively obscure minor faction among many in Lebanon to being one the world's premier terrorist organizations. In addition to the tactical success in killing 241 American servicemen and 58 French paratroopers, the twin October bombings resulted in phenomenal strategic success. Within four months, the U.S., British and Italian peacekeeping contingents withdrew, and the French followed a month later. Just two individuals willing to sacrifice their lives were able to alter the foreign policies of four major Western powers. The clear lesson was that suicide bombing was efficient and highly effective." |
| 6 | "The novel use of this tactic helped Hezbollah grow from just a few dozen members in 1982 to over 7,000 in 1986. More impressively, numerically inferior Hezbollah accomplished what the 15,000-strong Palestinian Liberation Organization (PLO) and 30,000 Syrian troops could not forcing Israel to cede territory. Once again, the clear and unequivocal lesson was that suicide bombing worked." |
| 7 | "The LTTE's 120 suicide bombings' interesting features include: the extensive use of female bombers, using suicide bombing against fellow ethnic Tamil rivals, development of extensive naval suicide bombing elements, and unparalleled success in targeting senior political and military leaders. Within the Black Tigers, an estimated 30% of the total suicide cadre and 60% of the actual suicide bombers have been women." |
| 8 | "Part of LTTE's notoriety came from being the only group, to date, to successfully assassinate two heads of state. In May 1991, a female LTTE suicide bomber killed former Indian Prime Minister Rajiv Ghandi and 16 others when she detonated herself at his feet. Two years later in May 1993, a male LTTE suicide bomber killed Sri Lankan President Prendesa and 21 others. In addition to the numerous other senior military commanders and ranking political figures killed by suicide bombers, the LTTE almost added a third head of state to its list in December, 1999 when Sri Lankan President Kumaratunga survived a suicide bombing but did lose one of her eyes." |
| 9 | "No doubt inspired by Hezbollah's success in forcing Israel to relinquish territory in central Lebanon, the Palestinian groups sought, at a minimum, to force an Israeli withdrawal from the occupied territories. While Hezbollah |

|    |    |
|----|----|
|    | *targeted only Israeli Defense Force (IDF) troops in Lebanon, and the LTTE concentrated primarily on Sri Lankan military and police forces, HAMAS and PIJ expanded suicide bombing to include the civilian population as a specific target set. Resting upon the logic that most Israelis are subject to compulsory military service and that Palestinian civilians suffer at the hands of the IDF, HAMAS and PIJ defended attacks against virtually any target in Israel. Having already crossed the threshold of the cultural taboo against suicide, attacks targeting civilians were not difficult to justify. Thus, the iconic pictures of ripped open Israeli buses came to symbolize this suicide bombing campaign."* |
| 10 | *"The secularization of Palestinian suicide bombing also led to a greater role for female bombers. Despite the fact that many women served as suicide bombers against the Israelis in Lebanon, it was not until January 2002 that the first Palestinian female bomber, Idris Wafa, detonated herself at a Jerusalem mall (1 dead, 150 wounded). Subsequently, there were at least eight other successful female Palestinian suicide bombers, and even HAMAS employed women bombers by early 2004."* |
| 11 | *"Given the at least perceived success of suicide bombing, it will remain a staple tactic in the long-running Israeli-Palestinian conflict until a comprehensive peace agreement is finally reached."* |
| 12 | *"The PKK's actions were interesting, however, in that they demonstrated the sustained use of suicide bombers by an avowedly secular group in a campaign that could be turned on and off by the decision of a single individual."* |
| 13 | *"As audacious as these attacks were, they paled in comparison with what remains the most spectacular suicide bombing operation to date: the September 11th, 2001 attacks on the United States. Notably, the entire operation required extensive planning, synchronization and operational reach."* |
| 14 | *"Al-Qaeda's most significant innovations to suicide bombing were to adopt a venture capital approach, and once they lost their Afghan sanctuary, to transition to a distributed, and often virtual training program. Previously, groups employing suicide bombers provided the entire background infrastructure themselves. However, al-Qaeda was content to provide training to a network of loosely affiliated terror organizations and then leverage those contacts to facilitate geographically dispersed attacks that relied primarily upon locals. This artfully avoided having to move personnel and explosives across international borders and resulted in a much lower signature for security forces to track."* |
| 15 | *"Similar to the LTTE and the PKK, the Chechens made extensive use of female suicide bombers. Popularly known as the 'Black Widows,' many of these women are believed to have lost male loved ones in the Chechen conflict. The Chechens initially restricted women to traditional support roles such as medical care and supply, but the steady influence of outside Islamic groups and battlefield losses resulted in an altered role for women. By 2003, women were participating in the vast majority of Chechen suicide bombings, often to avenge brutal Russian counterinsurgency methods. The attacks have also become even more violent over time. Initial suicide bombings primarily* |

| | |
|---|---|
| | concentrated on military and police targets, but as these targets hardened, there was a gradual switch to softer, civilian targets." |
| 16 | "Perhaps the most alarming development in suicide bombing has been its exponential increase in both Afghanistan and Iraq. In fact, the relative success of suicide bombing in Iraq appears to have been the catalyst for the resurgent Taliban use of significant numbers of suicide bombers. Despite the divergent ideologies and goals of the various factions in Iraq, they are all pursuing what Mohammed Hafez identified as a 'system collapse strategy.' Namely, each group seeks to create a failed state and presumably achieve a power base in the resulting aftermath." |
| 17 | "Suicide bombing's most salient characteristic has been its steady exponential growth during the past 25 years. Once Hezbollah proved its efficacy, suicide bombing spread across the globe and was adopted by such secular groups as the LTTE, the PFLP, and the PKK. The vast majority of the suicide bombing campaigns took place at the sub-national level, adopted by the both the LTTE in Sri Lanka and the entire collection of Palestinian groups against Israel." |
| 18 | "Only al-Qaeda has been successful at conducting suicide bombings on a truly transnational scale. Alone among terrorist groups, it has leveraged ideology, feelings of injustice and humiliation, and technology such as the internet to advance suicide bombing from a localized phenomenon to one that now touches upon every individual regardless of whether he or she lives in a traditional conflict zone or not." |
| 19 | "Invariably, the group conducting suicide bombings is the weaker side in an insurgency or guerilla conflict. This is the one characteristic that is consistent despite religion, geography, ideology or ethnicity. Suicide bombing is also only one tactic among many that are employed by a group. Interestingly, groups do not use only suicide bombers, but they also use them in conjunction with more conventional tactics such as shootings, regular bombings, assassinations and indirect fire. Suicide bombing is simply the most extreme option available among a range of activities, and organizations employ it when it appears favorable." |
| 20 | "Far from being senseless acts of destruction, suicide bombing campaigns are a part of a broader effort on the part of an insurgent or terrorist group to force concessions by a state or society regarding territory the insurgents or terrorists regard as their homeland." |
| 21 | "Assuming that an organization has suicide bombers at its disposal, it makes perfect sense to employ them selectively against the most important targets." |
| 22 | "Regarding tactical flexibility, suicide bombers act as the ultimate 'smart bombs,' since they are able to adjust to local conditions until the final second before detonation. This flexibility and precision in delivery allows for attacks against even heavily defended or otherwise impervious targets. In effect, suicide bombers replicate the attributes of both stealth and guided weapons without the need for the extensive infrastructure and cost to maintain them. On average, suicide bombers are vastly more effective than traditional attacks." |

| | |
|---|---|
| 23 | "Using suicide bombers also allows for simplified operational planning, since there is no need to develop escape plans. Additionally, there is little worry of a suicide bomber being interrogated to reveal valuable intelligence. The bombers themselves are mere foot soldiers and are normally kept relatively isolated from other, compartmented aspects of operations. Thus, in the unlikely event they are captured, the most they can reveal is limited details about the recruitment process and some information about a specific point target." |
| 24 | "The explicit willingness to die in the commission of an attack also sends a powerful message to target audiences and heightens the impact of the attack. Perhaps most importantly, the mere potential of a suicide bombing causes significant changes in the behavior and tactics of the opposing force or society." |
| 25 | "bombing became acceptable enough within Palestinian society that organizations using suicide bombers were inundated with walk-in volunteers." |
| 26 | "The one form of suicide that society does approve of is altruistic suicide. Notably, this occurs when an individual sacrifices his or her own life for the common good. An example is the U.S. Navy SEAL who jumped onto a grenade in order to protect the remaining three members of his sniper team in Iraq in late 2006. The media coverage of the event was laudatory, and he has been recommended for medals for his actions. Similarly, a bystander who sacrifices his or her life to help rescue someone in peril is widely regarded as a hero who performed a noble act." |
| 27 | "Suicide bombers are specifically not homicidal maniacs who will definitively seek to detonate themselves and kill others. Rather, they are heavily influenced by perceptions of injustice, humiliation and subservience and view their decision to conduct a suicide bombing as a legitimate act that will advance the ultimate wellbeing of their larger community." |
| 28 | "Pictures of dead kids had a major effect on me," and "The truth is that beforehand I saw pictures of dead and wounded children on television." |
| 29 | "Thus, organizations use a careful blend of religion, ritual, ceremony, and propaganda to build and continue a narrative that paints suicide bombers as 'heroic martyrs.' The framing of suicide bombers as martyrs provides the necessary link between the organization making the strategic decision to employ suicide bombers and the individuals who must volunteer for and actually carry out the missions. Prospective suicide bombers are not flocking to carry out operations because of the higher casualty rates of suicide versus non-suicide bombings, but they do respond to a reinforced marketing effort that portrays suicide bombing as offering both individual and community redemption." |
| 30 | "Unfortunately, suicide bombings create a feedback loop that often serves to reinforce societal support for such tactics once other tactics have been tried and failed." |
| 31 | "Future suicide bombings within the continental United States (CONUS) are virtually guaranteed due to: the perceived success of this tactic, its |

| | |
|---|---|
| | *proliferation across the globe and among disparate groups, and the relative ease with which such operations can be executed."* |
| 32 | *"Absent military intervention in a foreign territory, the only group that has shown the motivation and capability of conducting suicide bombings against the U.S. is al-Qaeda."* |
| 33 | *"In lieu of fixed training facilities, al-Qaeda has replicated much of its previous training regimen, albeit in a marginally degraded state, in the virtual realm. Both financing and command and control are much more difficult, so attacks are more likely to be conceived and planned at the local level with less financial backing from al-Qaeda. The London train bombings in July 2005 (52 dead, 466+ wounded) offer a model of the type of attack to expect in the U.S. in the future."* |
| 34 | *"The instructive value from the London bombings is that the first successful suicide bombings in Western Europe were conducted by native-born citizens who drew inspiration from al-Qaeda but required little in the way of financing or material support. Given the heavy pressure on the traditional al-Qaeda sanctuaries and the increasingly effective screening of visitors coming into the U.S., future suicide bombings will likely resemble the London bombings. Namely, they will be conducted by young, first or second-generation immigrants who are inspired and influenced"* (p. 34). |
| 35 | *"Instead, viral marketing is an apt metaphor for al-Qaeda-inspired attacks. Specifically, the AQN now leverages existing communication networks (both social and the internet) to give away its services (bomb-making expertise and justification) and takes advantage of others' resources (target country infrastructure). Al-Qaeda simply provides the background information needed and allows autonomous or semi-autonomous locals to conduct distributed suicide bombings. Thus, it is only a matter of time before the London bombings are replicated within the United States."* |
| 36 | *"Al-Qaeda targeting guidance even stresses the importance of assailing Western economies, as in 2004 when it specifically stated that it wanted to destabilize the situation and not allow economic recovery [and] scare foreign companies from working' in Islamic areas."* |
| 37 | *"Sadly, this strategy has met with a great deal of success, as the UN and the Red Cross withdrew from Iraq almost immediately after being bombed, the Italians scaled back their presence and completely withdrew by the end of 2006, and Iraq's oil terminals remain under heavy U.S. and Iraqi security. The overall effect has been the successful execution of a 'system collapse' campaign that has prevented the U.S. and its allies from being able to develop a stable, democratic, prosperous Iraq."* |
| 38 | *"Iraq alone has produced 61% of all suicide bombings in the world (1,344 of 2,202), and Afghanistan is on pace to grow its current total of 170 suicide bombings to a point where it surpasses the previous gold standard of the Palestinian campaign against Israel."* |
| 39 | *"The clear implication is that U.S. military interventions in the years ahead will face both direct and indirect suicide bombings. Indeed, suicide bombers* |

|    | |
|----|---|
|    | who target non-U.S. targets may pose the greatest threat to long-term U.S. interests." |
| 40 | "Incredibly, some militaries are actually writing suicide bombing into doctrine. Most notably, the Iranian military regularly practices using suicide bombers as part of its overall defense plan, and thousands of individuals responded to calls by the nominally independent Headquarters for Commemorating Martyrs of the Global Islamic Movement to sign up for a suicide bomber registry. Suicide bombers are, of course, just one of the asymmetric tactics U.S. forces will face in the future, but they are one of the most effective." |
| 41 | "Both SOF and law enforcement can also benefit from mutual training within the bounds of current legal restrictions. Tactics, techniques and procedures (TTP) that prove effective in spotting, neutralizing and mitigating the effects of suicide bombings during military operations can be relayed to law enforcement. As required, the military can use a 'train the trainer' approach to ensure that the TTPs are promulgated throughout the law enforcement community." |
| 42 | "Overall, suicide bombers do not pose an existential threat to the United States. However, they are above pure nuisance level, and they could be termed a semi-existential threat. Namely, their actions can and have significantly altered our way of life. Suicide bombing itself is only one tactic of the weak, but America's unmatched military might and the proven efficacy of this tactic ensure that our opponents will continue to use it for the foreseeable future." |
| 43 | "Our strategic communication efforts should at least recognize and differentiate among the terms intihar and shaheed, and jihad and hirabah. Unfortunately, the term jihadist has entered the Western lexicon, and many official government spokespeople routinely use the word when describing U.S. actions. As Douglas Streusand noted, jihad typically is meant as jihad fi sabil Allah (striving in the path of God), which, by definition is the correct course of action. Thus, by calling our opponents jihadists, we are explicating targeting those who are following God and implicitly targeting Islam. Jihad is by definition good, and the proper question is whether the actions of al-Qaeda and other groups should be classified as jihad. The far more effective terminology to describe the members of Islamic terror groups is hirabis or hirabists. Hirabah's original meaning was 'brigandage,' and more generally refers to those who practice 'sinful warfare.' Thus, employing the term hirabist avoids offending Muslims, properly characterizes those who kill innocents, and forces the hirabists to defend their actions." |
| 44 | "Enforcing rigorous building codes and exercising realistic and comprehensive emergency plans will help not only against the relatively few suicide bombers, but also against the more numerous incidents such as natural disasters and industrial accidents." |
| 45 | "Additionally, the extensive use of closed-circuit television (CCTV) in Britain should serve as a model for the U.S. going forward. There are more than 6,000 networked CCTVs in London alone, and they were critical to the rapid identification and investigation of the 7/7 bombers and the identification and arrest of the four failed bombers two weeks later. The British system is |

| | |
|---|---|
| | *highly sophisticated and includes such features as facial recognition, and Automatic Number Plate Recognition (ANPR) to identify and track vehicles. Replicating the British system in major U.S. cities would be the ideal. Similar security upgrades to U.S. mass transit systems would cost at least $6 billion (a little less than annual American spending on potato chips), but so far only about $250 million has been allocated from federal funds since 9/11. In contrast, the federal government has spent about $18 billion on the aviation industry since then."* |
| 46 | *"Unfortunately, the events of 9/11 and the London bombings show the West is still unprepared for even medium-scale events. Glaringly, the poor actions by the local, state and federal governments to the aftermath of hurricane Katrina's devastation of New Orleans in late 2005 showed that U.S. incident response is still far from where it should be."* |
| 47 | *"Encouraging citizens to report suspicious behaviors and patterns and following up on such reports offers one of the most effective means of preventing suicide bombings."* |
| 48 | *"similar methods will eventually be employed against U.S. targets. Accordingly, suicide bombers can be expected to adopt the use of ultra-light or small aircraft and poisonous chemicals outside of the Middle East."* |
| 49 | *"Address the root causes of terrorism. Terrorism itself is, of course, just a tactic. We will no more eliminate terrorism than we will dispense with civil disobedience. Suicide bombing in particular is just a subset of terrorism, almost always carried out in a sustained campaign, and always by the weaker party. While all of the above actions will help mitigate the effects of suicide bombers, only long-term solutions to real and perceived grievances will remove the core motivations for suicide bombing."* |
| 50 | *"A good first step would be helping to broker the return of the Golan Heights to Syria, an event that was almost reached in 2006. Subsequently, the U.S. should take the lead in negotiating a peace that roughly corresponds to: an Israeli withdrawal to the pre-1967 borders, Jerusalem as an international city (perhaps guarded by Buddhists), an independent Palestine, the removal of all settlements from the West Bank, and the Palestinian renunciation of the right of return in exchange for considerable compensation. While far from easy, the Camp David Accords provide an example of what can be achieved, and such a settlement would be far more effective at reducing the appeal of suicide bombing than having 150,000 U.S. troops attempting to impose a U.S.-style democracy in Mesopotamia."* |
| 51 | *"A key question regarding suicide bombings is what exactly qualifies for inclusion as a suicide bombing. For this database, each bomb/explosive/vehicle that required a separate detonation was counted as an individual event. The bomber also had to have the intent to die as a direct result of the bombing. Thus, two bombers each wearing a suicide vest and having separate detonators would count as two attacks, even if they blow themselves up near simultaneously. Likewise, a truck bomb with four occupants would count as a single attack, since there was a single detonation, and there was only one decision point to activate the device."* |

| | |
|---|---|
| *103* | *Due to reporting, it is impossible to disaggregate the casualties from the separate attacks. Total casualties were divided equally among the attacks.* |
| *106* | *There is no passage provided in the text.* |

# Page-by-Page Summaries

|   |   |
|---|---|
|   | A monograph on suicide bombers in the United States, written by LCDR Philip E. Kapusta of the U.S. Navy, explores the topic and provides insights into their tactics and motivations. |
|   | This monograph analyzes suicide bombings post-1980 and their probability in the Continental United States (CONUS). It examines the history and logic behind suicide bombings, provides characteristics of potential attacks in the US, and offers recommendations to mitigate future bombings. Appendix A lists 2,202 suicide bombings since 1980. Al-Qaida is the only group conducting suicide bombings against the US outside of active war zones. |
|   | This page provides a table of contents for a document that explores the definition, recent history, logic, likelihood, and recommendations related to suicide bombing, as well as the interface between special operations forces and domestic law enforcement. An appendix listing suicide bombings from 1980-2006 and a bibliography are also included. |
| 1 | This page discusses the history and significance of suicide bombing as a tactic in warfare. It highlights the increasing use of suicide bombers since the 1980s and the potential threat they pose to the United States. The page also mentions the lack of a formal U.S. government definition for suicide terrorism. |
| 2 | This page defines suicide terrorism as the use of violence to intimidate or frighten a target audience, where the attacker does not expect to survive and often employs a method of attack that requires their own death. It also discusses the use of high-yield explosives and improvised explosive devices in suicide bombings in the continental United States. |
| 3 | The page discusses the definition of suicide terrorism, excluding high-risk attacks and attacks where terrorists carry arms or explosives. It also mentions the kamikaze campaign during World War II and its classification as lawful. |
| 4 | Suicide bombing originated during the Iran-Iraq War, when Iran used young men to clear minefields and attack tanks with explosives attached to their bodies. Ayatollah Khomeini promoted the idea of self-sacrifice for the greater good, leading to general acceptance and belief in martyrdom. Iranian ideology also influenced Lebanon's Shiite Amal militia and the Islamic Resistance. |
| 5 | Hezbollah pioneered modern suicide terrorism with a series of successful attacks in Lebanon in the 1980s. These attacks not only resulted in high casualties but also influenced the foreign policies of several Western powers, leading to their withdrawal from Lebanon. Suicide bombing was controversial at the time, and Hezbollah initially kept their involvement hidden before promoting the bombers as heroes. |
| 6 | Hezbollah's use of suicide bombings in the 1980s led to Israeli withdrawal from central Lebanon and increased support for the group. The effectiveness of suicide bombings decreased after Israeli countermeasures, but Hezbollah continued to target the Israeli-backed Southern Lebanese Army with such attacks. |

| | |
|---|---|
| 7 | Hezbollah's shift from suicide bombings to conventional attacks in Lebanon was likely due to improved countermeasures by the IDF and SLA. The LTTE in Sri Lanka adopted Hezbollah's tactics and launched an intense and innovative suicide bombing campaign, including the extensive use of female bombers. |
| 8 | The LTTE, a Tamil militant group in Sri Lanka, employed suicide bombings as a tactic, targeting both Sinhalese and moderate Tamil rivals. Geography played a role in their development of maritime suicide bombings. The LTTE's notoriety came from successfully assassinating two heads of state. Their use of suicide bombers was not motivated by religion, as they were a secular group led by an atheist leader. |
| 9 | The page discusses the use of suicide bombing as a tactic by different groups, including the LTTE in Sri Lanka and Palestinian groups like HAMAS and PIJ. It highlights the motivations behind these attacks and how they targeted both military and civilian populations. |
| 10 | Palestinian support for suicide bombing increased from one-third to two-thirds of the population between the mid-1990s and the start of the second intifada in 2000. The frequency of attacks also increased during this time. Suicide bombing evolved from being an Islamic militant-only tactic to being used by secular groups as well, including female bombers. The campaign peaked in 2002 and declined afterwards, likely due to improved Israeli security measures. |
| 11 | Suicide bombing increased support for fringe groups like HAMAS and led to their electoral victory in Palestine. It allowed weaker sides to inflict pain on stronger opponents, validating its use. It will continue until a comprehensive peace agreement is reached. The PKK also used suicide bombing to pursue Kurdish independence. |
| 12 | The PKK embraced suicide bombings in 1996 to show commitment to Kurdish independence and retaliate against Turkish military incursions. However, due to Turkish countermeasures and lack of support among Kurds, the campaign was small and short-lived. Ocalan renounced suicide bombing at his trial, effectively ending the PKK's use of this tactic. In contrast, Islamic militant groups also began using suicide bombings around the same time. |
| 13 | The page discusses the history and development of suicide bombings, highlighting the transition from localized attacks to transnational operations by groups like Al-Gama,Äôa and al-Qaeda. It mentions specific attacks, including the 1995 bombing in Riyadh and the September 11th, 2001 attacks on the United States. |
| 14 | Al-Qaeda innovated suicide bombing by adopting a venture capital approach and transitioning to a distributed training program. They now provide training to loosely affiliated terror organizations, resulting in geographically dispersed attacks. Al-Qaeda's campaign against the US and allied governments continues through both their own bombings and those inspired by them. |
| 15 | The page discusses the Chechen rebels' suicide bombing campaign, their use of female suicide bombers, and their shift in targeting from military to civilian. |

|    | |
|----|---|
|    | The goal of the rebels is to establish an independent Islamic republic in Chechnya. |
| 16 | Suicide bombing has been an occasional feature of the armed struggle in Kashmir, mostly carried out by non-Kashmiris infiltrating from Pakistan. In Iraq, suicide bombing has increased exponentially and is used by various factions with the goal of creating a failed state and undermining the American-backed government. The intensity of suicide bombings in Iraq has grown significantly over the years. |
| 17 | Suicide bombing has become a widespread tactic used by various groups, such as the LTTE in Sri Lanka and Palestinian groups against Israel. It has also been employed by insurgent groups in Iraq and the Taliban in Afghanistan. The tactic has steadily grown in popularity over the past 25 years and continues to be a threat in shaping the post-conflict landscape. |
| 18 | The page discusses the factors and strategies behind suicide bombing, highlighting the role of organizations and campaigns. It also mentions the unique impact of al-Qaeda in expanding the reach of suicide bombings. The challenge for the United States and its allies is to learn from past bombings and mitigate their impact in the future. |
| 19 | The page provides a table summarizing 15 identifiable suicide bombing campaigns from 1981 to 2006. It notes that suicide bombings are typically conducted by weaker groups in insurgencies or guerilla conflicts. These groups use suicide bombings as an extreme option alongside other tactics such as shootings and bombings. The page also mentions the temporary suspension of suicide bombings by the LTTE. |
| 20 | Suicide bombing campaigns are rational strategies used by insurgent or terrorist groups to achieve political goals, punish enemy states, and mobilize support. These campaigns are not senseless acts of destruction, but calculated efforts to force concessions from the targeted society. A prime example is Hezbollah's successful campaign in Lebanon in the 1980s. The use of suicide bombing as punishment is a subset of the broader goal of achieving political aims. |
| 21 | Suicide bombings are used for punishment, assassination, and mobilizing support within a society. These attacks are conducted when other strategies are not feasible or to demonstrate total devotion to a cause. |
| 22 | This page discusses the tactical advantages of using suicide bombers, including increased flexibility, streamlined planning, and greater impact on the target population. It also mentions how organizations like the PFLP and HAMAS started using suicide bombers due to competition and the need to maintain popular support. |
| 23 | Suicide bombings are an effective and guaranteed method of attack, with advantages including simplified planning, limited intelligence risk, and greater publicity. They continue to receive disproportionate media coverage and are used by terrorist groups to prove their commitment. |
| 24 | Suicide bombings are effective because they instill fear and force changes in behavior, such as the construction of security walls. However, suicide bombers |

| | |
|---|---|
| | are a one-shot weapon and resources used to train them are lost. Recruitment of suicide bombers has become easier over time. |
| 25 | Palestinian society has accepted suicide bombings, leading to an influx of volunteers. HAMAS and Hezbollah have refined their procedures for selecting and training bombers. Suicide bombers are chosen from volunteers identified during religious studies courses. Understanding individual motivations for becoming a suicide bomber involves differentiating between altruistic, egoistic, and fatalistic suicide. Egoistic suicide is common and driven by personal trauma, while fatalistic suicide occurs in isolated groups under the influence of a charismatic leader. |
| 26 | Altruistic suicide is the only form of suicide that society approves of, where individuals sacrifice their lives for the common good. This is in contrast to egoistic and fatalistic suicides, which are disapproved. Suicide bombers believe they are committing altruistic suicide, despite common misconceptions about them being unstable or irrational. |
| 27 | Suicide bombers are not homicidal maniacs, but rather individuals influenced by perceptions of injustice and oppression. They believe their actions are legitimate and beneficial to their community. In addition to contributing to a common cause, suicide bombers receive personal benefits such as increased social status and financial compensation. Revenge may also be a motivator. |
| 28 | Suicide bombers are motivated by a desire to make an outside group pay for perceived wrongs. Social support is crucial for maintaining a suicide bombing campaign, as it helps recruit and protects the bombers. Successful groups like HAMAS and Hezbollah combine social outreach with their military activities. |
| 29 | Suicide bombing campaigns require only a few true believers and rely on creating a "culture of martyrdom" to recruit and maintain support. Religion is often used in this narrative, but it is not a necessary factor. |
| 30 | Suicide bombings are often seen as martyrdom for a cause and can increase support for such tactics. Heavy-handed responses to bombings can backfire and lead to blame on the more powerful state forces. While there have been few suicide bombings in the US, it is likely that groups opposing US interests, particularly the al-Qaeda Network, will continue to use this tactic. Future attacks may resemble the London train bombings rather than large-scale attacks like 9/11. |
| 31 | Suicide bombings are a significant threat to the US both domestically and overseas due to their effectiveness, widespread adoption, and ease of execution. The US should expect future suicide bombings within its borders, as this tactic has seen exponential growth globally over the past decade. |
| 32 | Al-Qaeda is the only group that has conducted suicide bombings against the US. Other groups may emerge, but efforts to prevent future attacks should focus on al-Qaeda. Attack methodology varies, with different groups specializing in specific types of bombings. Since 9/11, al-Qaeda's operations have changed significantly due to losing its sanctuary in Afghanistan. |
| 33 | Al-Qaeda is now primarily an ideological entity that motivates and inspires attacks. They favor vehicle-borne explosives for their own attacks, while |

|    | attacks inspired by al-Qaeda are often carried out by recent immigrants using person-borne devices. Al-Qaeda has shifted to virtual training and attacks are more likely to be planned locally. The London train bombings serve as a model for future attacks in the US, where home-grown citizens conducted the bombings with self-financing and homemade bombs. Some of the bombers may have received |
|----|---|
| 34 | The London bombings in 2005 were carried out by native-born citizens who were inspired by al-Qaeda and protested against British foreign policies. The bombings highlighted the potential for future attacks by young, first or second-generation immigrants who are influenced by extremist ideologies. |
| 35 | Al-Qaeda is still capable of carrying out attacks, particularly in the Middle East, and has evolved its methods to use viral marketing and leverage existing communication networks. The group has shown ingenuity in its attacks, such as using airplanes on 9/11 and large vehicle-borne improvised explosive devices in previous bombings. |
| 36 | Al-Qaeda has a history of targeting symbolic and economic targets, with a shift towards economic targets over time. They have also targeted the same location multiple times if previous attempts were unsuccessful. Oil facilities and Western economies are particularly vulnerable. Previous plots may be revisited in future attacks. |
| 37 | Al-Qaeda in Iraq uses suicide bombings to target US, Iraqi, and foreign entities, causing strategic effects such as the withdrawal of organizations and the destabilization of Iraq. Their success will likely lead to further expansion of this tactic within the Middle East. |
| 38 | The glorification of suicide bombers in the Muslim world has led to a significant increase in suicide bombing campaigns. Iraq and Afghanistan are now responsible for the majority of suicide bombings worldwide. |
| 39 | The page discusses the increase in suicide bombings against American targets overseas, particularly after 9/11. It highlights the shift in tactics from targeting embassies and military forces to specifically targeting the US. The implications are that US military interventions will continue to face suicide bombings, both directly and indirectly. |
| 40 | The page discusses the use of suicide bombers as an effective asymmetric tactic, the potential long-term impact of the U.S. withdrawal from Iraq, and the limited interaction between Special Operations Forces (SOF) and domestic law enforcement regarding suicide bombers. |
| 41 | The page discusses the benefits of intelligence sharing and training between Special Operations Forces (SOF) and law enforcement agencies in regards to suicide bombings. It suggests a "pull" system for accessing information and highlights the value of transferring knowledge and technology between the two groups. However, it argues against placing additional requirements on SOF and suggests that other agencies have enough resources to handle homeland defense. |
| 42 | The page discusses the military response to suicide bombings in the US, suggesting that Special Operations Forces (SOF) should be primarily deployed |

|    | overseas. It also recommends adopting language that frames the debate on suicide bombings in a favorable way. |
|----|---|
| 43 | The page discusses the use of terminology related to terrorism and suggests using alternative terms such as "hirabists" instead of "jihadists" and "intihar" instead of suicide bombers. It also emphasizes the importance of proper language in strategic communication efforts and emergency planning for multiple suicide bombings. |
| 44 | The page discusses the need for timely communication, redundant communication systems, and population evacuation measures in response to threats such as suicide bombings. It also emphasizes the importance of preparation, immediate response, and reconstruction in threat mitigation. The example of the HSBC Bank bombing in Istanbul is given to illustrate the effectiveness of low-cost security measures. |
| 45 | The page discusses the impact of building design on casualties in terrorist attacks and suggests replicating the sophisticated CCTV system in Britain in major US cities to enhance security. It also highlights the discrepancy in funding between aviation industry and mass transit security upgrades. |
| 46 | The page discusses the need for improved emergency response to suicide bombings, citing examples of past failures. It emphasizes the importance of realistic emergency exercises and the need to prepare the public for such events. The reconstruction aspect is deemed less of a concern due to the robust US infrastructure. |
| 47 | Suicide bombings pose a persistent threat to American presence overseas. Americans can be taught to identify and report suspicious behaviors to prevent such attacks. Force protection plans should anticipate suicide bombers targeting official US buildings. Tactics and techniques used by organizations employing suicide bombers tend to radiate outward from the Middle East. |
| 48 | The page discusses the potential use of small aircraft and poisonous chemicals by suicide bombers outside of the Middle East, the need to improve intelligence collection and analysis, and the preference for a unified intelligence community similar to the British model. It also suggests forging good ties with immigrant and Islamic communities to help identify suspicious behavior. |
| 49 | Addressing the root causes of terrorism, such as real and perceived grievances, is necessary to eliminate the core motivations for suicide bombing. Long-term solutions that do not involve concessions, such as achieving energy independence and brokering a comprehensive peace settlement in the Israeli-Palestinian conflict, would remove the need for direct military intervention in the Middle East. The US could allocate funds for alternative energy development to end dependence on foreign oil imports. |
| 50 | The page discusses the need for greater diplomatic efforts and a comprehensive settlement in the Middle East, particularly regarding the Israeli-Palestinian conflict. It suggests specific steps, such as returning the Golan Heights to Syria and negotiating a peace agreement based on pre-1967 borders, Jerusalem as an international city, an independent Palestine, and removal of settlements from the West Bank. The page highlights the potential |

| | | |
|---|---|---|
| | | effectiveness of such a settlement in reducing terrorism compared to military intervention. |
| | 51 | This appendix provides a list of suicide bombings from 1980 to 2006, with details such as date, organization, location, country, target, casualties, and source. It explains the criteria for inclusion and addresses questions about failed attacks and ambiguous cases. The data is sourced from multiple references and may contain variations in casualty counts. |
| | 52 | This page provides a list of terrorist attacks carried out by various groups in Lebanon and other countries. The attacks involve car bombs, truck bombs, and other explosive devices targeting embassies, military posts, and government officials. The attacks resulted in numerous casualties and deaths. |
| | 53 | This page provides a list of terrorist attacks carried out by various groups in different countries, including details such as location, method of attack, and number of casualties. |
| | 54 | The page provides a list of terrorist attacks that occurred between January 1995 and April 1996. The attacks took place in various countries such as Israel, Algeria, Sri Lanka, and Pakistan, and involved different methods such as car bombs, belt bombs, and boat bombs. The attacks targeted military personnel, civilians, buses, and government buildings. |
| | 55 | The page lists various terrorist attacks, including bombings and attacks on naval vessels, in Sri Lanka, Turkey, Israel, Lebanon, Germany, Tanzania, Kenya, Algeria, and Gaza. |
| | 56 | The page provides a list of terrorist attacks from various locations including Israel, Turkey, Sri Lanka, and India. The attacks involve different methods such as car bombs, belt bombs, and grenades, targeting government, police, military, and civilian locations. |
| | 57 | This page lists various terrorist attacks in Sri Lanka, Russia, Yemen, Pakistan, India, and other countries, including details such as the location, target, number of casualties, and the type of bomb used. |
| | 58 | The page provides a list of terrorist attacks from April to October 2001, including the date, location, type of attack, casualties, and other details. |
| | 59 | The page provides a list of terrorist attacks with details such as date, location, perpetrator, target, casualties, and method of attack. |
| | 60 | The page provides a list of terrorist attacks that occurred between March and July 2002, detailing the date, location, type of attack, number of casualties, and other relevant information. Attacks range from bombings at hotels, restaurants, and markets to bus and car bomb explosions. Various militant groups such as Hamas, PIJ, Fatah, and al-Qaeda are mentioned. |
| | 61 | This page provides a list of terrorist attacks from July 2002 to March 2003, including details such as the location, type of attack, number of casualties, and the perpetrator. |
| | 62 | The page provides a list of terrorist attacks, including the date, location, type of attack, number of casualties, and other details. |

| | |
|---|---|
| 63 | This page contains a list of terrorist attacks that occurred in various locations including Russia, Kenya, Indonesia, Iraq, Israel, and Turkey. The attacks involved different methods such as bombings and shootings, targeting different types of places like restaurants, hotels, embassies, and military sites. |
| 64 | The page lists various terrorist attacks that occurred between November 2003 and January 2004 in different locations such as Turkey, Iraq, Israel, Pakistan, Afghanistan, and Indonesia. The attacks involved truck bombs, car bombs, belt bombs, and other explosives targeting embassies, military bases, police stations, and civilian areas. Multiple terrorist groups are mentioned, including al-Qaeda, Taliban, Hamas, and others. |
| 65 | The page lists various terrorist attacks, including bombings and car bombs, that occurred in different locations such as Jerusalem, Iraq, Russia, and Pakistan. The attacks targeted government/police institutions, military bases, religious sites, and civilian areas. Multiple bombers were involved in some incidents, and some attacks were thwarted or resulted in the arrest of suspects. |
| 66 | This page lists various terrorist attacks that occurred in different locations, including Uzbekistan, Iraq, Spain, and Pakistan. The attacks involve different types of bombs, such as car bombs and belt bombs, targeting government/police entities, military personnel, and civilians. |
| 67 | The page provides a list of bombings that occurred in Iraq, Pakistan, Sri Lanka, Russia, Uzbekistan, and Israel between June and August 2004, targeting military, government/police, and civilian locations. Various extremist groups were responsible for these attacks, resulting in numerous casualties. |
| 68 | This page lists various terrorist attacks that occurred in different countries, including Russia, Iraq, Israel, Indonesia, and Pakistan. The attacks involved different methods such as car bombs, belt bombs, and grenade attacks, targeting airplanes, schools, government/police institutions, and military convoys. |
| 69 | The page provides a list of bombings that occurred in various locations, including Iraq, Egypt, Afghanistan, and Israel, between October 2 and November 2, 2004. The bombings targeted military, government/police, and civilian sites, resulting in numerous casualties. |
| 70 | The page provides a list of car bomb attacks in Iraq and other countries during November 2004, including the location, target, casualties, and perpetrators. |
| 71 | This page provides a list of bombings in Iraq and Saudi Arabia between December 1, 2004, and January 6, 2005, including the locations, targets, and casualties. |
| 72 | The page lists various bombings and attacks in Iraq and Afghanistan, targeting civilians, government/police, military, and religious sites. The attacks involve car bombs, belt bombs, and other explosives, resulting in casualties and damage. |

| | |
|---|---|
| 73 | The page lists various bombings in Iraq and Lebanon, targeting civilians, military personnel, government buildings, mosques, and other locations. The attacks involved car bombs, belt bombs, and other explosives. |
| 74 | This page lists a series of terrorist attacks in various locations, including Iraq, Israel, Qatar, Pakistan, and Afghanistan. The attacks involve car bombs, belt bombs, and truck bombs targeting military, government/police, and civilian locations. |
| 75 | The page provides a list of car bomb attacks in Iraq between March 30 and April 19, 2005. The attacks targeted military, government/police, and civilian locations, resulting in casualties and damage. |
| 76 | The page provides a list of car bomb attacks in Iraq, including the date, location, target, casualties, and other details. |
| 77 | The page lists various bombings and attacks in Iraq, Russia, Afghanistan, and Turkey, including the locations, targets, and casualties. |
| 78 | The page provides a list of car bomb attacks in Iraq and other locations, including the date, location, target, casualties, and responsible group. |
| 79 | The page provides a list of car bomb attacks in Iraq and other locations, including the dates, locations, targets, and casualties. |
| 80 | The page contains a list of car bombings and other attacks in Iraq and other countries, including the dates, locations, and targets of each attack. |
| 81 | The page provides a list of bombings that took place in various locations in Iraq, Israel, and England during July 2005. The bombings targeted government/police institutions, military patrols, and civilian areas, resulting in numerous casualties. |
| 82 | The page provides a list of bombings and attacks in Iraq, Afghanistan, Egypt, England, Israel, India, and Russia between July 17th and August 5th, 2005. The attacks targeted government/police, military, and civilian locations. Car bombs, belt bombs, and bus bombs were used, resulting in casualties and damage. |
| 83 | This page lists various car bomb attacks in Iraq and Afghanistan targeting military, government, and police entities. The attacks resulted in casualties and foiled attempts. |
| 84 | The page lists various car bomb incidents in Iraq and one in Pakistan between September 7th and September 25th, 2005. The targets include restaurants, government/police buildings, military patrols, religious sites, and markets. |
| 85 | The page provides a list of bombings and attacks in Iraq and Afghanistan, including details such as location, type of attack, and target. |
| 86 | The page provides a list of car bombings and other attacks in Iraq, Kashmir, Russia, Afghanistan, and Israel, including details such as locations, targets, and casualties. |

| | |
|---|---|
| 87 | The page provides a list of terrorist attacks in Iraq, Afghanistan, Jordan, Bangladesh, and Israel from November to December 2005, including details such as location, type of attack, casualties, and target. |
| 88 | The page provides a list of bombings that occurred in various locations, including Iraq, Afghanistan, Bangladesh, and Russia, between December 6, 2005, and January 3, 2006. The bombings targeted government, police, military, and civilian locations, resulting in casualties and damage. |
| 89 | The page lists various bombings and attacks in Iraq, Afghanistan, Sri Lanka, China, and Israel, targeting government/police, military, and civilian locations. The attacks involved car bombs, belt bombs, boat bombs, and bus bombs. Casualties include police officers, military personnel, and civilians. |
| 90 | Summary of the page: The page lists various bombings that took place in different countries, including Iraq, Afghanistan, and Pakistan, between 6th and 13th March 2006. The bombings targeted different locations such as restaurants, military bases, markets, and government/police checkpoints, resulting in numerous casualties. |
| 91 | This page contains a list of bombings in Iraq, Afghanistan, Sri Lanka, and China, targeting various locations such as schools, military patrols, religious sites, and markets. It includes information on the number of casualties, the type of bomb used, and the organizations responsible for the attacks. |
| 92 | This page contains a list of bombings that occurred in various locations, including Iraq, Afghanistan, Sri Lanka, and Russia. The bombings targeted military, government, and police institutions, resulting in numerous casualties. |
| 93 | Between May and June 2006, there were multiple car bomb attacks in Afghanistan and Iraq targeting government, military, and civilian locations. The attacks resulted in numerous casualties and were carried out by various groups including the Taliban. |
| 94 | This page lists a series of bombings and attacks in Iraq, Afghanistan, Sri Lanka, Russia, and Pakistan between June 17 and July 10, 2006. Targets included government/police, military, civilians, and religious sites. Several attacks were foiled or resulted in arrests. |
| 95 | This page lists various bombings and attacks in Iraq, Afghanistan, and Pakistan from July 10 to July 25, 2006, targeting government/police, military, and civilian locations. The bombings involve different types of explosives such as car bombs, belt bombs, and truck bombs. The casualties range from 0 to 105. |
| 96 | This page provides a list of bombings and attacks in Iraq, Afghanistan, Pakistan, and Sri Lanka, detailing the location, target, casualties, and perpetrators. |
| 97 | The page provides a list of terrorist attacks in Iraq and Afghanistan, including the date, location, target, number of casualties, and type of attack. |
| 98 | This page lists various terrorist attacks carried out by different groups in countries such as Yemen, Iraq, Afghanistan, and Somalia. The attacks |

| | | |
|---|---|---|
| | | involved car bombs, belt bombs, and other explosive devices targeting military, government, police, and civilian locations. |
| | 99 | The page provides a list of bombings in Iraq and Afghanistan from September to October 2006, including the locations, targets, and number of casualties. |
| | 100 | The page provides a list of bombings in Iraq, Afghanistan, Sri Lanka, and Pakistan between October 17, 2006, and November 11, 2006. The bombings targeted military, government/police, and civilian locations, resulting in numerous casualties. |
| | 101 | The page lists various terrorist attacks that occurred in Iraq, Afghanistan, Pakistan, and Somalia in November 2006. Attacks targeted government/police, military, and civilian locations using car bombs or belt bombs. The attacks resulted in multiple casualties. |
| | 102 | The page provides a list of terrorist attacks that occurred in various locations, including Sri Lanka, Pakistan, Iraq, Afghanistan, and other countries. The attacks involved car bombs, belt bombs, and other explosive devices targeting military, government/police, and civilian targets. The casualties range from zero to multiple deaths and injuries. |
| | 103 | The page provides information on various attacks and campaigns in different countries, including Iraq, Lebanon, Sri Lanka, Egypt, Russia, and Bangladesh. It also includes abbreviations for different groups involved in these conflicts. |
| | 104 | The page provides a list of various organizations, military forces, and abbreviations related to conflict and terrorism, along with their corresponding acronyms. |
| | 105 | The PDF contains a list of abbreviations for various news sources. |
| | 106 | This page lists various news agencies and publications from around the world, including links to their websites. |
| | 107 | This page is a bibliography of various sources related to terrorism, including studies on mass casualty bombings, the root causes of terrorism, suicide terror, and suicide bombings in Operation Iraqi Freedom. |
| | 109 | The page contains a list of various sources related to terrorism, including publications, databases, and books. |
| | 110 | The page provides citations for various sources related to terrorism and warfare, including books and articles. |
| | 111 | The page contains a list of various sources related to suicide terrorism, including books, journals, and articles, that provide information on topics such as the history, tactics, and impacts of suicide bombings. |
| | 112 | Various sources on terrorism, including books, articles, and government documents, are listed. Topics include the globalization of terror, suicide bombings, counter-terrorism strategies, and military terminology. |

# Suicide Bombers in CONUS

A Monograph

by

LCDR Philip E. Kapusta

U.S. Navy

School of Advanced Military Studies

United States Army Command and General Staff College

Fort Leavenworth, Kansas

AY 06-07

Approved for Public Release; Distribution is Unlimited

| REPORT DOCUMENTATION PAGE | | Form Approved OMB No. 0704-0188 |
|---|---|---|

Public reporting burden for this collection of information is estimated to average 1 hour per response, including the time for reviewing instructions, searching existing data sources, gathering and maintaining the data needed, and completing and reviewing this collection of information. Send comments regarding this burden estimate or any other aspect of this collection of information, including suggestions for reducing this burden to Department of Defense, Washington Headquarters Services, Directorate for Information Operations and Reports (0704-0188), 1215 Jefferson Davis Highway, Suite 1204, Arlington, VA 22202-4302. Respondents should be aware that notwithstanding any other provision of law, no person shall be subject to any penalty for failing to comply with a collection of information if it does not display a currently valid OMB control number. **PLEASE DO NOT RETURN YOUR FORM TO THE ABOVE ADDRESS.**

| 1. REPORT DATE (DD-MM-YYYY) 07-05-2007 | 2. REPORT TYPE AMSP Monograph | 3. DATES COVERED (From - To) July 2006 – Feb 2007 |
|---|---|---|
| 4. TITLE AND SUBTITLE Suicide Bombers in CONUS | | 5a. CONTRACT NUMBER |
| | | 5b. GRANT NUMBER |
| | | 5c. PROGRAM ELEMENT NUMBER |
| 6. AUTHOR(S) LCDR Philip Kapusta (U.S. Navy) | | 5d. PROJECT NUMBER |
| | | 5e. TASK NUMBER |
| | | 5f. WORK UNIT NUMBER |
| 7. PERFORMING ORGANIZATION NAME(S) AND ADDRESS(ES) Advanced Military Studies Program 250 Gibbon Avenue Fort Leavenworth, KS 66027-2134 | | 8. PERFORMING ORGANIZATION REPORT NUMBER |
| 9. SPONSORING / MONITORING AGENCY NAME(S) AND ADDRESS(ES) Command and General Staff College 1 Reynolds Avenue Fort Leavenworth, KS 66027 | | 10. SPONSOR/MONITOR'S ACRONYM(S) CGSC |
| | | 11. SPONSOR/MONITOR'S REPORT NUMBER(S) |

**12. DISTRIBUTION / AVAILABILITY STATEMENT**
Approved for Public Release; Distribution is Unlimited

**13. SUPPLEMENTARY NOTES**

**14. ABSTRACT**
This monograph analyzes recent (post-1980) suicide bombings and determines the probability of the same in the Continental United States (CONUS). Analysis includes a brief history of modern suicide bombing and an examination of the strategic, tactical, social and individual logic of suicide bombing. It addresses the probable characteristics of suicide bombings against the U.S., both within CONUS and abroad. The monograph also makes recommendations about what can be done to mitigate future bombings. Appendix A lists 2,202 suicide bombings since 1980, and as of early 2007 is the best available open source suicide bombing database in the world.

The vast majority of suicide bombings (98%) are part of an organized campaign. The only group that conducts suicide bombings against the U.S. outside of active war zones is Al-Qaida. Al-Qaida attacks have evolved to the point where there are two different strains: al-Qaida-sponsored and al-Qaida-inspired. Both are likely in CONUS within the mid-future.

**15. SUBJECT TERMS**
Suicide bomb(s), suicide bomber(s), suicide bombing(s), terror, terrorism, terrorist(s), CONUS, al-Qaida, al-Qaeda

| 16. SECURITY CLASSIFICATION OF: | | | 17. LIMITATION OF ABSTRACT | 18. NUMBER OF PAGES | 19a. NAME OF RESPONSIBLE PERSON Kevin C.M. Benson, COL, US Army |
|---|---|---|---|---|---|
| a. REPORT UNCLASS | b. ABSTRACT UNCLASS | c. THIS PAGE UNCLASS | UNLIMITED | 112 | 19b. TELEPHONE NUMBER (include area code) 913-758-3302 |

Standard Form 298 (Rev. 8-98)
Prescribed by ANSI Std. Z39.18

# SCHOOL OF ADVANCED MILITARY STUDIES

## MONOGRAPH APPROVAL

LCDR Philip E. Kapusta

Title of Monograph: Suicide Bombers in CONUS

Approved by:

_____  Monograph Director
Timothy Challans, PH.D.


_____  Director,
Kevin C.M. Benson, COL, AR           School of Advanced
                                     Military Studies


_____  Director,
Robert F. Baumann, Ph.D.             Graduate Degree
                                     Programs

# Abstract

SUICIDE BOMBERS IN CONUS by LCDR Philip E. Kapusta, USN, 50 pages.

This monograph analyzes recent (post-1980) suicide bombings and determines the probability of the same in the Continental United States (CONUS). Analysis includes a brief history of modern suicide bombing and an examination of the strategic, tactical, social and individual logic of suicide bombing. It addresses the probable characteristics of suicide bombings against the U.S., both within CONUS and abroad. The monograph also makes recommendations about what can be done to mitigate future bombings. Finally, Appendix A lists 2,202 suicide bombings since 1980, and as of early 2007 is the best available open source suicide bombing database in the world.

Suicide attackers have been a part of warfare for over two millennia, but the coupling of suicide attackers and explosives greatly increased the importance and effectiveness of this tactic in the $20^{th}$ century. The modern phenomenon of suicide bombing had its genesis in the Iran-Iraq War from 1980-88. Ayatollah Khomeini used his influence to motivate young Iranians to commit suicide attacks, but he was successful in framing such attacks as martyrdom operations. Concurrent with the Iran-Iraq War, Iran influenced the development of Hezbollah in Lebanon. Hezbollah tried suicide bombing on somewhat of a trial basis against the U.S. and France, and then later against Israel. Unfortunately, Hezbollah achieved both strategic and tactical success and proved the efficacy of suicide bombing.

Not surprisingly, other groups such as the Liberation Tigers of Tamil Eelam (LTTE), the Palestinians and the People's Liberation Army of Kurdistan (PKK) started employing suicide bombers in the 1980s and 1990s. As suicide bombing spread geographically and ideologically, it also increased in sophistication. It advanced from being a simple bomb delivered by truck, to include suicide vests, boat bombs, and eventually airplanes. Target sets similarly expanded. Once the taboo against suicide was overcome, previous distinctions among civilian non-combatants and uniformed military members became meaningless.

The vast majority of suicide bombings (98%) are part of an organized campaign. Thus, there is a logic for the individuals blowing themselves up, since they believe that they are acting for the common good. The scale of campaigns has also steadily increased. While Hezbollah mounted some 50 attacks in Lebanon over years, suicide bombers in Iraq commonly conduct 50 attacks in a single month. Another trait that holds constant regardless of religion, geography or nature of the conflict is that the side employing suicide bombers is always the weaker side. Given the U.S. conventional military dominance for the foreseeable future, suicide bombing will be a staple tactic of its opponents. For the most part, suicide bombings will be confined to those periods when the U.S. is actively militarily intervening overseas.

The only group that conducts suicide bombings against the U.S. outside of active war zones is Al-Qaida. Its methodology has morphed over time from being a traditional terrorist organization that conducted attacks with its own operatives, to being a "venture capitalist" that sponsored and financed others, to its present form of being a viral marketer. Al-Qaida still plans and attempts its own attacks, and these Al-Qaida-sponsored attacks tend to be large-scale, involve multiple, simultaneous attackers, and require extensive planning and coordination. Al-Qaida-inspired attacks, however, usually feature first or second-generation attackers operating within their parent country, are often self-financed, and use person-borne devices with locally procured explosives. There will still be Al-Qaida-sponsored suicide bombings every few years, but the more likely and numerous suicide bombings in CONUS will be Al-Qaida-inspired.

TABLE OF CONTENTS

| | |
|---|---:|
| SUICIDE BOMBING DEFINED | 1 |
| RECENT HISTORY OF SUICIDE BOMBING | 4 |
| LOGIC OF SUICIDE BOMBING | 18 |
| LIKELIHOOD OF SUICIDE BOMBING IN CONUS | 30 |
| SOF INTERFACE WITH DOMESTIC LAW ENFORCEMENT | 40 |
| RECOMMENDATIONS | 42 |
| APPENDIX A: SUICIDE BOMBINGS (1980-2006) | 51 |
| BIBLIOGRAPHY | 107 |

# SUICIDE BOMBING DEFINED

[You can] "never understand anything about the allure of martyrdom… until you realize that someone who has decided to take this path as his own sees himself not only as an avenging Ninja, but also as something of a movie star, maybe even a sex symbol – a romantic figure at the very least, larger than life." *The Road to Martyr's Square*[1]

Suicide attackers such as the Jewish Zealots and Sicarii (4 BC to 70 AD) and the Ismaili Assassins (11th and 12th centuries) have been a part of warfare for over two millennia.[2] However, the coupling of suicide attackers and explosives greatly increased the importance and effectiveness of this tactic in the 20th century. Most notably, the use of suicide bombers started increasing exponentially from the early 1980s through the present day. Several groups that habitually employ suicide bombers are hostile to the United States, and they possess both the intent and the capability to conduct attacks within the continental United States (CONUS). Since defense of the homeland is the number one priority for the Department of Defense (DOD), understanding and countering suicide bombers is of significant importance to the U.S. military. This monograph assesses the likelihood and probable characteristics of future suicide bombers in CONUS.

DOD defines terrorism as "the use of unlawful violence or threat of violence to inculcate fear; intended to coerce or to intimidate governments or societies in the pursuit of goals that are generally political, religious, or ideological."[3] Interestingly, there is no formal U.S. government definition for suicide terrorism. Instead, definitions for suicide terrorism can be culled from the relatively large field of literature on the subject. For example, Dr. Boaz Ganor, executive director of the International Policy Institute for Counter-Terrorism in Israel, defines a suicide attack as an "operational method in which the very act of the attack is dependent upon the death of the

---

[1] Anne Marie Oliver and Paul Steinberg, *The Road to Martyr's Square*, (Oxford: Oxford University Press, 2005), 72.
[2] Mia Bloom, *Dying to Kill*, (Columbia University Press, New York, 2005), 4.
[3] Joint Publication 1-02, Department of Defense Dictionary of Military and Associated Terms, 12 April 2001, as amended through 14 April 2006.

perpetrator."[4] Terrorism researcher Robert Pape offers a subtly different definition of suicide terrorism as "the use of violence to intimidate or frighten a target audience where the attacker(s) does not expect to survive the mission and often employs a method of attack that requires his or her death in order to succeed."[5] Similarly, Dr. Robert Bunker and John Sullivan offer that, "Suicide bombing is the act of blowing oneself up while trying to kill (destroy) or injure (damage) a target. The target might be military or civilian or both."[6] Finally, Yoram Schweitzer defines suicide terror, "as a politically motivated violent attack perpetrated by a self-aware individual (or individuals) who actively and purposefully causes his own death through blowing himself up along with his chosen target. The perpetrator's death is a precondition for the success of the mission."[7]

In order to be of maximum use for U.S. government counter-terrorism efforts, this monograph will conform closely with the DOD definition and define suicide terrorism as: "unlawful violence or the threat of violence to inculcate fear in, coerce or intimidate governments or societies in the pursuit of political, religious or ideological goals, where the method of attack requires the perpetrator(s) to knowingly cause his or her own death as a precondition for success." Specifically, this monograph will examine suicide bombing in the continental United States (CONUS), where bombing is defined as: "a method of attack using high-yield explosives (i.e. trinitrotoluene (TNT)), improvised explosive devices (IED) or vehicle-borne improvised explosive devices (VBIED)." The inclusion of improvised explosives in the definition captures the use of unorthodox tactics such as deliberately crashing vehicles into targets to cause

---

[4] Boaz Ganor, "Suicide Terrorism: an Overview," (15 February 2000): 1; available at http://www.ict.org.il/articles/articledet.cfm?articleid=128 ; Internet; accessed 9 September 2006.
[5] Robert Pape, *Dying to Win*, (New York: Random House, 2005), 9.
[6] Robert J. Bunker, Ph.D. and John P. Sullivan, *Suicide Bombings in Operation Iraqi Freedom*, (Military Review, Jan-Feb 2005), 69.
[7] Yoram Schweitzer, "Suicide Terrorism: Development & Characteristics," (21 April 2000): 1; available at http://www.ict.org.il/articles/articledet.cfm?articleid=112 ; Internet; accessed 9 September 2006.

explosions as in the 9/11 attacks, whereby the terrorists may cause an explosion and do not have to be in physical possession of an explosive device at the start of the operation.

Notably, the above definition of suicide terrorism excludes extremely high-risk attacks where the possibility of death for the attacker is great but not necessarily a pre-condition of the operation. For example, the 1972 attack at Tel Aviv's Lod airport by three Japanese Red Army members (24 dead, 78 wounded) would not qualify as suicide terrorism, since the perpetrators were able to execute a successful attack and at least theoretically all could have remained alive at the end. Indeed, one of the attackers, Kozo Okamoto, was captured while attempting to flee the scene and was sentenced to life imprisonment before being released in 1983 during a prisoner exchange.[8] It also does not include attacks where the terrorists carry arms or explosives to kill themselves if the operation fails, since their deaths are not preconditions for success. In contrast, the 9/11 attacks would be considered suicide terrorism, since there was no way for the hijackers to crash their planes into the selected targets without also causing their own deaths.

Defining the violence as "unlawful" also excludes such actions as the massive Japanese *kamikaze* (divine wind) campaign near the end of World War II. To put the *kamikaze* effort in perspective, in one month (April 1945), the Battle of Okinawa saw over 2,000 *kamikaze* attacks and U.S. casualties of almost 5,000 dead, another 5,000 wounded, 36 ships sunk and 368 ships damaged.[9] This amounts to almost as many attacks in one month as all suicide bombings from 1980-2006, and almost as many U.S. casualties as were suffered during the Pearl Harbor and 9/11 attacks combined. However, the Japanese tactic of using suicidal attackers was regarded as lawful, since it consisted of uniformed military forces attacking opposing military forces, and no Japanese leaders were charged with war crimes for ordering *kamikaze* attacks.

---

[8] Rui Kotani, "In the Spotlight: Japanese Red Army (JRA)," (9 October 2003); 2; available at http://www.cdi.org/friendlyversion/printversion.cfm?documentID=1771 ; Internet; accessed 9 September 2006.

[9] Laura Lacey, "The Battle of Okinawa," (2003): 1; available at http://www.militaryhistoryonline.com/wwii/okinawa/default.aspx/ ; Internet; accessed 9 September 2006.

# RECENT HISTORY OF SUICIDE BOMBING

"The price we had to pay in Beirut was so great, the tragedy at the barracks was so enormous...we had to pull out. We couldn't stay there and run the risk of another suicide attack on the Marines." President Ronald Reagan in *An American Life*[10]

The modern phenomenon of suicide bombing had its genesis in the Iranian Revolution and the Iran-Iraq War 1980-88. Early in the war, Iran adopted innovative measures to combat Iraq's conventional military superiority. Significantly, the Iranians employed legions of young men to clear minefields with their bodies and/or directly assault Iraqi tanks with explosives attached to their bodies. The participants went far beyond simply conducting risky military attacks with a high probability of death - a common enough scenario in militaries the world over. Rather, the young Iranians entered battle with "keys to paradise" around their necks, fully expected to die, and, in fact, believed that they would ascend directly to paradise only if they were killed in the engagement.[11]

Suicide attacks were far from the norm for the Iranian military at the onset of the war, and their adoption rested in great part upon Ayatollah Khomeini's actions to promote them. He used his powerful religious authority to replace the normally strong Islamic prohibition against suicide (*intihar*) with the idea that the young men were instead conducting a praiseworthy act of self-sacrifice (*istishad*) for the greater good. This distinction is roughly equivalent to the Judeo-Christian difference between those who commit suicide and those who are martyred. Despite some initial skepticism, the Iranian population gradually reached a point of general acceptance and belief that the young men were martyrs.[12]

Concurrent with the Iran-Iraq War, Iran exported features from its Islamic revolution to turbulent Lebanon. There, Iranian ideology influenced both the Shiite Amal militia and the Islamic Resistance, the predecessor of Hezbollah (Party of God). Specifically, Amal executed the

---

[10] U.S. Army TRADOC, *Suicide Bombing in the COE*, (Fort Leavenworth, KS: 15 Aug 2005), II-1.
[11] Bunker and Sullivan, 70.
[12] Ami Pedahzur, *Suicide Terrorism*, (Great Britain: Polity Press, 2005), 160.

first confirmed vehicular suicide bombing in December, 1981 against the Iraqi Embassy in Lebanon (27 dead, 100+ wounded).[13] Almost a year passed before the next attack; when 15-year-old Ahmad Qasir detonated his car bomb at the Israeli military base in Tyre, Lebanon on 11 November, 1982 (62 dead, 28 wounded).[14] Hezbollah then inaugurated what is often thought of as the modern era of suicide terrorism by using a vehicle-borne suicide bomber to destroy the U.S. Embassy in Lebanon on April 18th, 1983 (63 dead, 100 wounded). Six months later on October 23rd, Hezbollah conducted near-simultaneous suicide bombings against the U.S. Marine and the French peacekeeping troop barracks in Lebanon (241 dead, 81 wounded and 58 dead, 15 wounded respectively). Hezbollah followed up these attacks two weeks later with another suicide bombing of the Israeli headquarters in Tyre, Lebanon that killed 58, including 28 Israelis.[15] Suicide terrorism, with its unmistakable Iranian fingerprints, arrived on the world stage.

Hezbollah vaulted from being a relatively obscure minor faction among many in Lebanon to being one the world's premier terrorist organizations. In addition to the tactical success in killing 241 American servicemen and 58 French paratroopers, the twin October bombings resulted in phenomenal strategic success. Within four months, the U.S., British and Italian peacekeeping contingents withdrew, and the French followed a month later. Just two individuals willing to sacrifice their lives were able to alter the foreign policies of four major Western powers.[16] The clear lesson was that suicide bombing was efficient and highly effective.

Interestingly, suicide tactics were exceptionally controversial at the time, and Hezbollah initially carefully guarded its role in the attacks. For example, Ahmad Qasir's identity as the bomber in the 1982 Tyre attack was kept secret for two years before a well-executed marketing campaign secured his status as a hero in both Lebanon and Iran. The Iranians went on to erect a

---

[13] Bunker and Sullivan, 71.
[14] Pedahzur, 118.
[15] Ibid., 49.
[16] U.S. Army TRADOC, I-3.

memorial for him in Tehran, and Hezbollah now annually commemorates his attack.[17] However, Hezbollah leaders were also careful never to issue an official religious ruling (*fatwa*) legitimizing suicide attacks. Along with Iranian leaders, Hezbollah officials publicly extolled and justified suicide attacks as legitimate. Nonetheless, they were careful not to commit themselves fully to an official endorsement, and Hezbollah could have reversed its position in the face of widespread condemnation or opposition.[18]

Instead, Hezbollah found growing acceptance, if not full support, for its campaign as it launched nine more suicide bombing attacks against the Israelis through the middle of 1985. In the face of this campaign, the Israelis withdrew from central Lebanon and contented themselves with loosely controlling southern Lebanon from a series of 45 fortified bases and support from the Israeli-backed Southern Lebanese Army (SLA). The Israeli withdrawal amounted to yet another victory for Hezbollah and further validated using suicide bombers. The novel use of this tactic helped Hezbollah grow from just a few dozen members in 1982 to over 7,000 in 1986. More impressively, numerically inferior Hezbollah accomplished what the 15,000-strong Palestinian Liberation Organization (PLO) and 30,000 Syrian troops could not – forcing Israel to cede territory.[19] Once again, the clear and unequivocal lesson was that suicide bombing worked.

The Israelis repositioned into more defensible garrisons with reduced resupply requirements and simultaneously increased their vehicles' armor and improved convoy tactics. Thus, suicide bomber effectiveness against the remaining Israelis fell dramatically, and Hezbollah effectively ended its suicide bomber campaign against the Israeli Defense Force (IDF). However, the SLA became the new focus of an even more robust suicide bomber campaign, as Hezbollah targeted the SLA with some 20 suicide bomb attacks from July, 1985 through November of 1986. Thereafter, Hezbollah largely switched to attacking IDF and SLA forces with more conventional

---

[17] Pedahzur, 160.
[18] Pape, 138.
[19] Ibid., 131-132.

means such as: mortar fire, rockets, ambushes, and concealed roadside explosives. The switch from primarily using suicide bombers to more conventional attacks was likely due to the combination of Hezbollah's increased operational capability and improved countermeasures on the part of the IDF and the SLA.[20]

Despite the fact that many of the suicide bombers in Lebanon were females, Christians and/or Communists, suicide bombing was viewed as a Shiite Muslim phenomenon at the time. However, just as the Hezbollah campaign was ramping down at the end of 1986, the Hindu-dominated Liberation Tigers of Tamil Eelam (LTTE) introduced suicide bombing to the ongoing Tamil-Sinhalese civil war in Sri Lanka. After emerging as the winner of a brutal struggle for primacy among more than 20 Tamil resistance groups in the mid-1980s, the LTTE studied and adopted Hezbollah's proven suicide bombing tactics. In fact, the first LTTE suicide bombing was almost an exact replica of the bombing of the U.S. Marine barracks four years earlier in Beirut: on July 5th, 1987, Captain Miller of the LTTE's special Black Tiger suicide unit drove a truck bomb into an army camp and killed 40 Sri Lankan soldiers and wounded 70 others.[21]

Captain Miller's attack was just the opening salvo in the LTTE's long-running and innovative suicide bombing campaign that ultimately eclipsed Hezbollah's in intensity and scale. The LTTE's 120 suicide bombings' interesting features include: the extensive use of female bombers, using suicide bombing against fellow ethnic Tamil rivals, development of extensive naval suicide bombing elements, and unparalleled success in targeting senior political and military leaders. Within the Black Tigers, an estimated 30% of the total suicide cadre and 60% of the actual suicide bombers have been women. This is both to conserve male manpower for direct combat and because of the greater ease with which women can conceal suicide bombs and pass

---

[20] Pedahzur, 50-51.
[21] Christoph Reuter, *My Life Is a Weapon*, (Princeton, NJ: Princeton University Press, 2004), 156-158.

through security checkpoints.[22] Although the vast majority of the LTTE's attacks were directed against the Sinhalese, the LTTE also employed suicide bombing against moderate Tamil rivals,[23] as with at least three suicide bombings targeting fellow Tamil politicians in 1999.

Geography no doubt played a significant role in the LTTE's development of an effective maritime suicide bombing capability. The Tamil minority is concentrated along the northern coast of Sri Lanka, and the LTTE needed a way to maintain contact with the ethnic Tamils living in South India.[24] Thus, it was a short bridge from maintaining maritime lines of communication to building an attack capacity, and naval suicide bombings that employed both divers and suicide boats became signature LTTE tactics. Similar to Hezbollah, the LTTE used suicide bombings to rise from being one small, obscure guerilla movement among many to being the sole armed opposition group within its minority population. Part of LTTE's notoriety came from being the only group, to date, to successfully assassinate two heads of state. In May 1991, a female LTTE suicide bomber killed former Indian Prime Minister Rajiv Ghandi and 16 others when she detonated herself at his feet. Two years later in May 1993, a male LTTE suicide bomber killed Sri Lankan President Prendesa and 21 others. In addition to the numerous other senior military commanders and ranking political figures killed by suicide bombers, the LTTE almost added a third head of state to its list in December, 1999 when Sri Lankan President Kumaratunga survived a suicide bombing but did lose one of her eyes.[25]

The final significant lesson from the LTTE's use of suicide bombers is its secular nature. The Tamils are majority Hindu, but there is a sizable 15% Christian Tamil minority, and Tamil propaganda makes little mention of religious motivations. Indeed, the atheist Prabhakaran has led the LTTE since its inception as a group of left-wing students. Although the LTTE did attack Buddhist targets, this was more symptomatic of the relentless and indiscriminate nature of their

---

[22] Ibid., 160-161.
[23] Bloom, 61.
[24] Walter Laqueur, *No End to War*, (New York: Continuum, 2004), 80.
[25] Schweitzer, 3.

attacks than a religious ideology. Specifically, the LTTE attacked not only Sinhalese Buddhists, but also fellow Hindus and occasionally Muslims and Christians.[26] The defining characteristic of the LTTE has been the calibrated use of suicide bombing as an effective tactic by the militarily inferior side in a long-running insurgency.

The next major development in the progression of suicide bombing was its adoption as a tactic by Palestinians. Hard-line religious groups such as Harakat al-Muqawama al-Islamiyyah (HAMAS) and Palestinian Islamic Jihad (PIJ) were the first to employ suicide bombers beginning in 1993. Although the use of suicide bombers in Israel was probably inevitable, it was likely accelerated by Israel's decision to deport 415 HAMAS and PIJ activists to Lebanon at the end of 1992. Hezbollah sheltered and cared for them on a mountainside until international pressure forced Israel to allow them back into the occupied territories after only nine months. During the activists' time in Lebanon, Hezbollah provided them with military, religious and operational training in addition to food and shelter. Thus, when the HAMAS and PIJ militants returned to the West Bank and Gaza, the pump was primed for the use of suicide bombers against Israel proper.[27]

No doubt inspired by Hezbollah's success in forcing Israel to relinquish territory in central Lebanon, the Palestinian groups sought, at a minimum, to force an Israeli withdrawal from the occupied territories. While Hezbollah targeted only Israeli Defense Force (IDF) troops in Lebanon, and the LTTE concentrated primarily on Sri Lankan military and police forces, HAMAS and PIJ expanded suicide bombing to include the civilian population as a specific target set. Resting upon the logic that most Israelis are subject to compulsory military service and that Palestinian civilians suffer at the hands of the IDF, HAMAS and PIJ defended attacks against virtually any target in Israel. Having already crossed the threshold of the cultural taboo against suicide, attacks targeting civilians were not difficult to justify. Thus, the iconic pictures of ripped open Israeli buses came to symbolize this suicide bombing campaign.

---

[26] Laqueur, 80-82.
[27] Bloom, 122-123.

Palestinian acceptance of suicide bombing was hardly instantaneous or fixed. As Mia Bloom noted, there were two distinct periods that correlated strongly with the progress of peace talks. Throughout the mid-1990s, when just HAMAS and PIJ were conducting suicide bombings, Palestinian support for this tactic never rose above one-third of the population. However, by the start of the second *intifada* in late 2000, more than two-thirds of Palestinians were supportive of suicide bombings.[28] Attack frequency correlated with social support: suicide bombings against Israel averaged only five a year from 1993 through 2000, but there were an average of 47 attacks a year from 2001 through 2003.

Another notable feature of Palestinian suicide bombing post-2000 was its evolution from being an Islamic militant-only endeavor to its use by such secular groups as Fatah (al-Aqsa Martyrs' Brigade faction) and the Marxist-based Popular Front for the Liberation of Palestine (PFLP). The secularization of Palestinian suicide bombing also led to a greater role for female bombers. Despite the fact that many women served as suicide bombers against the Israelis in Lebanon, it was not until January 2002 that the first Palestinian female bomber, Idris Wafa, detonated herself at a Jerusalem mall (1 dead, 150 wounded). Subsequently, there were at least eight other successful female Palestinian suicide bombers, and even HAMAS employed women bombers by early 2004.[29]

The Palestinian campaign peaked in 2002, and by 2006, there were only five successful suicide bombings against Israel. Interestingly, the campaign's intensity declined despite a lack of any meaningful progress on a political settlement. Improved Israeli security measures no doubt accounted for some of the decline. By 2003, Israel finished construction of the first section of its planned security fence,[30] and armed guards searched patrons at most major public venues. Similar to its retrenchment in Lebanon, Israel also took steps to consolidate its more vulnerable

---

[28] Ibid., 23.
[29] Mohammed Hafez, *Manufacturing Human Bombs*, (Washington, D.C.: U.S. Institute of Peace, 2006), 20.
[30] Pape, 240.

positions by withdrawing entirely from the Gaza Strip and from some isolated West Bank settlements. Other Israeli countermeasures such as targeted assassinations, home demolitions, checkpoints and closures likely increased Palestinian support for suicide bombing.[31]

One result of Palestinian suicide bombing was the increased power of and support for once fringe groups. HAMAS, in particular, leveraged its employment of suicide bombers in conjunction with its social outreach network to gain popular support. In 1999, there was genuine hope for the peace process, and HAMAS enjoyed less than 12% popular support. However, groups opposed to the peace process often used suicide bombings to scuttle any forward progress while bolstering their own credentials.[32] Thus, by 2006, HAMAS posted a decisive electoral victory over the notoriously corrupt Fatah and become the freely chosen Palestinian government.

Again, the clear lesson for the groups employing suicide bombing was that it was effective. Relatively small organizations were able to play a spoiler role in the peace process while simultaneously enhancing their own legitimacy. Suicide bombing also conferred a sense of power to the weaker side. Despite a massive Israeli overmatch in terms of conventional military strength, suicide bombing allowed the Palestinians to inflict significant pain and suffering on the general Israeli population. The abrupt Israeli withdrawal from the Gaza Strip also seemed to validate the use of suicide bombers. Although numerous factors contributed to the Israeli decision, suicide bombing advocates could only claim vindication and feel validation. Given the at least perceived success of suicide bombing, it will remain a staple tactic in the long-running Israeli-Palestinian conflict until a comprehensive peace agreement is finally reached.

Another group that started its suicide bombing campaign in the mid-1990s was the Kurdistan Workers' Party (PKK). Started as a left-wing group in 1978, the PKK blended Marxist ideology with the desire for Kurdish independence under the charismatic leadership of Abdullah

---

[31] Mohammed Hafez, "Symbolic Dimensions of Suicide Terrorism" in *Root Causes of Suicide Terrorism*, (New York: Routledge, 2006), 73.
[32] Bloom, 24-25.

Ocalan. PKK military arms began actively fighting the Turks in 1984, but they did not employ suicide bombings until 1996. Explanations for the decision to embrace suicide bombing include both a desire to demonstrate total commitment to the cause of Kurdish independence and a need to strike back after successful Turkish military incursions into Kurdish areas. Likely influenced by both considerations, Ocalan himself was instrumental in the PKK adopting this tactic.[33]

Partly resulting from effective, if heavy-handed, Turkish countermeasures, the PKK's campaign was relatively small and short-lived. Specifically, the PKK executed only 22 suicide bomb attacks, of which about two-thirds were successful. Due to intense Turkish military pressure and low popular support among the Kurds the PKK purported to represent, Ocalan was forced to flee to a variety of nations before finally being captured in Kenya and extradited to Turkey to stand trial. At his trial, Ocalan renounced suicide bombing and called upon the remaining PKK members to halt their attacks. Because of his virtually unchallenged leadership, his edict was dutifully obeyed, and the PKK's suicide bombing campaign effectively came to an end. Overall, the PKK accomplished very little by employing suicide bombers, mostly because of its lack of genuine support among the Kurds. The Kurds generally viewed the suicide bombings as the PKK's attempt to remain relevant, and the Kurds also tended to blame the PKK for subsequent Turkish security actions instead of rallying to the PKK's cause. The PKK's actions were interesting, however, in that they demonstrated the sustained use of suicide bombers by an avowedly secular group in a campaign that could be turned on and off by the decision of a single individual.[34]

At the same time that the PKK started its campaign in the mid-1990s, various Islamic militant groups also began incorporating suicide bombing into their operations. For example both Al-Gama'a al-Islamiya and the Armed Islamic Group (GIA) conducted scattered suicide bombings against Egyptian and Algerian targets respectively. Both groups largely abandoned

---
[33] Pedahzur, 86-91.
[34] Ibid., 91-95.

suicide bombing after only a few attacks, but the stage was set for the further proliferation of suicide bombing. While the GIA operated almost exclusively within Algeria, Al-Gama'a's attacks in such widespread locations as Pakistan and Croatia previewed the geographic dispersal of suicide bombings. Previously, groups such as Hezbollah, the LTTE and HAMAS attacked only within narrow geographic confines. This changed as truly transnational organizations started to adopt the tactic.[35]

Although little noted at the time, al-Qaeda initiated its suicide bombing campaign against the United States and its allies when it bombed a U.S. defense contractor building in Riyadh on November 13th, 1995 (5 dead, 11 wounded).[36] Al-Qaeda suicide bombing has typically been characterized by several distinctive features: meticulous and lengthy planning, a preference for simultaneous and spectacular attacks, and the first truly trans-national suicide bombing capability. Indeed, it was three years until the next al-Qaeda suicide bombing operation, the simultaneous bombings of the U.S. embassies in Kenya and Tanzania (291 dead, 4,000+ wounded and 10 dead, 77 wounded respectively). Much as Hezbollah made a name for itself with a limited number of suicide bombings, so too did al-Qaeda emerge from relative obscurity to become one of the world's most prominent terrorist groups. Even though two more years passed until al-Qaeda's next suicide bombing against the *U.S.S. Cole* in Yemen in October 2000 (17 dead, 39 wounded), it had already vaulted to the top of the list of threats against the United States.[37]

As audacious as these attacks were, they paled in comparison with what remains the most spectacular suicide bombing operation to date: the September 11th, 2001 attacks on the United States. Notably, the entire operation required extensive planning, synchronization and operational reach. Just two days prior, al-Qaeda managed to assassinate Northern Alliance leader Shah Masoud when two suicide bombers posing as journalists detonated their bomb hidden inside

---

[35] Ibid.), 104-105.
[36] Pape, 270.
[37] Yoram Schweitzer, "Al-Qaeda and Epidemic of Suicide Attacks," in *Root Causes of Suicide Terrorism*, (New York: Routledge, 2006), 142-143.

a camera. Presumably, al-Qaeda sought to cripple the Northern Alliance to mitigate potential American military reaction to the upcoming 9/11 attacks. Although Masoud's assassination did not ultimately prevent al-Qaeda from losing its Afghan safe haven, three out of four hijacked aircraft hit their assigned targets on 9/11, and this operation alone accounts for 20% of all suicide bombing fatalities since 1980.[38]

Al-Qaeda's most significant innovations to suicide bombing were to adopt a venture capital approach, and once they lost their Afghan sanctuary, to transition to a distributed, and often virtual training program. Previously, groups employing suicide bombers provided the entire background infrastructure themselves. However, al-Qaeda was content to provide training to a network of loosely affiliated terror organizations and then leverage those contacts to facilitate geographically dispersed attacks that relied primarily upon locals. This artfully avoided having to move personnel and explosives across international borders and resulted in a much lower signature for security forces to track.

Al-Qaeda continued to conduct its own suicide bombings after its expulsion from Afghanistan, but the overall campaign is now more accurately described as al-Qaeda inspired. By replacing its Afghan training camps with ideological and technical material on the internet and the occasional traveling expert, al-Qaeda replicated a significant portion of its pre-9/11 capability. This was reflected by the July 2005 suicide bombings in England against three trains and one bus (52 dead, 466+ wounded). British citizens who operated relatively independently and likely received general assistance from al-Qaeda during visits to Pakistan perpetrated these attacks. Similarly, Jemaah Islamiyah began employing suicide bombers to strike Western-related targets in Southeast Asia based on its association with Al-Qaeda.[39] Thus, al-Qaeda's campaign against the United States and allied governments continues in the form of both al-Qaeda-only bombings

---

[38] Ibid., 142-143.
[39] Ibid., 144-145.

and a series of suicide bombings by associated groups that have received varying degrees of ideological, financial and technical assistance.

Another Islamic group that initiated a clearly identifiable suicide bombing campaign was the Chechen rebels. Operating under a variety of names such as the Riyadh-as-Saliheen Martyrs' Brigade (RaS), the Special Purpose Islamic Regiment, and the International Islamic Brigade (IIB), the Chechens alternately claimed or denied credit for numerous suicide attacks that targeted both Russian military and civilian targets. Chechen rebels continue to seek to pressure Russian leaders to make concessions, with the overall goal of establishing an independent Islamic republic in Chechnya. Much like al-Qaeda, the Chechens tended to favor fewer, more spectacular attacks. They averaged only about 10 attacks a year from 2000 through 2006. However, nearly all attacks featured large vehicle-borne bombs or coordinated assaults with multiple suicide bombers (73% of all attacks).[40]

Similar to the LTTE and the PKK, the Chechens made extensive use of female suicide bombers. Popularly known as the "Black Widows," many of these women are believed to have lost male loved ones in the Chechen conflict. The Chechens initially restricted women to traditional support roles such as medical care and supply, but the steady influence of outside Islamic groups and battlefield losses resulted in an altered role for women. By 2003, women were participating in the vast majority of Chechen suicide bombings, often to avenge brutal Russian counterinsurgency methods. The attacks have also become even more violent over time. Initial suicide bombings primarily concentrated on military and police targets, but as these targets hardened, there was a gradual switch to softer, civilian targets.[41] Much like the Israeli-Palestinian conflict, the Chechen campaign can only be expected to continue until a comprehensive settlement is attained.

---

[40] Pape, 185.
[41] Bloom, 153-155.

In Kashmir, groups such as Lashkar-e-Taiba (LET) and Jaish-e-Muhammed (JEM) also adopted suicide bombing in their fight against India. However, suicide bombing has been more of an occasional feature of a long-running armed struggle rather than the centerpiece. Thus, JEM led its December, 2001 assault on the Indian Parliament with a car bomb, but it was just part of the overall operation. The main reason for only 20 suicide bombings over the past decade is the lack of infrastructure and societal support with Kashmir itself. Virtually all of the suicide bombings have been by non-Kashmiris infiltrating in from Pakistan. Given the opposition to suicide bombing by such truly indigenous Kashmiri groups as Hizbul Mujahideen, suicide bombing in Kashmir is likely to remain the near-exclusive domain of militants from Pakistan and be accordingly rare.[42]

Perhaps the most alarming development in suicide bombing has been its exponential increase in both Afghanistan and Iraq. In fact, the relative success of suicide bombing in Iraq appears to have been the catalyst for the resurgent Taliban use of significant numbers of suicide bombers. Despite the divergent ideologies and goals of the various factions in Iraq, they are all pursuing what Mohammed Hafez identified as a "system collapse strategy." Namely, each group seeks to create a failed state and presumably achieve a power base in the resulting aftermath. Thus, organizations that employ suicide bombers such as the Ba'athists, the Ansar al-Sunna Army, and the Mujahideen Shura Council can be grouped within a single campaign with the goal of undermining the nascent American-backed Iraqi government.[43]

A distinguishing characteristic of the suicide bombing campaign in Iraq has been its unrivaled intensity. It grew from a few scattered bombings during the conventional month-long combat phase in Operation Iraqi Freedom (OIF), to include 217 suicide bombings in 2004, 646 attacks in 2005 and another 423 suicide bombings in 2006. It easily surpassed the campaigns by

---

[42] Mia Bloom, "Motivations for Suicide Terrorism," in *Root Causes of Suicide Terrorism*, (New York: Routledge, 2006), 29-30.
[43] Mohammed Hafez, "Suicide Terrorism in Iraq," in *Studies in Conflict & Terrorism, 29*, (Routledge, 2006), 595.

both the LTTE in Sri Lanka and the entire collection of Palestinian groups against Israel. The campaign in Iraq has also been exceptionally brutal and bloody. Seemingly no target is out-of-bounds: mosques, markets, churches, crowds of civilians, and humanitarian organizations have all been targeted. Of course, Coalition forces in Iraq rapidly strengthened their vehicles, tactics and bases to thwart suicide bombers, making attacks against soft targets and Iraqi security forces more profitable by comparison. In contrast to the Ba'athists, who mainly target Coalition military forces, some groups are specifically looking to inflame sectarian tension, making Iraqi civilians the desired target.[44] Thus, some two-and-a-half decades after its emergence on the world stage, suicide bombing remains a viable tactic and has already played a significant role in shaping the eventual form of the post-OIF Iraq.

Much as insurgent groups in Iraq employ suicide bombings to cause a system collapse in Iraq, the Taliban have recently adopted a similar strategy. Suicide bombings in Afghanistan skyrocketed from only a single case in 2001 during the initial war, to just two cases in both 2002 and 2003, to five bombings in 2004, to 27 suicide bombers in 2005, to an unprecedented 133 in 2006. The global proliferation and acceptance of suicide bombing is clearly evident, given its near absence during the 10-year war against Soviet occupation little more than a decade earlier. The Taliban's campaign also serves as an example of a more traditional, sub-national suicide bombing campaign against a foreign occupation. To a greater extent than Iraq, the future of Afghanistan is still in the balance, but suicide bombing will remain a key tactic employed by those seeking to avoid the emergence a stable, moderately Western-friendly government.

Suicide bombing's most salient characteristic has been its steady exponential growth during the past 25 years. Once Hezbollah proved its efficacy, suicide bombing spread across the globe and was adopted by such secular groups as the LTTE, the PFLP, and the PKK. The vast majority of the suicide bombing campaigns took place at the sub-national level, adopted by the

---

[44] Ibid., 608.

weaker party operating within a relatively small geographic area. Occupation, or at least perceived occupation as in Sri Lanka, was usually a critical ingredient.[45] Religion played an important role in suicide bombing, including developing a culture that supported the use of the tactic, but it was not necessarily a causal factor.[46]

Only al-Qaeda has been successful at conducting suicide bombings on a truly transnational scale. Alone among terrorist groups, it has leveraged ideology, feelings of injustice and humiliation, and technology such as the internet to advance suicide bombing from a localized phenomenon to one that now touches upon every individual regardless of whether he or she lives in a traditional conflict zone or not.[47] The challenge for the United States and its allies will be to draw the right the lessons from suicide bombings past to best mitigate their impact and ultimately their use in the future.

## LOGIC OF SUICIDE BOMBING

**STRATEGIC LOGIC** – Virtually every suicide bombing is conducted by an organization and takes place within the context of an overall campaign. Of the 2,202 suicide bombings listed in this monograph, 2,157, or 98%, fall within an identifiable campaign. Rare is the individual who spontaneously decides to become a suicide bomber. In fact, only 45 of the identified suicide bombings were conducted by lone individuals or unwitting bombers. Some reports out of Iraq indicate that in 2006 insurgents started to kidnap people, booby-trap their cars, release the kidnap victims and then detonate their cars when they reached viable targets such as police checkpoints. It is unclear if using kidnap victims is a result of a shortage of suicide bombers or simply to create a less suspicious car bomb, but the use of such tactics would

---

[45] Assaf Moghadam, "Suicide Terrorism, Occupation, and the Globalization of Martyrdom," in *Studies in Conflict & Terrorism, 29,* (Routledge, 2006), 720-721.
[46] Hafez, *Manufacturing Human Bombs*, 10.
[47] Moghadam, 721-723.

doubtless increase the numbers of unwitting bombers.[48] However, an operational capability to create unwitting bombers point to a highly sophisticated network that is at least as dangerous as one conducting a conventional suicide bombing campaign. The following table summarizes suicide bombings from 1981 through 2006 and groups them into 15 identifiable campaigns:

| Campaign | Country | Attacks | Dead | Wounded | Ongoing? |
|---|---|---|---|---|---|
| Hezbollah v. U.S./France | Lebanon | 5 | 389 | 318 | No |
| Hezbollah v. Israel/SLA | Lebanon | 49 | 497 | 945 | No |
| Liberation Tigers of Tamil Eelam | Sri Lanka | 120 | 1,431 | 4,671 | Yes |
| HAMAS/PIJ/PFLP/Fatah v. Israel | Israel | 237 | 739 | 5,003 | Yes |
| Egyptian militants v. Egypt govt | Egypt | 11 | 110 | 357 | Yes |
| Chechen militants v. Russia govt | Russia | 59 | 603 | 1,637 | Yes |
| Al-Qaeda network v. Western govt | Global | 62 | 3,750 | 9,573 | Yes |
| PKK v. Turkish govt | Turkey | 27 | 31 | 206 | No |
| Kashmiri separatists v. India govt | Kashmir/India | 26 | 115 | 387 | Yes |
| Pakistani militants v. Pakistan govt | Pakistan | 28 | 469 | 1,246 | Yes |
| Taliban v. U.S./ Afghan govt | Afghanistan | 170 | 391 | 1,076 | Yes |
| Iraq militants v. U.S./Iraqi govt | Iraq | 1,344 | 7,825 | 20,332 | Yes |
| IMU v. Uzbek govt | Uzbekistan | 8 | 20 | 44 | Yes |
| JMB v. Bangladesh govt | Bangladesh | 7 | 46 | 276 | Yes |
| ICU v. Somali govt | Somalia | 4 | 8 | 28 | Yes |
| None | | 45 | 315 | 854 | |
| **Total** | | **2,202** | **16,739** | **46,899** | |

Invariably, the group conducting suicide bombings is the weaker side in an insurgency or guerilla conflict. This is the one characteristic that is consistent despite religion, geography, ideology or ethnicity. Suicide bombing is also only one tactic among many that are employed by a group. Interestingly, groups do not use only suicide bombers, but they also use them in conjunction with more conventional tactics such as shootings, regular bombings, assassinations and indirect fire. Suicide bombing is simply the most extreme option available among a range of activities, and organizations employ it when it appears favorable.[49] The LTTE, for example, largely suspended its use of suicide bombers from the end of 2001 until early 2006. This was

---

[48] David Rising, "Iraqis Using Kidnap Victims as Bombers," (21 September 2006) available at: http://www.washingtonpost.com/wp-dyn/content/article/2006/09/21/AR2006092101009.html : internet; accessed 12 November, 2006.

[49] Bloom, "Motivations for Suicide Terrorism," 28.

during a period when the armed struggle continued, but LTTE leaders judged that they could achieve their political aims without suicide bombings. However, once the LTTE was frustrated with the slow pace of negotiations, it made the decision to readopt suicide bombing as part of its tactical repertoire (14 attacks in 2006).

Although the individual bomber is, by definition, expendable, groups conducting suicide bombing campaigns have objectives that extend far beyond the attacks themselves. Organizations employing suicide bombers pursue rational goals that include: achieving political goals, punishing enemy states or societies, attacking specific targets, and mobilizing support for their cause.[50]

Far from being senseless acts of destruction, suicide bombing campaigns are a part of a broader effort on the part of an insurgent or terrorist group to force concessions by a state or society regarding territory the insurgents or terrorists regard as their homeland. Using what would be recognized as a rational cost-benefit analysis, the group decides that suicide bombing is the best method to achieve its goals. The prototypical example is Hezbollah's highly successful campaign to drive the U.S. and France from Lebanon in the early 1980s. With just five suicide bombings, a small, little-known militia movement was able to compel the withdrawal of the entire U.N. peacekeeping force and reverse the foreign policy of four major Western governments. Significantly, Hezbollah also halted its suicide bombing campaign once it met its political aims.

Suicide bombing used as punishment on a state or society is largely a subset of the larger goal of achieving political goals. However, Pape describes the subtle distinction between punishment and denial as coercive strategies. Specifically, a punishment strategy seeks to impose a prohibitively high cost on a rival society for a given course of action. In contrast, a denial strategy seeks to illustrate to a target society that it cannot achieve its objectives, regardless of level of effort. Since, to date, groups using suicide bombers have always been the weaker side,

---

[50] U.S. Army TRADOC, II-1.

they must rely upon a punishment framework. They simply do not possess the strength to pursue a credible denial strategy.[51] Although the long-term goal remains to force political concessions, some suicide bombings are conducted purely for punishment motivations, as when HAMAS conducted three attacks in the aftermath of Israel's assassination of leading bomb maker Yahya Ayyash ("The Engineer") in 1996. HAMAS specifically stated that its attacks were in response to the killing, and although they fit within the larger effort against Israel, these particular attacks were launched in direct response to Israeli actions.

Some high value targets are protected to the point that only a suicide bomber has a reasonable chance. A prime example is al-Qaeda's assassination of Northern Alliance leader Ahmad Shah Masoud in Afghanistan on 9 September, 2001 (2 dead, 2 wounded). Knowing that the U.S. would likely respond to the 9/11 attacks with military action against their sanctuary in Afghanistan, al-Qaeda presumably sought to remove the most capable opposition figure. However, he was closely guarded, and al-Qaeda spent months infiltrating two members into his camp. The bombers posed as journalists and detonated a bomb hidden in their camera once they gained access to interview Masoud.[52] Assuming that an organization has suicide bombers at its disposal, it makes perfect sense to employ them selectively against the most important targets. Indeed, 5.31% of suicide bombings (117 of 2,202) have been assassinations or attempted assassinations.

Finally, an organization may pursue suicide bombing in order to mobilize support within a society. This is particularly evident when there are multiple organizations pursuing the same goal, as in the Palestinian territories. Specifically, groups often resort to suicide bombing in order demonstrate their total devotion to their cause and to "outbid" other groups. A prime example is the Marxist-Leninist Popular Front for the Liberation of Palestine (PFLP). The PFLP refrained from suicide bombings until October, 2001, when it adopted the tactics and language of the more

---

[51] Pape, 29-30.
[52] Ami Pedahzur, 20.

successful HAMAS, Palestinian Islamic Jihad (PIJ) and other groups that had gained popular support. Founded in 1967, the PFLP did not perceive the need to use suicide bombers until 34 years later when it was losing "market share" to other organizations that were regarded as more committed and effective in large part because of their willingness to employ suicide bombers.[53] Similarly, two years after HAMAS' spiritual leader Sheikh Yassin "categorically renounced the use of women as suicide bombers," the group reversed itself and started to use female bombers. Although HAMAS justified this change in part due to the tactical advantages of infiltrating women into Israel, a significant concern was that other Palestinian groups had started using female bombers and HAMAS had to use this previously excluded resource in order to maintain popular support.[54]

**TACTICAL LOGIC -** The numerous tactical advantages of using suicide bombers versus trying to deliver bombs and maintain a reasonable chance of escape argue strongly in favor of opting for the suicide bomber. Specifically, suicide bombers offer: increased tactical flexibility and effectiveness, streamlined operational planning, less likelihood of intelligence leaks, expanded target sets, limited vulnerability, and increased publicity and psychological impact on the target population.[55]

Regarding tactical flexibility, suicide bombers act as the ultimate "smart bombs," since they are able to adjust to local conditions until the final second before detonation. This flexibility and precision in delivery allows for attacks against even heavily defended or otherwise impervious targets. In effect, suicide bombers replicate the attributes of both stealth and guided weapons without the need for the extensive infrastructure and cost to maintain them. On average, suicide bombers are vastly more effective than traditional attacks. Attacks classified as suicide assaults accounted for only 3% of terrorist attacks from 1980-2001, but they caused a full 48% of

---

[53] Bloom, *Dying to Kill*, 33-34.
[54] Debra Zedalis, "Female Suicide Bombers," (Carlise, PA: Strategic Studies Institute, June 2004), 7.
[55] Bunker and Sullivan, 73.

all deaths at terrorist hands (even excluding the 9/11 attacks).[56] It only makes sense to employ the most effective weapon available, and there is no question about the proven efficacy of suicide bombers relative to other forms of attack.

Using suicide bombers also allows for simplified operational planning, since there is no need to develop escape plans. Additionally, there is little worry of a suicide bomber being interrogated to reveal valuable intelligence. The bombers themselves are mere foot soldiers and are normally kept relatively isolated from other, compartmented aspects of operations. Thus, in the unlikely event they are captured, the most they can reveal is limited details about the recruitment process and some information about a specific point target.

Once the bomber is dispatched, some form of success is virtually guaranteed. Unlike a conventional bomb, there is no window of vulnerability during which the bomb can be detected and disarmed. Even if security forces detect the bomber before he or she reaches the intended target, the bomber can still activate the device and potentially cause significant damage and casualties.[57]

Suicide bombings offer the additional advantages of greater publicity and psychological effect upon the target populations. The globalization of media and the 24-hour news cycle serve to ensure coverage of successful suicide bombings, and they produce greater coverage and dissemination than non-suicide attacks of similar scale. Despite thousands of conventional terrorist attacks against Israel, suicide bombings continue to receive a disproportionate share of press reporting. This, in turn, helps spur terrorist groups that are in competition with other groups for popular support and resources to employ suicide bombers to prove their commitment and

---

[56] Robert A. Pape, "The Strategic Logic of Suicide Terrorism," *American Political Science Review*, Vol 97, No 3 (August 2003), 5.
[57] Bunker and Sullivan, 70.

effectiveness.[58] The explicit willingness to die in the commission of an attack also sends a powerful message to target audiences and heightens the impact of the attack.

Perhaps most importantly, the mere potential of a suicide bombing causes significant changes in the behavior and tactics of the opposing force or society. Two poignant examples are the Israeli construction of its security wall and the interaction of U.S. forces in Iraq. Israel accelerated the deployment of its massive security system of fences, walls and intrusion prevention devices almost exclusively because of suicide bombers. Interestingly, Israel did not feel the need to construct such a barrier system during five decades of infiltration by Palestinian guerillas. Yet Israel was willing to undertake its largest and most expensive infrastructure project to prevent suicide bombings.[59] Likewise, massive blast barriers encircle every U.S. bases in Iraq, and every outpost maintains extensive entry control mechanisms. While these tactics are effective at mitigating the suicide bombers, they dramatically decrease contact and rapport between the local populace and Coalition troops. Assuming that the local people are the real prize during an insurgency, the insurgent garners an enormous advantage by forcing the government forces to adopt restrictive force protection measures.

The only drawback from a tactical perspective is that the suicide bomber is a "one-shot" weapon. All of the resources used to train and prepare the bomber are lost once he or she is employed. Terrorist groups must strike a balance between using individuals who are smart and sophisticated enough to blend into the target society long enough to execute their mission and simultaneously be expendable. Unfortunately, this is a minimal consideration for most groups, since there appears to be no shortage of willing and able bombers.

For example, recruitment of Palestinian suicide bombers was once an involved affair requiring months of training, indoctrination and preparation. Over time, however, suicide

---

[58] Bloom, *Dying to Kill*, 39, 79.
[59] Israeli Ministry of Defense, "Execution Aspects of the Security Fence," available at: http://www.securityfence.mod.gov.il/Pages/ENG/execution.htm ; internet; accessed 20 Jan 07.

bombing became acceptable enough within Palestinian society that organizations using suicide bombers were inundated with walk-in volunteers. HAMAS refined its procedures such that the suicide bombers themselves require only a few days of preparation. Separate cells conduct reconnaissance, prepare the bomb itself, and facilitate delivering the bomber to the target. The bombers are culled from the numerous volunteers identified during HAMAS-sponsored religious studies courses.[60] Similarly, Hezbollah reported a decade after it stopped dispatching suicide bombers in southern Lebanon that its stable of volunteers had actually increased. Thus, the decision to devote resources to identify, assess and recruit suicide operatives had changed to the point that all it needed to do was select the cream of the crop from the numerous applicants.[61]

**INDIVIDUAL LOGIC** – The most important concept for understanding individual motivations for becoming a suicide bomber is to differentiate altruistic suicide from egoistic or fatalistic suicide. Egoistic suicide is the most common form, and it involves a person who is both detached from society and suffers a personal trauma such as divorce or the loss of a loved one. Most people weather these travails with the help of friends, faith and family. A very small minority decide the pain is too great and commit suicide in order to escape their own pain. Individuals normally plan and execute their suicide attempts in private without the intent to harm anyone else. In contrast, fatalistic suicides occur among those who live among a small group within a physically isolated compound, commonly under the influence of a charismatic leader. The group commits suicide *en masse*, typically under the threat of intrusion by outsiders or the predicted Apocalypse. The mass suicide by over 900 followers of Jim Jones in Guyana in 1978 and the 77 followers of David Koresh who burned to death in Texas in 1993 are prime examples of fatalistic suicide. Group members form societal bonds, but only within their small, select

---

[60] Pape, *Dying to Win*, 232.
[61] Pedahzur, 160.

faction. Not surprisingly, society disapproves of both egoistic and fatalistic suicides and exerts considerable pressure to deter such actions.[62]

The one form of suicide that society does approve of is altruistic suicide. Notably, this occurs when an individual sacrifices his or her own life for the common good. An example is the U.S. Navy SEAL who jumped onto a grenade in order to protect the remaining three members of his sniper team in Iraq in late 2006. The media coverage of the event was laudatory, and he has been recommended for medals for his actions.[63] Similarly, a bystander who sacrifices his or her life to help rescue someone in peril is widely regarded as a hero who performed a noble act. Significantly, a person who commits altruistic suicide displays a high level of social connection – the direct opposite of those attempting egoistic suicide. Another key distinction of altruistic suicide is that the actor is forced to make a decision to give his or her life. Absent a specific danger or event, the altruistic individual would continue living: the person committing egoistic suicide specifically seeks to end his or her life.

Most of the research on suicide in the West focuses on egoistic suicide, and this frames our concept of who commits suicide. Specifically, such individuals are perceived to be those with a psychopathology, poor coping skills and limited attachment to society. This helps to explain the common description of suicide bombers as nihilistic, unstable, irrational or deranged. In fact, the opposite is usually true of suicide bombers. Substantial research indicates that suicide bombers display none of the dysfunctional and suicidal attributes normally associated with suicidal acts.[64]

Suicide bombers clearly believe that they are committing a form of altruistic suicide in furtherance of the common good. Far from seeking to wantonly destroy society, their social

---

[62] Pape, *Dying to Win*, 173-179.
[63] Thomas Watkins, "SEAL Falls on Grenade to Save Comrades," (13 October, 2006), internet; available at http://www.shoutwire.com/viewstory/34138/SEAL_Falls_on_Grenade_to_Save_Comrades ; accessed 20 January, 2007.
[64] Scott Atran, "Genesis and Future of Suicide Terrorism," (4) internet, available at http://www.interdisciplines.org/terrorism/papers/1/printable/paper ; accessed 9 September, 2006.

bonds are so strong and nurtured by recruiters that they honestly believe in the goodness of their act. Importantly, one must avoid the fundamental attribution error of focusing on personality traits to the exclusion of situational factors when assessing suicide bombers. Suicide bombers are specifically not homicidal maniacs who will definitively seek to detonate themselves and kill others. Rather, they are heavily influenced by perceptions of injustice, humiliation and subservience and view their decision to conduct a suicide bombing as a legitimate act that will advance the ultimate wellbeing of their larger community.[65]

In addition to contributing to a common cause, there are personal benefits that accrue to a suicide bomber, particularly within Muslim society. Assuming that the bomber is generally considered a martyr (*shahid*), the act is accepted as the fulfillment of a religious command and is specifically not suicide. Accordingly, the social status of the bomber and the bomber's family increases. The bomber's family also typically receives financial compensation, often in the range of thousands of dollars. For Muslims, a *shahid* is granted eternal life in paradise, the service of 72 virgins, and the ability to secure a place in heaven for 70 of his or her relatives. Not surprisingly, suicide bombers' pre-attack wills are often upbeat and exhort family to be happy because the bomber will ascend directly to heaven and there will be a family reunion there.[66]

A final individual motivation may be revenge. This can be a result of personal loss or broader revenge for an aggrieved society. For example, many of the female Black Widow suicide bombers from Chechnya lost close relatives at the hands of security forces, and 27-year-old Palestinian lawyer Hanadi Jaradat detonated herself in Haifa, Israel's Maxim restaurant (21 dead, 60 wounded) in October, 2003 after her brother and cousin were killed by Israeli security forces.[67] A personal connection is not required, and numerous bombers report being motivated by the perceived loss and suffering of their identified community. Specifically, two failed

---

[65] Ibid., 3.
[66] Ganor, 2.
[67] Hafez, *Manufacturing Human Bombs*, 49.

Palestinian suicide bombers reported: "Pictures of dead kids had a major effect on me," and "The truth is that beforehand I saw pictures of dead and wounded children on television."[68] Although there may be a belief that a suicide bombing will contribute in some small part to an eventual reversal of the apparent wrongs, the dominant motivation may be to make an outside group pay for having committed these wrongs in the first place.

## SOCIAL LOGIC

An important condition that must be met to allow a suicide bombing campaign to continue is a critical mass of social support that views the use of the tactic as a legitimate tactic to meet common goals. Specifically, insurgent and terrorist groups require some level of popular support to maintain their recruiting base, preserve operational security, and, most critically for suicide bombing campaigns, to have their suicide bombers widely regarded as martyrs in pursuit of community aims.[69]

All terrorist and insurgent groups require some level of popular support, even if it is coerced, in order to operate. By definition, the groups are fighting against a power structure and must take operational risks and expose themselves to general members of the populace. Local inhabitants possess enormous quantities of information that would be valuable to the legitimate security forces, so the terrorists and insurgents must be intimidating or popular enough that the civilians do not relay this information to the security organs. Not surprisingly, the more successful groups such as HAMAS and Hezbollah have used a combination of social outreach programs in conjunction with their military arms. This both helps maintain popular support and provides a wealth of data and connections to facilitate recruiting.

A good deal of group exposure takes place during recruiting activities, which require at least a small portion of the population to move beyond simple tacit support to take active measures. However, the pitifully small numbers required for a suicide bombing campaign means

---

[68] Bloom, "Motivations for Suicide Terrorism," 36.
[69] Pape, *Dying to Win*, 81.

that very few have to be committed to the extreme point of being willing to detonate themselves. For example, Hezbollah's entire campaign against Israel and the Southern Lebanese Army (SLA) from 1982 through 1999 consisted of only 49 bombings, and the average campaign has consisted of only 130 bombings. Thus, only a few true believers are required, and for the vast majority of groups opting to conduct suicide bombings, they have encountered little difficulty in recruiting more than enough actual bombers.

In order to maintain support and recruits, groups that employ suicide bombers must follow the additional step of ensuring that its members who deliberately take their own lives in the course of bombing the enemy are seen in a specific manner. In particular, developing what Mohammed Hafez describes as the "culture of martyrdom" is a critical enabler, without which the campaign will be unsustainable. Thus, organizations use a careful blend of religion, ritual, ceremony, and propaganda to build and continue a narrative that paints suicide bombers as "heroic martyrs." The framing of suicide bombers as martyrs provides the necessary link between the organization making the strategic decision to employ suicide bombers and the individuals who must volunteer for and actually carry out the missions. Prospective suicide bombers are not flocking to carry out operations because of the higher casualty rates of suicide versus non-suicide bombings, but they do respond to a reinforced marketing effort that portrays suicide bombing as offering both individual and community redemption.[70]

Significantly, groups typically employ religion in constructing their martyrdom narrative, but this is not a causal factor. Islamic culture, in particular, seems receptive to the ideal of redemptive self-sacrifice, but it is not a necessary pre-condition. For example, the LTTE were able to conceive of and execute a decades-long suicide bombing campaign that featured the eventual liberation their homeland as a centerpiece without reference to religious martyrdom.

---

[70] Mohammed Hafez, "Symbolic Dimension of Suicide Terrorism," in *Root Causes of Suicide Terrorism*, (New York: Routledge, 2006), 75-76.

Rather, LTTE suicide bombers were cast as martyrs for the greater cause of an independent Tamil homeland.

Unfortunately, suicide bombings create a feedback loop that often serves to reinforce societal support for such tactics once other tactics have been tried and failed. Terrorists and insurgents are very sensitive to this and are usually careful to calibrate their campaign to ensure a continued base of support within the larger community. For instance, HAMAS initially limited its targeting of Israeli civilians, but it soon reversed its position as support for suicide bombings grew within the Palestinian population. In large part, the increase in support resulted from the very actions the Israelis took to counter the suicide bombers. Heavy-handed responses to suicide bombers may enjoy limited effectiveness in the short run, but over time the civilian populations tend to blame the more powerful state forces for oppressive security measures. Ultimately, it is, of course, popular support that both the insurgent and the government vie for, and this is the true key to ending suicide bombings.[71]

## LIKELIHOOD OF SUICIDE BOMBING IN CONUS

Because there have been so few (5) suicide bombings within the U.S., any predictions must by necessity analyze worldwide patterns and extrapolate lessons from them. Fortunately, the 2,202 bombings over the past 25 years (appendix A) offer enough data to draw meaningful conclusions:

Over the near to mid-term, suicide bombing will remain a staple tactic of numerous groups that oppose U.S. interests, but only the al-Qaeda Network (AQN) has shown the will and operational reach to conduct suicide bombings within CONUS. The AQN remains fully committed to and capable of attacking U.S. interests, both abroad and to a much lesser extent within the U.S. Future AQN attacks will likely resemble the London train bombings more than previous grandiose AQN-directed attacks such as the 9/11 attacks due to the morphing of AQN

---

[71] Bloom, *Dying to Kill*, 88-94.

operational procedures and its loss of sanctuary in Afghanistan. The only other realistic sources of suicide bombers in CONUS are Hezbollah and Iran's Islamic Revolutionary Guards Corps-Quds Force (IRGC-QF) in response to events in the Middle East.

Significantly, the U.S. should also expect suicide bombings against its forces wherever it intervenes militarily and against its direct and indirect interests overseas. Since U.S. conventional military power is unmatched, adversaries will naturally seek some way to overcome this disparity. Suicide bombing offers one proven and cost-effective method to counter this U.S. strength. High-profile suicide bombings against U.S.-affiliated civilian targets abroad will also continue given its widespread proliferation, adoption, and acceptance as a legitimate tactic by terrorist groups and significant segments of civilization.

## FUTURE SUICIDE BOMBINGS IN CONUS

Future suicide bombings within the continental United States (CONUS) are virtually guaranteed due to: the perceived success of this tactic, its proliferation across the globe and among disparate groups, and the relative ease with which such operations can be executed. As noted in the below table and drawn from the data in Appendix A, suicide bombings have seen exponential growth over the past decade, and they will continue for the foreseeable future:

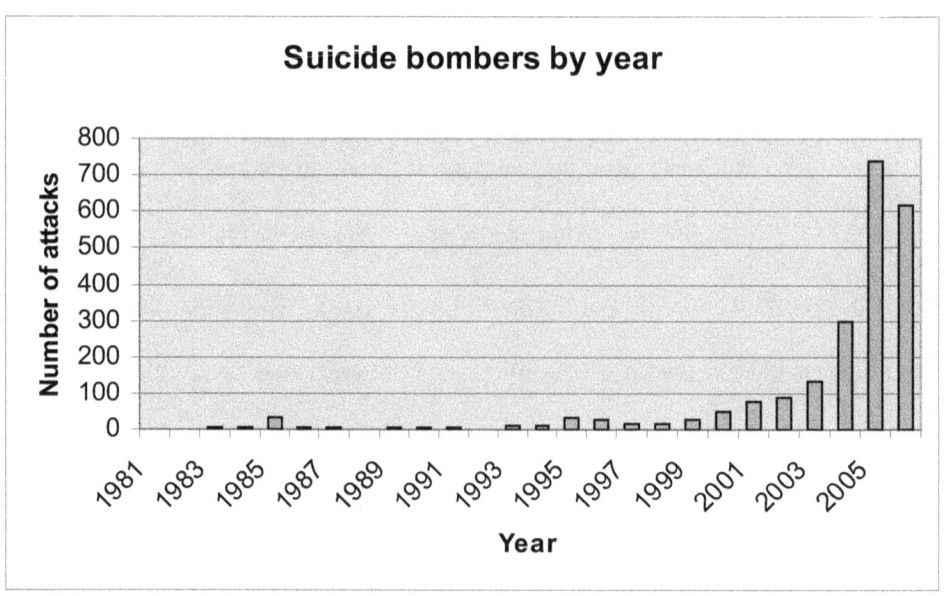

Absent military intervention in a foreign territory, the only group that has shown the motivation and capability of conducting suicide bombings against the U.S. is al-Qaeda. Before 9/11, suicide bombers targeted the U.S. only eight times, split evenly between four attacks by Hezbollah in Lebanon and four attacks by al-Qaeda. These attacks accounted for just 3.2% of all suicide bombings in the world (8 of 251). Of note, suicide bombings by Hezbollah against the U.S. stopped in 1984 once U.S. forces withdrew from Lebanon. From 1985-2001, of the at least 19 groups using suicide bombers, the sole organization directly targeting the U.S. was al-Qaeda. Even post-9/11, the AQN remains the only organization targeting the U.S. with suicide bombers outside of the active combat zones of Afghanistan and Iraq. Thus, efforts to mitigate future suicide bombers in CONUS should focus on the AQN and its operational characteristics. Additional groups with the means and motive to attack the U.S. homeland might materialize, but there will likely be a considerable warning period as they emerge and grow in capability.

Attack methodology also follows patterns, and groups tend to specialize in specific types of suicide bombing. For example, only 16% of all Palestinian suicide bombings (38 of 237) involved car or truck bombs. A person wearing a suicide belt or carrying a bag delivered the remainder. This is likely a result of Israeli security measures that made it more cost effective and practical to concentrate on person-borne devices. Likewise, the LTTE pioneered the use of suicide boats. Because of the maritime geography of Sri Lanka, 38.3% of all LTTE suicide bombings (46 of 120) involved boat bombs or suicide divers delivering mines.

Prior to 9/11, a- Qaeda attacks were characterized by: centralized planning, large-scale operations, multiple simultaneous bombings, and targeting the U.S. directly. The dual bombings of the U.S. embassies in Tanzania and Kenya in 1998 are textbook examples. However, since 9/11, al-Qaeda operations have morphed significantly. Al-Qaeda lost its sanctuary in Afghanistan, and thus its ability to maintain both large-scale training camps that processed thousands of recruits and a relatively effective command and control structure. Consequently, al-

Qaeda is now more of ideological entity that provides the motivation, justification and inspiration for attacks.

AQN attacks fall into two distinct categories: al-Qaeda-sponsored attacks and al-Qaeda-inspired attacks. Al-Qaeda itself tends to favor vehicle-borne explosives. A full 64.5% of its suicide bombings (40 of 62) entailed delivery by some form of vehicle, and until May of 2003 al-Qaeda only used non-vehicle bombings in the two special cases of assassinating Ahmad Shah Masoud and attempting to detonate a shoe bomb aboard an airliner. This makes sense when viewed within the context of al-Qaeda's penchant for large-scale attacks, since vehicles can carry vastly more explosives than an individual. In contrast, al-Qaeda-inspired attacks are more likely to be performed by recent immigrants who live in the target countries, procure the explosives locally, are largely self-financed, use person-borne devices, and have only a tenuous connection to al-Qaeda.

In lieu of fixed training facilities, al-Qaeda has replicated much of its previous training regimen, albeit in a marginally degraded state, in the virtual realm. Both financing and command and control are much more difficult, so attacks are more likely to be conceived and planned at the local level with less financial backing from al-Qaeda. The London train bombings in July 2005 (52 dead, 466+ wounded) offer a model of the type of attack to expect in the U.S. in the future.

In contrast to the 9/11 attacks when al-Qaeda infiltrated its operatives into the U.S., home-grown British citizens conducted the London bombings. Three of the bombers were second-generation Pakistanis, and the fourth was a convert to Islam who was originally born in Jamaica. The operation appears to have been self-financed by the bombers themselves for only £8,000 (~$16,656), and they constructed the bombs themselves using commercially available materials in a small apartment that they rented for the purpose. Although it is possible that they obtained the bomb-making formula and procedures entirely from the internet, it is more likely that a more experienced bomb-builder gave them some training and/or assistance, possibly in Pakistan or Afghanistan. At least three of the bombers traveled to Pakistan and possibly went into Afghanistan, but their travels were not suspicious enough to raise red flags among the British intelligence services. Two of the bombers (Mohammad Sidique Khan and Shehzad Tanweer) came to the attention of British authorities at the periphery of other investigations into violent extremists, but at the time neither was marked for additional investigation or surveillance.[72]

On 7 July, 2005, the four bombers traveled into London's King's Cross station and boarded separate trains. At about 0850, three of the bombers detonated themselves aboard underground metro trains. Symbolically, the explosions appear to have been planned to form the crude shape of a cross radiating outward from King's Cross. The fourth bomber exploded himself almost an hour later on the upper deck of a London bus after purchasing a battery, likely after his bomb failed to detonate in the underground. Later, so-called martyrdom videos made by Khan and Tanweer made it clear that the suicide bombings were carried out in protest of British foreign policies. Both al-Qaeda itself and the AQN-linked Abu Hafs al-Masri Brigade claimed responsibility for the attacks. Two weeks later, another group of four young British Muslims attempted to detonate suicide bombs on three trains and a bus in London. Fortunately, the bombs failed, and only the detonators exploded. Authorities arrested all four would-be bombers within a week, and they made statements indicating that their bombing attempts were also in protest of British actions in Iraq and Afghanistan.

The instructive value from the London bombings is that the first successful suicide bombings in Western Europe were conducted by native-born citizens who drew inspiration from al-Qaeda but required little in the way of financing or material support. Given the heavy pressure on the traditional al-Qaeda sanctuaries and the increasingly effective screening of visitors coming into the U.S., future suicide bombings will likely resemble the London bombings. Namely, they will conducted by young, first or second-generation immigrants who are inspired and influenced

---

[72] House of Commons, "Report of the Official Account of the Bombings in London on 7th July 2005," (HC 1087, London, 11 May 2006), 13-23.

by al-Qaeda, but they will be able to procure and finance the necessary materials without extensive outside help.

Al-Qaeda will still carry out directly sponsored attacks, but these attacks will likely be concentrated in the Middle East, where its infrastructure and influence is strongest. The large U.S. troop presence in the region provides an ample array of targets that allows al-Qaeda to maintain a high enough operational tempo to demonstrate that it is standing up to the U.S. and retaining its relevance. Unfortunately, al-Qaeda has advanced beyond its previous innovation of using a venture capital approach to sponsor terrorism. No longer do groups have to plan attacks and ask for al-Qaeda financing. Instead, viral marketing is an apt metaphor for al-Qaeda-inspired attacks. Specifically, the AQN now leverages existing communication networks (both social and the internet) to give away its services (bomb-making expertise and justification) and takes advantage of others' resources (target country infrastructure).[73] Al-Qaeda simply provides the background information needed and allows autonomous or semi-autonomous locals to conduct distributed suicide bombings. Thus, it is only a matter of time before the London bombings are replicated within the United States.

### AQN ATTACKS AGAINST THE U.S.

The AQN has also shown both ingenuity and thoughtful targeting in its attacks. Specifically, the use of airplanes on 9/11 made use of the large commercial aviation infrastructure to create *de facto* cruise missiles without a need for a large investment by al-Qaeda. The hijackers also took advantage of well-known security loopholes that allowed small edged weapons onto aircraft and instructed aircrews and passengers to comply with hijackers. Other AQN attacks displayed similar ingenuity. The twin embassy bombings in Kenya and Tanzania in 1998 employed large vehicle-borne improvised explosive devices (VBIED), and al-Qaeda's next

---

[73] Dr. Ralph F. Wilson, "The Six Simple Principles of Viral Marketing," (1 Feb, 2000, Web Marketing Today) internet: available at: http://www.wilsonweb.com/wmt5/viral-principles.htm accessed 12 Mar 2007.

attack against the U.S. featured a boat bomb against a U.S. Navy warship in Yemen in 2000. Each attack featured a different target set (embassies, warship, commercial and government buildings) and different delivery means (truck, boat and airplanes). Unfortunately, security enhancements have traditionally lagged al-Qaeda's assessed operational and planning capability, so al-Qaeda suicide bombings have highlighted new vulnerabilities while the old ones were still being addressed.

Al-Qaeda attacks show a general pattern of striking targets of symbolic and economic importance, with a gradual shift in favor of the economic targets. For example, al-Qaeda's first four suicide bombings were against U.S. government and military targets, the 9/11 attacks were split evenly between government and civilian targets, and outside of Iraq, 79.2% of post-9/11 attacks (42 of 53) have been against other than government targets. Notably, the AQN has publicly identified oil as a particular vulnerability, and 2006 witnessed suicide bombings against oil refineries in both Yemen and Saudi Arabia, in addition to the maritime suicide bombing of a French oil tanker off the coast of Yemen in 2002. Al-Qaeda targeting guidance even stresses the importance of assailing Western economies, as in 2004 when it specifically stated that it wanted to "…destabilize the situation and not allow economic recovery…[and] scare foreign companies from working" in Islamic areas.[74]

Al-Qaeda has also shown a distinct tendency to attack the same target multiple times when the first assaults are not successful. For example, the 9/11 attacks were necessary only because the first bombing in 1993 failed to collapse one tower of the World Trade Center. Similarly, the bombing of *U.S.S. Cole* replicated an earlier attempted boat bombing of the *U.S.S. Sulllivans* that failed when the suicide boat sank before reaching its target. Thus, it is very reasonable to expect that the AQN will attempt attacks against targets from previous plots such as: the Capitol building, the Sears Tower in Chicago, and hotels in Las Vegas.

---

[74] Intelcenter, "al-Qaeda Targeting Guidance v1.0," (2004, Intelcenter/Tempest Publishing, Alexandria, VA) internet: available at: http://www.asisonline.org/newsroom/aq.pdf accessed 1 Mar 07, 7.

Within Iraq, it is impossible to disaggregate all of the al-Qaeda in Iraq (Tan zim Qa'idah il-Jihad fi Bilad ir-Rafidayn) suicide bombings from the numerous other suicide bombings in the country. The U.S. presence in Iraq is almost entirely military and government, so virtually all direct attacks against the U.S. fall into these categories. However, it is very clear that al-Qaeda pursues both governmental and non-governmental targets against U.S., Iraqi and foreign entities with an eye toward generating strategic effects. Specifically, al-Qaeda claimed credit for such suicide bombings in Iraq as the attacks against the Italians, the Poles, the Red Cross, the United Nations (UN), oil pumping stations in the Gulf, and assassination attempts against multiple Iraqi leaders. Sadly, this strategy has met with a great deal of success, as the UN and the Red Cross withdrew from Iraq almost immediately after being bombed, the Italians scaled back their presence and completely withdrew by the end of 2006, and Iraq's oil terminals remain under heavy U.S. and Iraqi security. The overall effect has been the successful execution of a "system collapse" campaign that has prevented the U.S. and its allies from being able to develop a stable, democratic, prosperous Iraq.

Although al-Qaeda's has a limited ability to attack in the U.S., it can be expected to maintain and even expand its suicide bombing infrastructure within the Middle East. Given the perceived success of this tactic, it will continue to grow as a methodology. Al-Qaeda will attack the U.S. directly whenever it can, but it will also be content to conduct suicide bombings against targets that contribute to an indirect assault on U.S. interests. AQN attacks can also be expected to display high degrees of novelty, be primarily vehicle-borne, be of larger scale and feature multiple attackers when possible, and generally be of strategic rather than just tactical value.

### FUTURE SUICIDE BOMBINGS AGAINST U.S. TARGETS OCONUS

Thomas Friedman cogently noted that the number one selling book in China concerned how to get your child into Harvard University while the Muslim world lauded suicide bombers. Predictably, societies that venerate education will eventually build their own Harvards, and societies that glorify suicide bombers produce better and better suicide bombers. At the moment, the AQN and others have succeeded in glorifying suicide bombers in the Muslim world. This glorification is not universal, but it has achieved enough of a critical mass that suicide bombing campaigns are now orders of magnitude greater than previous efforts. Hezbollah started the modern era of suicide bombing with a campaign of just five bombings and then one of only 49 bombings. The LTTE more than doubled this effort with 120 attacks, and the various Palestinian factions then doubled the LTTE's efforts with 237 suicide bombs. Both campaigns remain ongoing, but they pale in comparison to the new levels of violence in Afghanistan and Iraq. Iraq alone has produced 61% of all suicide bombings in the world (1,344 of 2,202), and Afghanistan is on pace to grow its current total of 170 suicide bombings to a point where it surpasses the previous gold standard of the Palestinian campaign against Israel. Notably, militants in Afghanistan began using suicide bombing only after observing its success in Iraq. These two campaigns now account for more than two-thirds of all of the world's suicide bombings (68.8%), and both remain in full gear.[75]

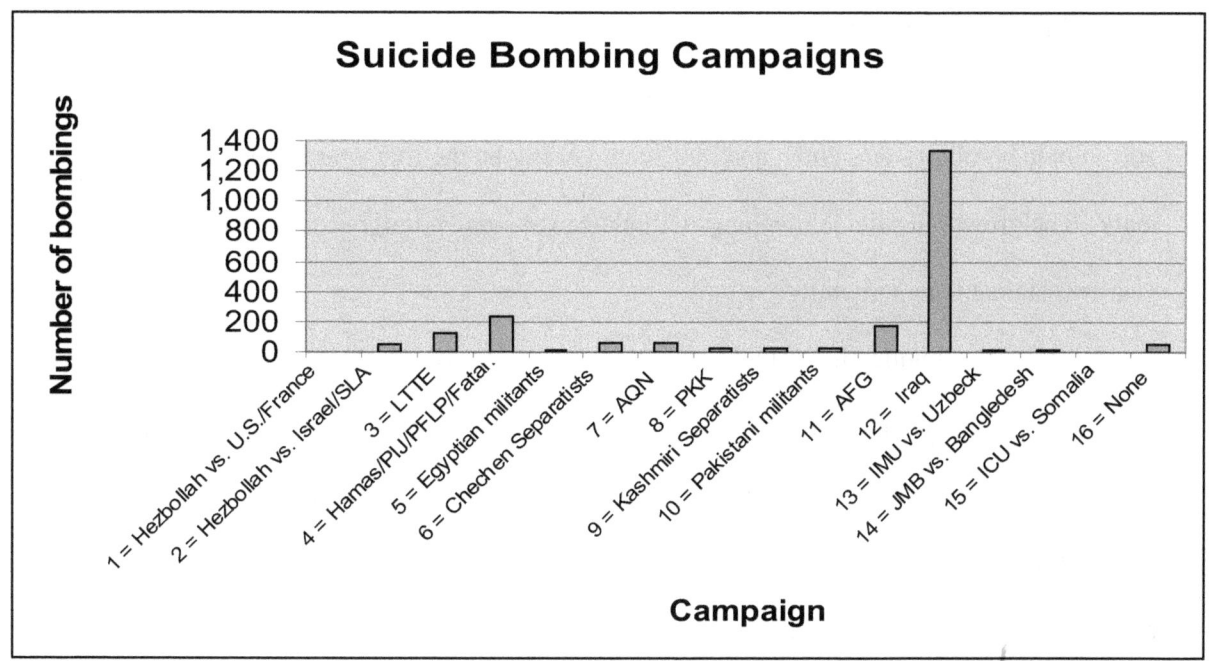

---

[75] The information in this paragraph, the above table, and the following two paragraphs is drawn from the list of suicide bombings presented in Appendix A.

Along with the overall growth of suicide bombings, suicide bombings against American targets overseas grew dramatically in the post-9/11 area, and they will be a staple of terrorist tactics for at least the near- to mid-term future. Of the eight suicide bombings against direct U.S. targets before 9/11, 62.5% were against embassies (5 of 8) and the other 37.5% (3 of 8) targeted U.S. military forces abroad. The attacks were also evenly split between Hezbollah and al-Qaeda with four each. Of course, Hezbollah would have presumably continued its campaign had the U.S. not withdrawn its forces from Lebanon.

After 9/11, suicide bombings directed specifically against U.S. targets took a brief hiatus, with only the failed attempt to down an airliner over the Atlantic at the end of 2001, and a single bombing in 2002 directed the U.S. Consulate in Pakistan (12 dead, 40 wounded). However, the U.S. invasion of Iraq in 2003 opened a new chapter in suicide bombing. Since Operation Iraqi Freedom (OIF) began, there have been at least 373 suicide bombings directed specifically against U.S. targets, with 97.6% of them (364 of 373) taking place in either Iraq or Afghanistan. The remaining 1,150 suicide bombings in Iraq and Afghanistan also indirectly target the U.S., since they aim to counter U.S. efforts to reshape those two societies. The first year to see more than 100 suicide bombings was 2003, and 2007 could easily be the first year to go over the 1,000 mark. The growth in suicide bombings will plateau at some point, but 1,000 suicide bombings a year is sustainable in perpetuity.

The clear implication is that U.S. military interventions in the years ahead will face both direct and indirect suicide bombings. Indeed, suicide bombers who target non-U.S. targets may pose the greatest threat to long-term U.S. interests. Documents captured in Iraq illustrated a thoughtful campaign to use suicide bombers to force various organizations such as the U.N. and the Red Cross to leave Iraq and force the U.S. to pay a higher and higher cost to remain. This strategy even extended to compelling Coalition nations to withdraw, so the suicide bomb attacks against the Italians, the Poles, and even the London 7/7 bombings should come as no surprise. Thus, although the military can take steps to mitigate the direct impact of suicide bombers, there will always be a plethora of alternative soft targets available to violent organizations that can achieve the effect of forcing a military withdrawal.

Incredibly, some militaries are actually writing suicide bombing into doctrine. Most notably, the Iranian military regularly practices using suicide bombers as part of its overall defense plan, and thousands of individuals responded to calls by the nominally independent Headquarters for Commemorating Martyrs of the Global Islamic Movement to sign up for a suicide bomber registry.[76] Suicide bombers are, of course, just one of the asymmetric tactics U.S. forces will face in the future, but they are one of the most effective.

Operation Iraqi Freedom's long-term impact is likely to be similar to that of the ill-fated Soviet invasion of Afghanistan. As of early 2007, there is mounting pressure to withdraw U.S. troops from Iraq, and it is very possible that they will be down to a minimal presence after the 2008 Presidential elections. Once U.S. troops withdraw, the insurgents and terrorists will regroup, but the experience, skills, and networks will remain and spread across the Middle East. Many of the Iraqis will likely stay in Iraq, but there will be another diaspora of combat-experienced radical Islamists throughout the region. As was seen after the Soviet withdrawal, these radicals will refit and then coalesce around new causes, but they will remain decidedly anti-Western. Without a major U.S. troop presence to target, many of the radicals will target other U.S. interests in the region. Thus, we can expect a continuation of the long-term effort to rid the region of Western influence, but many of the suicide bombings will be against softer targets such as commercial oil interests and U.S.-based hotel chains.

## SOF INTERFACE WITH DOMESTIC LAW ENFORCEMENT

Special Operations Forces (SOF) interaction with domestic law enforcement will likely remain limited with respect to suicide bombers. The two major areas for SOF and law

---

[76] Kenneth Katzman, "Iran's Influence in Iraq," (November 30, 2005, Congressional Research Service) internet: available at: http://lugar.senate.gov/iraq/pdf/CRS_IraqRS22323.pdfb accessed 19 Mar 2007, 6.

enforcement mutual assistance are intelligence sharing and training. SOF operating overseas are likely to encounter intelligence information regarding planned and past suicide bombings. Training SOF to recognize information that might be valuable to U.S. domestic law enforcement, collecting and analyzing this information, and then making it accessible to law enforcement are worthwhile goals to the extent that they can be accomplished without placing undue burdens on deploying units. Notably, a "pull" system that allows law enforcement to access information is desirable, since there are literally thousands of law enforcement jurisdictions in the U.S. Actively pushing information to every jurisdiction floods them with irrelevant data. However, law enforcement can search compiled information for items of particular interest and connect the pertinent dots based on local area knowledge that is not apparent from overseas.

Both SOF and law enforcement can also benefit from mutual training within the bounds of current legal restrictions. Tactics, techniques and procedures (TTP) that prove effective in spotting, neutralizing and mitigating the effects of suicide bombings during military operations can be relayed to law enforcement. As required, the military can use a "train the trainer" approach to ensure that the TTPs are promulgated throughout the law enforcement community. U.S. law enforcement has superb forensics capabilities that typically go beyond the normal military Sensitive Site Exploitation (SSE) procedures. Accordingly, there is significant value in transferring much of this knowledge and technology to the SOF community. To the extent possible, the military can also observe chain-of-custody requirements to aid in potential criminal prosecutions.

SOF are stretched thin enough in the Global War On Terror (GWOT) without additional requirements to defend the homeland against suicide bombers. There are also enough agencies with specific charters to protect the U.S. homeland without a need to dilute limited SOF assets. For example, the Department of Homeland Security (DHS) and the Federal Bureau of Investigation (FBI) have enough resources to devote to the issue, and specialized units such as the FBI's Hostage Rescue Team (HRT) provide the same capabilities that SOF could offer. SOF are better employed overseas conducting Direct Action (DA) against terrorists and executing Foreign Internal Defense (FID) and Irregular Warfare (IW) to strengthen partner capability instead of overlapping domestic law enforcement agencies.

After the first successful suicide bombings in U.S. mass transit systems and shopping malls, the military response will probably resemble that after 9/11. There will be a period of several months when National Guard and limited active duty specialists are deployed to augment security and screening at select locations. Over time, they will be phased out as both private and government active and passive screening systems grow. There will likely be pressure to deploy SOF to protect against suicide bombers. However, SOF are limited, duplicate existing law enforcement capabilities and are better deployed overseas. If truly desired, and for special events where a SOF capability provides value added, SOF could be deployed in a counter-terrorism (CT) role when actionable intelligence exists. To avoid potential legal constraints, the SOF personnel should be sworn as U.S. federal agents (i.e. Deputy U.S. Marshals) and act in a law enforcement capacity. For example, SOF teams could deploy to the Washington D.C. Metro system to augment existing law enforcement if there was a known cell of suicide bombers targeting the trains.

## RECOMMENDATIONS

Overall, suicide bombers do not pose an existential threat to the United States. However, they are above pure nuisance level, and they could be termed a semi-existential threat. Namely, their actions can and have significantly altered our way of life. Suicide bombing itself is only one tactic of the weak, but America's unmatched military might and the proven efficacy of this tactic ensure that our opponents will continue to use it for the foreseeable future. Although the U.S. cannot prevent all suicide bombings, it can take steps to mitigate their impact:

**Adopt language that frames the debate over suicide bombings in the most favorable terms.** For example, we should replace all references to *jihadists* with *hirabists* and all references to suicide or homicide bombers with *intihar* bombers. This will not win the GWOT by itself, but it will help ensure that we are not aiding the enemy with our own rhetoric. Specifically, our strategic communication efforts should at least recognize and differentiate among the terms *intihar* and *shaheed*, and *jihad* and *hirabah*. Unfortunately, the term j*ihadist* has entered the Western lexicon, and many official government spokespeople routinely use the word when describing U.S. actions.

As Douglas Streusand noted, *jihad* typically is meant as *jihad fi sabil Allah* (striving in the path of God), which, by definition is the correct course of action. Thus, by calling our opponents *jihadists*, we are explicating targeting those who are following God and implicitly targeting Islam. *Jihad* is by definition good, and the proper question is whether the actions of al-Qaeda and other groups should be classified as *jihad*. The far more effective terminology to describe the members of Islamic terror groups is *hirabis* or *hirabists*. *Hirabah*'s original meaning was "brigandage," and more generally refers to those who practice "sinful warfare." Thus, employing the term *hirabist* avoids offending Muslims, properly characterizes those who kill innocents, and forces the *hirabists* to defend their actions.[77]

Similarly, *intihar* can and should be introduced into the English vocabulary. It helps place the burden of justification on the bombers and their sponsors. Ironically, U.S. politicians are masters at language when it comes to domestic politics, as with the framing of the debate over the so-called "death tax" or "estate tax." However, this mastery of framing has yet to translate to the global stage. Adopting the proper language will at least prevent us from doing active harm to our cause as we are doing now, and it can help in the long-term war of ideas.

**Prepare emergency and building plans to account for multiple, near-simultaneous suicide bombers.** Although each incident is unique, there are common threads for every emergency management situation: the need to coordinate the actions of multiple agencies, the

---

[77] Gy Raz, "The War on the Word 'Jihad,'" (March 15, 2007, National Public Radio) internet: available at: http://www.npr.org/templates/story/story.php?storyId=6392989 accessed 15 Mar 2007, 1-2.

need for timely communication to both the responders and the public, the need for redundant communication systems, the need for population evacuation and control measures, and devising plans that address the concerns of the individuals involved and not just strive for efficiency. Enforcing rigorous building codes and exercising realistic and comprehensive emergency plans will help not only against the relatively few suicide bombers, but also against the more numerous incidents such as natural disasters and industrial accidents.

In general, threat mitigation encompasses three broad phases: preparation, immediate response, and reconstruction. Preparation entails the pre-hardening of the physical and human infrastructure in order to better withstand the effects of an attack. For example, many of the steps the British took to counter the threat posed by the Irish Republican Army should be adopted in the U.S. Building codes should immediately be amended to require such items as blast-resistant windows, doors and walls, setback distances commensurate with potential threat to the building, and vehicle and personnel access restrictions. All future construction can incorporate revised requirements, and existing buildings can be strengthened within reasonable cost and space limits. For example, it is impractical to achieve significant stand off distance for many buildings in urban centers, but bollards, benches and concrete planters can be added to sidewalks to maximize the existing space. This has the additional advantage of strengthening buildings against catastrophic weather events such as hurricanes and earthquakes.

The HSBC Bank bombing in Istanbul, Turkey on November 20$^{th}$, 2003 provides a good example of relatively low-cost security requirements that saved lives. The bank's windows were all coated with laminate film that prevented casualties from flying glass, and the building was constructed on a six-foot foundation that prevented direct vehicular access and helped vent the force of the explosion upward. Thus, even though the bomb was a very sizable 700kg charge and the bombers apparently tried to maximize casualties by waiting until a red light stopped traffic, no one inside the building died, and the building's structural integrity held.[78] In contrast, during the bombing of the Alfred P. Murrah Federal Building in Oklahoma City on 19 April 1995, the bomber (not suicide) was able to park the bomb (~1,800kg) within 10 feet of the building, and the building's partial collapse was responsible for 80% of the 168 deaths. Significantly, the foundation was not elevated, the ground floor was largely glass to add aesthetic appeal, and the there were only four freestanding support columns with no lateral support or designed redundancy on the bottom floor.[79] [80]

Additionally, the extensive use of closed-circuit television (CCTV) in Britain should serve as a model for the U.S. going forward. There are more than 6,000 networked CCTVs in London alone, and they were critical to the rapid identification and investigation of the 7/7 bombers and the identification and arrest of the four failed bombers two weeks later. The British system is highly sophisticated and includes such features as facial recognition, and Automatic Number Plate Recognition (ANPR) to identify and track vehicles.[81] Replicating the British system in major U.S. cities would be the ideal. Similar security upgrades to U.S. mass transit systems would cost at least $6 billion (a little less than annual American spending on potato chips)[82], but so far only about $250 million has been allocated from federal funds since 9/11. In contrast, the federal government has spent about $18 billion on the aviation industry since then.[83] At a minimum, the U.S. should start integrating networks of CCTV in major urban areas,

---

[78] Rodoplu, U, Arnold JL, Tokyay R, et al, "Mass-casualty terrorist bombings in Istanbul, Turkey, November, 2003: Reports of the events and the prehospital emergency response," *Journal of Prehospital and Disaster Medicine,* 2004; (19)2:133-145.

[79] R. Augustus Lim, "Anti Terrorism and Force Protection Applications in Facilities," (Gainesville, FL: University of Florida, June 2003), 41-43.

[80] National Research Council, "Protecting People and Buildings from Terrorism: Technology Transfer for Blast-effects Mitigation," (2001, National Academy Press, Washington, D.C.) available online at: http://books.nap.edu/books/0309082862/html accessed 19 Feb 2007, 2-6.

[81] Parliamentary Office of Science and Technology, "CCTV," (April 2002, London, England) available online at: http://www.parliament.uk/post/pn175.pdf accessed 27 Feb 07, 2.

[82] Food Management, "Executive Summary Candy & Snacks" (June 2004) available online at: http://www.food-management.com/article/5939 accessed 27 Feb 2007.

[83] Don Philpott, "London Bombings," (2005) available online at: http://www.homelanddefensejournal.com/pdfs/LondonBombing_SpecialReport.pdf accessed 27 Feb 2007, 2-3.

beginning with local police departments and with a requirement for all new commercial cameras (i.e. at banks) to feed into the system.

Immediate response to suicide bombings involves the actions taken by emergency services and the governments to secure blast sites, treat the victims of the blast, communicate instructions, evacuate people, safeguard evidence and initiate recovery efforts. Unfortunately, the events of 9/11 and the London bombings show the West is still unprepared for even medium-scale events. Glaringly, the poor actions by the local, state and federal governments to the aftermath of hurricane Katrina's devastation of New Orleans in late 2005 showed that U.S. incident response is still far from where it should be.

Emergency exercises should be as realistic as possible and incorporate lessons learned from previous suicide bombings. Many valuable procedures were worked out by the Israelis over the past decade and are readily available. However, New York City emergency communications were poor during the 9/11 attacks, despite the fact that the police and fire departments had the exact same problems during the 1993 World Trade Center bombing. Similarly, London's first responders suffered from inadequate communications systems, virtually non-existent crowd control plans, and an overwhelmed cell phone network during the 7/7 incidents. Incorporating updated scenarios that account for multiple bombers and exercise the full range of immediate response requirements will prove highly beneficial.

Reconstruction is the one area that does not need significant alteration. The U.S. infrastructure is robust and redundant enough that there will be ample resources to rebuild from all but the most massive and overwhelming attacks.

**Prepare the American public for suicide bombers within CONUS.** Akin to the preparation of the physical infrastructure, the American public should be inured to the concept that there will be multiple suicide bombings in the homeland. Since such events are entirely predictable, the time to start preparing the population is now. In contrast to the government's knee-jerk reactions that advised citizens to stockpile duct tape and plastic sheeting after the anthrax attacks in 2001, the script to respond to successful suicide bombings can be rational and sitting on the shelf.

Although Americans are somewhat more willing to report suspicious behavior in the post-9/11 era, unattended luggage in public U.S. places still receives far less scrutiny than it would in England. Most valuably, Americans can be taught to look for and report the telltale signs of potential suicide bombers, preferably during the preparation phase. For example, many of the peroxide and acetone-based chemicals commonly used in preparing homemade explosives produce distinct residues and odors. Encouraging citizens to report suspicious behaviors and patterns and following up on such reports offers one of the most effective means of preventing suicide bombings. The prime example is the well-publicized series of memos that noted an unusual pattern of Middle Eastern males taking flight classes prior to 9/11. Had multiple parties reported this pattern and it been analyzed under the mindset that suicide bombings were possible within the U.S., it is very possible that 9/11 could have been averted.

**Ensure that all force protection plans account for suicide bombers.** It has been almost 25 years since the U.S. embassy and the Marine barracks were bombed in Lebanon, so it should come as no surprise that suicide bombing is a real and persistent threat to official American presence overseas. Although there will be both AQN-sponsored and inspired attacks within the U.S., the vast majority of suicide bombings will continue to take place abroad. Accordingly, all future military interventions and placement of official U.S. buildings should be planned with the expectation that suicide bombers will target them.

Force protection planners must also account for the ingenuity of the organizations employing suicide bombers. While 9/11 is sometimes described as a failure of imagination, there is little doubt that suicide bombing will remain a viable tactic in the coming decades. The near-term question remains the delivery system employed. In general, tactics and techniques tend to radiate outward from the Middle East. Thus, we can observe Hezbollah's development of unmanned aerial vehicles (UAV) and Iraqi insurgents' use of chlorine bombs to predict that similar methods will eventually be employed against U.S. targets. Accordingly, suicide bombers can be expected to adopt the use of ultra-light or small aircraft and poisonous chemicals outside of the Middle East.

**Improve intelligence collection, analysis, and dissemination both domestically and abroad.** Aside from addressing the root causes of terrorism, this is the most effective step to reducing suicide bombers. Unfortunately, the creation of the Director of National Intelligence (DNI) in the wake of the 9/11 attacks was far from enough. Adding another layer of oversight to the 16 intelligence agencies did little to address systemic issues such as stove piping, a heavy reliance on technology versus human intelligence (HUMINT), and limited U.S. access to many poor and remote locations. Although the first DNI, John Negroponte, made limited progress on some issues, a good indication of the relative power of the DNI position is the fact that Ambassador Negroponte left his DNI position to become the Deputy Secretary of State in early 2007.

Ultimately, the British model of an agency for domestic intelligence (MI5) working closely with an agency for foreign intelligence (MI6) is preferable to the present U.S. fractured intelligence community. This will require legislative change similar to the Goldwater-Nichols Act that addressed systemic issues within the U.S. military. Sadly, there is presently no political will to affect this change, and it will not emerge until after another 9/11-scale attack against the U.S., most likely by suicide bombers.

In the interim, law enforcement agencies can concentrate on forging good ties with immigrant and Islamic communities. Although suicide bombing is not specifically a Muslim tactic, Muslims conduct 11 of the 12 ongoing campaigns, and all of the groups directly targeting the U.S. are Islamic. Since many of these communities are relatively insular within the U.S., community members are in a far better position than law enforcement to spot unusual or suspicious behavior. Nurturing relations that encourage community members to approach the authorities requires a thoughtful, sustained outreach program. While this is a significant effort over a period of years, the time to start is now.

**Address the root causes of terrorism.** Terrorism itself is, of course, just a tactic. We will no more eliminate terrorism than we will dispense with civil disobedience. Suicide bombing in particular is just a subset of terrorism, almost always carried out in a sustained campaign, and always by the weaker party. While all of the above actions will help mitigate the effects of suicide bombers, only long-term solutions to real and perceived grievances will remove the core motivations for suicide bombing.

Such solutions should specifically not be concessions, and they will most often be in the U.S.'s best interests. For example, achieving energy independence and brokering a comprehensive peace settlement regarding the Israeli-Palestinian conflict would remove the two issues that resonate most strongly in the Middle East. These two actions alone would eliminate the need for direct U.S. military intervention in the region and raise U.S. credibility. Although they seem daunting tasks, the U.S. could move much more proactively at relatively little cost.

Regarding energy, the U.S. government could allocate $8 billion (the rough cost of one month of military operations in Iraq)[84] to a series of substantial awards for alternative energy modeled after the X prize for space exploration. For example, there could be $1 billion prizes for whoever develops and agrees to license: a commercially viable electric car, photovoltaic cells that can power standard residential houses, wind turbines that can produce specified power, and geothermal systems that are commercially viable. The net effect would be to end U.S. dependence on foreign oil imports, and there would be no compelling national interest requiring direct military intervention in the Middle East.

---

[84] David Leonhardt, "What $1.2 Trillion Can Buy," (17 January 2007) available at: http://www.nytimes.com/2007/01/17/business/17leonhardt.html?ex=1326690000&en=7f221bfce7a6408c&ei=5090 : internet; accessed 3 May 2007.

Similarly, U.S. spokespersons often articulate that the GWOT is at most 20% military, but the diplomatic effort has so far lagged behind the application of force. Diplomatic initiatives on even half the scale of what has so far gone into military action would be most welcome. U.S. support for Israel colors virtually every action we undertake in the Middle East, and a comprehensive settlement would go far towards improving our image. A good first step would be helping to broker the return of the Golan Heights to Syria, an event that was almost reached in 2006. Subsequently, the U.S. should take the lead in negotiating a peace that roughly corresponds to: an Israeli withdrawal to the pre-1967 borders, Jerusalem as an international city (perhaps guarded by Buddhists), an independent Palestine, the removal of all settlements from the West Bank, and the Palestinian renunciation of the right of return in exchange for considerable compensation. While far from easy, the Camp David Accords provide an example of what can be achieved, and such a settlement would be far more effective at reducing the appeal of suicide bombing than having 150,000 U.S. troops attempting to impose a U.S.-style democracy in Mesopotamia.

# APPENDIX A: SUICIDE BOMBINGS (1980-2006)

This appendix lists all suicide bombings from 1 Jan, 1980 through 31 Dec, 2006, and all references are open source. The database is as complete and accurate as possible, but it is not guaranteed to be flawless. Accounts of many of the bombings are drawn from multiple sources, even though only two may be listed. Varied accounts of the same bombing were combined into a single description with more reputable news agencies (i.e. CNN, New York Times) given the greater weight. Casualty counts often vary, and the counts in this database sometimes use an average of the various reports. Casualty counts can vary as some minor wounds are counted or not counted in some accounts, and initial wounded may die because of their injuries.

A key question regarding suicide bombings is what exactly qualifies for inclusion as a suicide bombing. For this database, each bomb/explosive/vehicle that required a separate detonation was counted as an individual event. The bomber also had to have the intent to die as a direct result of the bombing. Thus, two bombers each wearing a suicide vest and having separate detonators would count as two attacks, even if they blow themselves up near simultaneously. Likewise, a truck bomb with four occupants would count as a single attack, since there was a single detonation, and there was only one decision point to activate the device. For a small number of attacks, it was not entirely clear they were suicide attacks. In these cases, this is noted in the comment section. Attacks reported as "possible" suicide bombings were not included, and "probable" suicide attacks were included.

Another question is when a failed attack should count as a suicide bombing. This database counts those attacks when the bomber had a complete, armed bomb and was attempting to deliver it to a target. Thus, a bomber who was arrested at a checkpoint on his or her way to conduct an attack would be entered. However, an individual who was arrested in a house with complete suicide vests would not count as a suicide bombing, even if there were unambiguous plans to employ them in the future.

Some attacks and reports make it impossible to disaggregate exact casualties. In these cases, the casualties are divided equally among the number of bombs, and it is noted by a caret symbol (^) in the target category.

**Description of data points:**
Date: The date the bombing took place.
Org: The organization that carried out the bombing (if known or claimed).
Location: The city, town or region in which the bombing took place.
Country: The country in which the bombing took place.
Target: The main target of the bombing (embassy, military, restaurant, etc.).
Dead: The number of people killed in the attack (not including the bomber(s)).
Wound: The number of people wounded in the attack.
US: Was the United States a direct target of the bombing (Yes or No)?
Weapon: The type of bomb used in the attack (car, truck, suicide belt, etc.). When the suicide bombing was part of a coordinated attack that also employed other weapons such as small arms or mortars, this noted in the comment section.
Camp: The campaign (if any) of which the bombing was a part.
Comment: Additional information related to the bombing. Most often, this includes a more exact description of the intended target and anything unusual or distinctive about the bombing (i.e. a specific mosque being bombed).
Source: An abbreviation listing the source(s) reporting the bombing. A complete key for the abbreviations is included at the end of the appendix.

| Date | Org. | Location | Country | Target | Dead | Wound | US | Weapon | Camp | Comment | Source |
|---|---|---|---|---|---|---|---|---|---|---|---|
| 15-Dec-81 | al-Dawa | Beirut | Lebanon | Embassy | 61 | 100 | N | Car bomb | x | Iraq Embassy | Pape/MIPT |
| 11-Nov-82 | Hezbollah | Tyre | Lebanon | Military | 62 | 28 | N | Car bomb | 2 | IDF HQ | Pape/ST |
| 18-Apr-83 | Hezbollah | Beirut | Lebanon | Embassy | 60 | 100 | Y | Car bomb | 1 | U.S. embassy | Pape/MIPT |
| 27-Jul-83 | ARA | Lisbon | Portugal | Embassy | 2 | 2 | N | Bag bomb | x | Armenians attack Turkish ambassador | MIPT/IT |
| 23-Oct-83 | Hezbollah | Beirut | Lebanon | Military | 241 | 81 | Y | Car bomb | 1 | U.S. military | Pape/MIPT |
| 23-Oct-83 | Hezbollah | Beirut | Lebanon | Military | 59 | 15 | N | Car bomb | 1 | French military | Pape/MIPT |
| 4-Nov-83 | Hezbollah | Tyre | Lebanon | Military | 39 | 0 | N | Car bomb | 2 | IDF post | Pape/MIPT |
| 12-Dec-83 | Hezbollah | Kuwait City | Kuwait | Embassy | 6 | 52 | Y | Truck bomb | 1 | U.S. embassy | Pape/MIPT |
| 13-Apr-84 | Hezbollah | Tyre | Lebanon | Military | 6 | 0+ | N | Truck bomb | 2 | IDF post/2 tanks destroyed | Pape/MIPT |
| 16-Jun-84 | Hezbollah | South Lebanon | Lebanon | Military | 5 | 9 | N | Car bomb | 2 | IDF post | Pape/ST |
| 20-Sep-84 | Hezbollah | Beirut | Lebanon | Embassy | 23 | 70 | Y | Truck bomb | 1 | U.S. embassy | Pape/ST |
| 5-Feb-85 | Hezbollah | Burj al Shimali | Lebanon | Military | 0 | 10 | N | Car bomb | 2 | IDF convoy, Sidon | Pape/MIPT |
| 8-Mar-85 | Hezbollah | South Lebanon | Lebanon | Military | 12 | 7 | N | Car bomb | 2 | IDF convoy | ST/NYT |
| 8-Mar-85 | Unknown | Dubai | UAE | Airplane | 0 | 0 | N | Suitcase | x | Failed to destroy Jordanian plane | MIPT/IT |
| 10-Mar-85 | Hezb/SSNP | South Lebanon | Lebanon | Military | 12 | 20 | N | Truck bomb | 2 | IDF post, Metulla crossing | Pape/MIPT |
| 12-Mar-85 | Hezbollah | Ras al-Ain | Lebanon | Military | 0 | 0 | N | Car bomb | 2 | IDF convoy, Jezzine | Pape/ST |
| 9-Apr-85 | Hezb/SSNP | Jezzin | Lebanon | Military | 2 | 2 | N | Car bomb | 2 | First female bomber/IDF post | Pape/ICT |
| 20-Apr-85 | Hezbollah | South Lebanon | Lebanon | Military | 12 | 100 | N | Truck bomb | 2 | IDF convoy, Qasimiyeh bridge | Pape/MIPT |
| 9-May-85 | Hezbollah | South Lebanon | Lebanon | Military | 2 | 4 | N | Suitcase | 2 | SLA checkpoint | Pape/ST |
| 25-May-85 | al-Dawa | Kuwait City | Kuwait | Govt/Police** | 5 | 12 | N | Car bomb | x | Emir, Kuwait | Pape/MIPT |
| 15-Jun-85 | Hezbollah | Beirut | Lebanon | Military | 23 | 17 | N | Car bomb | 2 | Lebanese Army post | Pape/ST |
| 9-Jul-85 | Hezbollah | South Lebanon | Lebanon | Military | 23 | 28 | N | Car bomb | 2 | SLA post, Hasbaya | Pape/ICT |
| 9-Jul-85 | Hezbollah | South Lebanon | Lebanon | Military | 0 | 6 | N | Car bomb | 2 | SLA post, Ras al-Biyada | Pape/ST |
| 15-Jul-85 | Hezbollah | Kfar Tibnit | Lebanon | Military | 10 | 11 | N | Car bomb | 2 | SLA post, Kifr Tibnit | Pape/ST |
| 17-Jul-85 | SSNP | South Lebanon | Lebanon | Military | 0 | 7 | N | Belt bomb | 2 | Premature detonation/police stop | DI |
| 31-Jul-85 | Hezb/SSNP | Arnoun | Lebanon | Military | 2 | 3 | N | Car bomb | 2 | IDF patrol, Arnun | Pape/MIPT |
| 6-Aug-85 | Hezbollah | Hasbaya | Lebanon | Military | 0 | 1 | N | Mule bomb | 2 | SLA post, Hasbaya | Pape/MIPT |
| 15-Aug-85 | Hezbollah | Beit Yahon gate | Lebanon | Military | 1 | 0 | N | Car bomb | 2 | IDF post | Pape/BG |
| 29-Aug-85 | Hezbollah | South Lebanon | Lebanon | Military | 15 | 24 | N | Car bomb | 2 | SLA post, Jezzine | Pape/ST |
| 3-Sep-85 | Hezbollah | South Lebanon | Lebanon | Military | 7 | 28 | N | Car bomb | 2 | SLA post, Honeh | Pape/ST |
| 11-Sep-85 | Hezbollah | Hasbaya | Lebanon | Military | 0 | 2 | N | Car bomb | 2 | SLA post/18-year-old female bomber | Pape/ICT |
| 12-Sep-85 | Hezb/SSNP | South Lebanon | Lebanon | Military | 20 | 17 | N | Car bomb | 2 | SLA post/female bomber | MIPT/ST |
| 17-Sep-85 | Hezbollah | South Lebanon | Lebanon | Military | 30 | 4 | N | Car bomb | 2 | SLA post, Taibe | Pape/MIPT |
| 18-Sep-85 | Hezbollah | South Lebanon | Lebanon | Military | 0 | 8 | N | Car bomb | 2 | SLA post, Tyre | Pape/ST |
| 11-Oct-85 | Hezbollah | South Lebanon | Lebanon | Military | 12 | 0+ | N | Car bomb | 2 | SLA post, Jezzine | Pape |
| 17-Oct-85 | Hezbollah | South Lebanon | Lebanon | Military | 6 | 9 | N | Grenades | 2 | SLA radio | Pape/ST |
| 3-Nov-85 | Hezbollah | South Lebanon | Lebanon | Military | 0 | 0 | N | Car bomb | 2 | Premature detonation | IT/UPI |
| 3-Nov-85 | Hezbollah | South Lebanon | Lebanon | Military | 0 | 0 | N | Mule bomb | 2 | SLA post, Khellet El-Khazem | Pape/IT |
| 4-Nov-85 | Hezb/SSNP | Arnoun | Lebanon | Military | 1 | 1 | N | Car bomb | 2 | SLA post, Arnun | Pape/MIPT |
| 12-Nov-85 | Hezbollah | Beirut | Lebanon | Govt/Police* | 5 | 13 | N | Car bomb | 2 | Militia leaders at St George Monastery | Pape/ST |
| 26-Nov-85 | Hezbollah | Jezzine | Lebanon | Military | 20 | 14 | N | Car bomb | 2 | SLA post, Jezzine | Pape/ICT |
| 8-Dec-85 | Unknown | South Lebanon | Lebanon | Military | 0 | 0 | N | Car bomb | 2 | UN forces foil attack on IDF | MIPT/IT |
| 7-Apr-86 | Hezbollah | South Lebanon | Lebanon | Military | 1 | 3 | N | Car bomb | 2 | SLA post, Hasbaya | Pape/ST |

| Date | Group | Location | Country | Target | Killed | Wounded | ? | Weapon | # | Notes | Source |
|---|---|---|---|---|---|---|---|---|---|---|---|
| 17-Jul-86 | Hezbollah | Jezzine | Lebanon | Military | 0 | 7 | N | Car bomb | 2 | Premature detonation | Pape/ICT |
| 20-Nov-86 | Hezbollah | South Lebanon | Lebanon | Military | 7 | 5 | N | Car bomb | 2 | SLA post, Tyre | Pape/MIPT |
| 5-Jul-87 | LTTE | Jaffna | Sri Lanka | Military | 40 | 60 | N | Truck bomb | 3 | Army camp/First LTTE suicide | Pape/SATP |
| 11-Nov-87 | LLO | Beirut | Lebanon | Airport | 6 | 73 | N | Suitcase | x | Possible unwitting bomber | ICT/ST |
| 14-Nov-87 | Hezbollah | Beirut | Lebanon | Hospital | 7 | 20 | N | Bag bomb | 2 | AUB hospital | ICT/ST |
| 19-Aug-88 | Hezbollah | South Lebanon | Lebanon | Military | 0 | 0 | N | Car bomb | 2 | IDF convoy/female bomber | MIPT/REUT |
| 19-Oct-88 | Hezbollah | Metulla | Lebanon | Military | 8 | 7 | N | Car bomb | 2 | IDF vehicle | Pape/MIPT |
| 9-Aug-89 | Hezbollah | South Lebanon | Lebanon | Military | 0 | 5 | N | Car bomb | 2 | IDF vehicle/2 bombers in car | Pape/MIPT |
| 31-Oct-89 | PFLP | Lebanon coast | Lebanon | Naval vessel | 0 | 3 | N | Boat bomb | 4 | IDF naval vessel | MIPT/SJMN |
| 9-Nov-89 | Hezbollah | South Lebanon | Lebanon | Military | 0 | 2 | N | Car bomb | 2 | IDF | MIPT/JP |
| 12-Jul-90 | LTTE | Trincomalee | Sri Lanka | Naval vessel | 6 | 0 | N | Boat bomb | 3 | 4 bombers in boat | Pape/SATP |
| 23-Nov-90 | LTTE | Manakulam | Sri Lanka | Military | 3 | 0 | N | Car bomb | 3 | Army camp | Pape/SATP |
| 24-Nov-90 | SBO/SSNP | South Lebanon | Lebanon | Military | 0 | 3 | N | Suitcase | 2 | IDF patrol | Pape/MIPT |
| 2-Mar-91 | LTTE | Columbo | Sri Lanka | Govt/Police* | 18 | 73 | N | Car bomb | 3 | Deputy Defense Minister | Pape/SATP |
| 19-Mar-91 | LTTE | Silavathurai | Sri Lanka | Military | 5 | 3 | N | Truck bomb | 3 | Army camp | Pape/SATP |
| 5-May-91 | LTTE | Trincomalee | Sri Lanka | Naval vessel | 5 | 4 | N | Boat bomb | 3 | 2 bombers in boat | Pape/SATP |
| 11-May-91 | LTTE | Kankesanthurai | Sri Lanka | Naval vessel | 3 | 0 | N | Boat bomb | 3 | 3 bombers in boat | SATP/IPCS |
| 21-May-91 | LTTE | Sriperumbudur | India | Govt/Police* | 17 | 21 | N | Belt bomb | 3 | Former Indian PM, Rajiv Ghandi | Pape/SATP |
| 21-Jun-91 | LTTE | Columbo | Sri Lanka | Military | 27 | 200 | N | Truck bomb | 3 | Defense Ministry | Pape/SATP |
| 17-Mar-92 | Hezbollah | Buenos Aries | Argentina | Embassy | 29 | 242 | N | Car bomb | 2 | Israeli Embassy | ST/TOL |
| 16-Nov-92 | LTTE | Columbo | Sri Lanka | Military* | 5 | 0 | N | Motorcycle | 3 | Sri Lankan Navy Chief | Pape/SATP |
| 16-Apr-93 | Hamas | Mehola junction | Israel | Restaurant | 2 | 5 | N | Car bomb | 4 | Detonated between two buses | ICT/ST |
| 1-May-93 | LTTE | Columbo | Sri Lanka | Govt/Police* | 23 | 60 | N | Bike bomb | 3 | Sri Lankan President Premedasa | Pape/SATP |
| 15-Aug-93 | Unknown | Cairo | Egypt | Govt/Police | 3 | 0+ | N | Motorcycle | 5 | Interior Minister, Egypt | Pape/ST |
| 29-Aug-93 | LTTE | Kilaly | Sri Lanka | Naval vessel | 12 | 3 | N | Boat bomb | 3 | Sri Lankan patrol boat | Pape/WE |
| 12-Sep-93 | Hamas | Gaza | Gaza | Bus | 0 | 2 | N | Car bomb | 4 | Car collided with bus/no detonation | MEJ/ST |
| 14-Sep-93 | Unknown | Gaza | Gaza | Govt/Police | 0 | 0 | N | Belt bomb | 4 | Police station | JP/TIME |
| 26-Sep-93 | Hamas | Gaza | Gaza | Military | 0 | 0 | N | Car bomb | 4 | Failed car bomb attack | MEJ/AP |
| 4-Oct-93 | Hamas | Beit El | West Bank | Bus | 0 | 30 | N | Car bomb | 4 | Close to No 173 bus | MEJ/ST |
| 11-Nov-93 | LTTE | Jaffna | Sri Lanka | Naval vessel | 0 | 0 | N | Boat bomb | 3 | Damaged two Dvora patrol boats | Pape/IPCS |
| 12-Dec-93 | PIJ | Gaza | Gaza | Military | 0 | 1 | N | Car bomb | 4 | IDF vehicle | MEJ/AP |
| 6-Apr-94 | Hamas | Afula | Israel | Bus | 8 | 51 | N | Car bomb | 4 | Bus with high school students | Pape/MEJ |
| 13-Apr-94 | Hamas | Hadera | Israel | Bus | 5 | 30 | N | Belt bomb | 4 | At Central Bus Station | Pape/ICT |
| 18-Jul-94 | Ansar Allah | Buenos Aries | Argentina | Civilian | 96 | 236 | N | Van bomb | 2 | Jewish community buildings | MIPT/CNN |
| 19-Jul-94 | Ansar Allah | Colon | Panama | Airplane | 20 | 0 | N | Bomb | 2 | Target 12 Jewish pax | JA/MIPT |
| 2-Aug-94 | LTTE | Palaly | Sri Lanka | Airplane | 0 | 0 | N | Grenades | 3 | Damaged helicopter | Pape/IPCS |
| 10-Aug-94 | LTTE | Kankesanthurai | Sri Lanka | Naval vessel | 0 | 3 | N | Mines | 3 | Sri Lankan warship (4,000 tons) | Pape/NYT |
| 19-Sep-94 | LTTE | Mannar Island | Sri Lanka | Naval vessel | 25 | 17 | N | Mines | 3 | Sri Lankan warship | Pape/ST |
| 19-Oct-94 | Hamas | Tel Aviv | Israel | Bus | 22 | 46 | N | Belt bomb | 4 | No 5 bus | Pape/ICT |
| 24-Oct-94 | LTTE | Columbo | Sri Lanka | Govt/Police* | 59 | 300 | N | Belt bomb | 3 | Presidential candidate Dissanayake | Pape/SATP |
| 8-Nov-94 | LTTE | Vettilaikerni | Sri Lanka | Naval vessel | 0 | 5 | N | Boat bomb | 3 | Sri Lankan landing craft/Bay of Bengal | ST/RMN |
| 11-Nov-94 | PIJ | Netzarim junction | Gaza | Military | 3 | 12 | N | Bike bomb | 4 | Near IDF checkpoint | Pape/ICT |
| 24-Dec-94 | Hamas | Jerusalem | Israel | Bus | 0 | 13 | N | Belt bomb | 4 | ICC bus stop | Pape/ICT |
| 22-Jan-95 | PIJ | Beit Lid junction | Israel | Bus^ | 9 | 34 | N | Belt bomb | 4 | 2 bombers/bus stop | Pape/ICT |

| Date | Group | Location | Country | Target | Killed | Wounded | ? | Weapon | Bombers | Notes | Source |
|---|---|---|---|---|---|---|---|---|---|---|---|
| 22-Jan-95 | PIJ | Beit Lid junction | Israel | Bus^ | 9 | 35 | N | Belt bomb | 4 | 2 bombers/targeted responders | Pape/ICT |
| 30-Jan-95 | GIA | Algiers | Algeria | Civilian | 42 | 75 | N | Truck bomb | x | Crowd | Pape/ST |
| 28-Feb-95 | Chechen sep | Rabat | Morocco | Embassy | 0 | 0 | N | Belt bomb | 6 | Russian Consulate | MIPT/BG |
| 9-Apr-95 | Hamas/PIJ | Gaza | Gaza | Bus | 8 | 40 | N | Car bomb | 4 | Target settler bus | Pape/MEJ |
| 18-Apr-95 | LTTE | Trincomalee | Sri Lanka | Naval vessel | 12 | 22 | N | Divers | 3 | 2 vessels attacked | Pape/SATP |
| 25-Apr-95 | Hezbollah | Bint Jbeil | Lebanon | Military | 0 | 22 | N | Belt bomb | 2 | IDF convoy | Pape/TOL |
| 24-Jun-95 | Hamas | Neve Dekalim | Gaza | Military | 0 | 3 | N | Mule bomb | 4 | IDF convoy | Pape/MEJ |
| 16-Jul-95 | LTTE | Jaffna | Sri Lanka | Naval vessel | 0 | 4 | N | Divers | 3 | Sri Lankan Navy command ship | Pape/ST |
| 24-Jul-95 | Hamas | Ramat Gan | Israel | Bus | 6 | 32 | N | Belt bomb | 4 | "Dan Cooperative" bus | Pape/ICT |
| 7-Aug-95 | LTTE | Columbo | Sri Lanka | Govt/Police | 22 | 40 | N | Cart bomb | 3 | Government Building/motorcade | Pape/SATP |
| 7-Aug-95 | GIA | Boufarik | Algeria | Civilian | 8 | 25 | N | Car bomb | x | 3 bombers in car | ST/ERRI |
| 21-Aug-95 | Hamas | Jerusalem | Israel | Bus | 4 | 100 | N | Belt bomb | 4 | No. 26 bus/Ramat Eshkol area | Pape/ICT |
| 31-Aug-95 | BKI | Chandigarh | India | Govt/Police* | 16 | 24 | N | Belt bomb | x | Punjab Chief Minister Beant Singh | Pape/LAT |
| 3-Sep-95 | LTTE | Trincomalee | Sri Lanka | Naval vessel | 0 | 0 | N | | 3 | | ST |
| 10-Sep-95 | LTTE | Kankesanthurai | Sri Lanka | Naval vessel | 0 | 0 | N | Diver | 3 | Damaged Dvora patrol boat | IPCS/ST |
| 20-Sep-95 | LTTE | Kankesanthurai | Sri Lanka | Naval vessel | 0 | 0 | N | | 3 | | ST |
| 2-Oct-95 | LTTE | Kankesanthurai | Sri Lanka | Naval vessel | 0 | 0 | N | Diver | 3 | Damaged Dvora patrol boat | IPCS/ST |
| 17-Oct-95 | LTTE | Trincomalee | Sri Lanka | Naval vessel | 9 | 0 | N | Divers | 3 | Damaged patrol boat | Pape/IPCS |
| 20-Oct-95 | LTTE | Columbo | Sri Lanka | Oil refinery | 23 | 25 | N | Mines | 3 | 2 oil depots | Pape/ST |
| 20-Oct-95 | al-Gamaah | Rijeka | Croatia | Govt/Police | 0 | 29 | N | Car bomb | 5 | Police HQ/for imprisoned militant | ST/DOS |
| 1-Nov-95 | Hamas/PIJ | Gush Katif | Gaza | Bus | 0 | 0 | N | Car bomb | 4 | 2 bombers partially foiled | MEJ/ST |
| 1-Nov-95 | Hamas/PIJ | Gush Katif | Gaza | Bus | 0 | 11 | N | Car bomb | 4 | 2 bombers partially foiled | MEJ/ST |
| 11-Nov-95 | LTTE | Columbo | Sri Lanka | Military | 0 | 2 | N | Belt bomb | 3 | 2 bombers/Army HQ | Pape/SATP |
| 11-Nov-95 | LTTE | Columbo | Sri Lanka | Military | 23 | 4 | N | Belt bomb | 3 | 2 bombers/target crowd from 1st bomb | Pape/IPCS |
| 13-Nov-95 | al-Qaeda | Riyadh | Saudi Arabia | Military | 5 | 11 | Y | Car bomb | 7 | U.S. military base | Pape/ST |
| 19-Nov-95 | al-Gamaah | Islamabad | Pakistan | Embassy | 16 | 60 | N | Truck bomb | 5 | Egyptian embassy | Pape/ICT |
| 24-Nov-95 | LTTE | Columbo | Sri Lanka | Military | 16 | 52 | N | Belt bomb | 3 | Sri Lankan Army HQ | SATP/SPUR |
| 5-Dec-95 | LTTE | Batticaloa | Sri Lanka | Govt/Police | 23 | 41 | N | Truck bomb | 3 | Police camp/3 bombers in truck | Pape/SATP |
| 11-Dec-95 | LTTE | Columbo | Sri Lanka | Military | 17 | 59 | N | Belt bomb | 3 | Sri Lankan Army HQ | SATP/SPUR |
| 21-Dec-95 | Al-jihad | Peshawar | Pakistan | Market | 45 | 100 | N | Car bomb | 10 | Probable suicide bomber/Saddar area | ST/CNN |
| 30-Dec-95 | LTTE | Batticaloa | Sri Lanka | Military | 0 | 2 | N | Belt bomb | 3 | Kallidi district | SATP/SPUR |
| 8-Jan-96 | LTTE | Batticaloa | Sri Lanka | Civilian | 0 | 3 | N | Belt bomb | 3 | Market | Pape/ST |
| 31-Jan-96 | LTTE | Columbo | Sri Lanka | Bank | 91 | 1400 | N | Truck bomb | 3 | Central Bank/3 bombers in truck | Pape/SATP |
| 13-Feb-96 | LTTE | Trincomalee | Sri Lanka | Naval vessel | 0 | 0 | N | Divers | 3 | | Pape |
| 25-Feb-96 | Hamas | Ashkelon | Israel | Bus | 2 | 25 | N | Belt bomb | 4 | Hitching post/bomber in IDF uniform | Pape/ICT |
| 25-Feb-96 | Hamas | Jerusalem | Israel | Bus | 26 | 80 | N | Belt bomb | 4 | No 18 bus/Hamas later denied credit | Pape/ICT |
| 3-Mar-96 | Hamas | Jerusalem | Israel | Bus | 19 | 6 | N | Belt bomb | 4 | No 18 bus | Pape/ICT |
| 4-Mar-96 | PIJ/Hamas | Tel Aviv | Israel | Mall | 20 | 75 | N | Belt bomb | 4 | Dizengoff Center Mall | Pape/ICT |
| 20-Mar-96 | Hezbollah | Taibeh | Lebanon | Military | 1 | 7 | N | Belt bomb | 2 | IDF convoy | Pape/ST |
| 1-Apr-96 | LTTE | Vettilaikerni | Sri Lanka | Naval vessel | 10 | 12 | N | Boat bomb | 3 | Dvora fast attack boat | Pape/SATP |
| 12-Apr-96 | LTTE | Columbo | Sri Lanka | Naval vessel | 0 | 0 | N | Boat bomb | 3 | Raid on ships in port | ST/IPSN |
| 25-Apr-96 | Unknown | Jerusalem | Israel | Bus | 0 | 0 | N | Belt bomb | 4 | Detonated while trying to arm bomb | TR/SEA |
| 29-Apr-96 | Unknown | Bhai Pheru | Pakistan | Bus | 52 | 26 | N | Bag bomb | 10 | Ignited bus' fuel tank | JA/ST |

| Date | Group | Location | Country | Target | Killed | Wounded | ? | Weapon | ? | Notes | Source |
|---|---|---|---|---|---|---|---|---|---|---|---|
| 11-Jun-96 | LTTE | Jaffna | Sri Lanka | Naval vessel | 0 | 4 | N | Mines | 3 | Sank gunboat | Pape/FWS |
| 30-Jun-96 | PKK | Tunceli | Turkey | Military | 9 | 30 | N | Belt bomb | 8 | Female PKK bomber at parade | Pape/ICT |
| 3-Jul-96 | LTTE | Jaffna | Sri Lanka | Govt/Police** | 37 | 50 | N | Belt bomb | 3 | Govt motorcade/Housing Minister | Pape/SAT |
| 18-Jul-96 | LTTE | Mullaitivu | Sri Lanka | Naval vessel | 35 | | N | Mines | 3 | Gunboat | Pape/ST |
| 24-Jul-96 | LTTE | Dehiwala | Sri Lanka | Train | 63 | 366 | N | Bag bomb | 3 | Up to 4 bombers | ST/SPI |
| 6-Aug-96 | LTTE | North of Sri Lanka | Sri Lanka | Naval vessel | 0 | 4 | N | Boat bomb | 3 | | ST |
| 14-Aug-96 | LTTE | Columbo | Sri Lanka | Civilian | 0 | 0 | N | Belt bomb | 3 | South Korean offices | ICT/ST |
| 25-Oct-96 | LTTE | Trincomalee | Sri Lanka | Naval vessel | 12 | 11 | N | Boat bomb | 3 | Gunboat | Pape/SAT |
| 25-Oct-96 | PKK | Adana | Turkey | Govt/Police | 5 | 15 | N | Belt bomb | 8 | Police HQ | Pape/ICT |
| 29-Oct-96 | PKK | Sivas | Turkey | Govt/Police | 4 | 9 | N | Belt bomb | 8 | Female/pregnancy disguise/police car | Pape/ICT |
| 25-Nov-96 | LTTE | Trincomalee | Sri Lanka | Govt/Police** | 1 | 0 | N | Belt bomb | 3 | Police chief | Pape/SAT |
| 8-Dec-96 | LTTE | Trincomalee | Sri Lanka | Naval vessel | 0 | 0+ | N | Mines | 3 | | Pape |
| 17-Dec-96 | LTTE | Ampara | Sri Lanka | Govt/Police* | 1 | 2 | N | Motorcycle | 3 | Police chief Upali Sahabandu | Pape/SAT |
| 25-Dec-96 | None | Frankfurt | Germany | Religious site | 2 | 10 | N | Grenades | x | Female/Luthern church | CNN/NYT |
| 6-Mar-97 | LTTE | China Bay | Sri Lanka | Airplane | 0 | 1 | N | Grenades | 3 | Air base | Pape/SAT |
| 21-Mar-97 | Hamas | Tel Aviv | Israel | Restaurant | 3 | 48 | N | Belt bomb | 4 | Apropo restaurant | Pape/MEJ |
| 23-Mar-97 | LTTE | Mullaitivu | Sri Lanka | Naval vessel | 0 | 0 | N | Boat bomb | 3 | 2 boat bombs destroyed | SATP/SPUR |
| 1-Apr-97 | PIJ | Gush Katif | Gaza | Bus | 0 | 0 | N | Belt bomb | 4 | Coordinated attack | ICT/MEJ |
| 1-Apr-97 | PIJ | Netzarim junction | Gaza | Military | 0 | 7 | N | Belt bomb | 4 | Coordinated attack | ICT/MEJ |
| 19-May-97 | Amal | Tyre coast | Lebanon | Naval vessel | 0 | 0 | N | Boat bomb | 2 | Fishing boat disguise/shot at a distance | ST/TOL |
| 30-Jul-97 | Hamas | Jerusalem | Israel | Mall^ | 7 | 88 | N | Belt bomb | 4 | 2 bombers/Mahane Yehuda market | Pape/ICT |
| 30-Jul-97 | Hamas | Jerusalem | Israel | Mall^ | 7 | 88 | N | Belt bomb | 4 | 2 bombers/Mahane Yehuda market | Pape/ICT |
| 4-Sep-97 | Hamas | Jerusalem | Israel | Mall^ | 2 | 66 | N | Belt bomb | 4 | 3 bombers/Ben-Yehuda Ped mall | Pape/ICT |
| 4-Sep-97 | Hamas | Jerusalem | Israel | Mall^ | 2 | 67 | N | Belt bomb | 4 | 3 bombers/Ben-Yehuda Ped mall | Pape/ICT |
| 4-Sep-97 | Hamas | Jerusalem | Israel | Mall^ | 2 | 67 | N | Belt bomb | 4 | 3 bombers/Ben-Yehuda Ped mall | Pape/ICT |
| 15-Oct-97 | LTTE | Columbo | Sri Lanka | Bank | 18 | 110 | N | Truck bomb | 3 | World Trade Center, Columbo | Pape/SAT |
| 19-Oct-97 | LTTE | Northern coast | Sri Lanka | Naval vessel | 7 | 21 | N | Boat bomb | 3 | Gunboat | Pape/SAT |
| 14-Nov-97 | LTTE | Columbo | Sri Lanka | Power plant | 0 | 0 | N | Belt bomb | 3 | Kelanitissa power plant | SATP/SPUR |
| 28-Dec-97 | LTTE | Maagalle | Sri Lanka | Govt/Police** | 0 | 0 | N | Truck bomb | 3 | Navy Chief, south Sri Lanka | Pape/SAT |
| 25-Jan-98 | LTTE | Kandy | Sri Lanka | Religious site | 15 | 34 | N | Truck bomb | 3 | Buddhist shrine/Temple of Tooth Relic | Pape/SAT |
| 6-Feb-98 | LTTE | Columbo | Sri Lanka | Military | 9 | 7 | N | Truck bomb | 3 | Air Force HQ | Pape/SAT |
| 23-Feb-98 | LTTE | Point Pedru | Sri Lanka | Naval vessel | 79 | 0 | N | Boat bomb | 3 | 8 suicide boats attack two ships | Pape/SAT |
| 5-Mar-98 | LTTE | Columbo | Sri Lanka | Civilian | 36 | 257 | N | Bus bomb | 3 | Train station | Pape/SAT |
| 12-Mar-98 | LTTE | Columbo | Sri Lanka | Naval vessel | 50 | 200 | N | Boat bomb | 3 | Sri Lankan Navy boat on patrol | Pape/ST |
| 14-May-98 | LTTE | Jaffna | Sri Lanka | Military* | 2 | 0 | N | Belt bomb | 3 | Army Brigadier Wijeyarante | Pape/SAT |
| 19-Jul-98 | Hamas | Jerusalem | Israel | Mall | 0 | 1 | N | Car bomb | 4 | Failed car bomb/driver injured | ST/MIPT |
| 7-Aug-98 | al-Qaeda | Dar es-Salaam | Tanzania | Embassy | 10 | 77 | Y | Car bomb | 7 | U.S. embassy | Pape/MIP |
| 7-Aug-98 | al-Qaeda | Nairobi | Kenya | Embassy | 291 | 4000 | Y | Truck bomb | 7 | U.S. embassy | Pape/MIP |
| 17-Aug-98 | LTTE | Batticaloa | Sri Lanka | Bank | 0 | 11 | N | Motorcycle | 3 | 4 injured were police | ST/MIPT |
| 31-Aug-98 | GIA | Algiers | Algeria | Mall | 25 | 61 | N | Belt bomb | x | GIA suspected/Bab El Oued market | ST/MIPT |
| 11-Sep-98 | LTTE | Jaffna | Sri Lanka | Govt/Police* | 18 | 12 | N | Belt bomb | 3 | Mayor of Jaffna | Pape/SAT |
| 29-Oct-98 | Hamas | Gush Katif | Gaza | Bus | 1 | 8 | N | Car bomb | 4 | Jeep blocked bomber from bus | ICT/HAA |
| 30-Oct-98 | LTTE | Mullaitivu | Sri Lanka | Naval vessel | 18 | 0 | N | Boat bomb | 3 | Gunboat escort MV Lanka Muditha | Pape/BBC |

| Date | Group | Location | Country | Target | Killed | Wounded | ? | Weapon | # | Notes | Source |
|---|---|---|---|---|---|---|---|---|---|---|---|
| 6-Nov-98 | PIJ | Jerusalem | Israel | Mall | 0 | 20 | N | Car bomb | 4 | 2 bombers in car | ICT/MEJ |
| 17-Nov-98 | PKK | Yuksekova | Turkey | Govt/Police | 0 | 6 | N | Belt bomb | 8 | Police station/missed military convoy | Pape/ICT |
| 1-Dec-98 | PKK | Lice | Turkey | Mall | 0 | 15 | N | Grenades | 8 | Military-visited supermarket | Pape/ICT |
| 24-Dec-98 | PKK | Van | Turkey | Military | 1 | 22 | N | Belt bomb | 8 | Near barracks | Pape/ICT |
| 4-Mar-99 | PKK | Batman | Turkey | Govt/Police | 0 | 4 | N | Belt bomb | 8 | Likely early detonation/police station | Pape/ICT |
| 11-Mar-99 | PKK | Dahuk | Iraq | Govt/Police | 2 | 6 | N | Belt bomb | 8 | Turkish Intel | Pape/MIPT |
| 18-Mar-99 | LTTE | Columbo | Sri Lanka | Govt/Police | 5 | 8 | N | Belt bomb | 3 | Mount Livinia Police Station | Pape/SATP |
| 20-Mar-99 | Unknown | Hazayi | Turkey | Unknown | 0 | 0 | N | Grenades | 8 | Female arrested before detonation | MIPT/SLPD |
| 20-Mar-99 | PKK | Van province | Turkey | Civilian | 1 | 3 | N | Belt bomb | 8 | Police station | MIPT/ST |
| 27-Mar-99 | PKK | Istanbul | Turkey | Civilian | 0 | 10 | N | Grenades | 8 | Taksim square/stopped by police | Pape/ICT |
| 3-Apr-99 | Unknown | Tunceli | Turkey | Unknown | 0 | 0 | N | Belt bomb | 8 | Premature detonation | MIPT/AP |
| 4-Apr-99 | PKK | Bingol | Turkey | Govt/Police** | 1 | 20 | N | Belt bomb | 8 | Governor Kamci targeted | Pape/MIPT |
| 9-Apr-99 | PKK | Yuksekova | Turkey | Govt/Police* | 1 | 4 | N | Belt bomb | 8 | Governor Canpolat targeted | Pape/ICT |
| 11-Apr-99 | LTTE | Kandy | Sri Lanka | Bus | 2 | 20 | N | Belt bomb | 3 | Passenger bus | SPUR/ST |
| 29-May-99 | LTTE | Batticaloa | Sri Lanka | Govt/Police* | 2 | 0 | N | Bike bomb | 3 | Rival Tamil leader "Razeek" | Pape/SATP |
| 2-Jun-99 | Unknown | Sirnak | Turkey | Unknown | 0 | 0 | N | Belt bomb | 8 | Detonated after police stop | MIPT/TRT |
| 5-Jul-99 | PKK | Adana | Turkey | Civilian | 0 | 17 | N | Belt bomb | 8 | Police Station/female bomber | Pape/ICT |
| 7-Jul-99 | PKK | Iluh/Batman | Turkey | Civilian | 0 | 0 | N | Grenades | 8 | Police killed bomber | Pape/ST |
| 25-Jul-99 | LTTE | Trincomalee | Sri Lanka | Naval vessel | 1 | 20 | N | Belt bomb | 3 | Attack on Navy ferry | SATP/ICT |
| 29-Jul-99 | LTTE | Columbo | Sri Lanka | Govt/Police* | 3 | 6 | N | Belt bomb | 3 | Tamil politician Dr. Thiruchelvam | Pape/SATP |
| 4-Aug-99 | LTTE | Vavuniya | Sri Lanka | Govt/Police | 10 | 18 | N | Bike bomb | 3 | Anti-terrorist police vehicle | Pape/SATP |
| 9-Aug-99 | LTTE | Vakarai | Sri Lanka | Military* | 1 | 4 | N | Belt bomb | 3 | Military commander | Pape/SATP |
| 16-Aug-99 | LTTE | Northern coast | Sri Lanka | Naval vessel | 10 | 2 | N | Boat bomb | 3 | Dvora gunboat | Pape/TN |
| 28-Aug-99 | PKK | Tunceli | Turkey | Govt/Police | 0 | 0 | N | Belt bomb | 8 | Governor's office | Pape/MIPT |
| 2-Sep-99 | LTTE | Vavuniya | Sri Lanka | Civilian | 3 | 0 | | Belt bomb | 3 | Rival Tamil leader Manikkadasan | Pape/IPCS |
| 4-Sep-99 | LeT | Handwara | Kashmir/India | Military | 1 | 1 | N | Grenades | 9 | Border Security Force camp | ST/TOI |
| 8-Dec-99 | LTTE | Point Pedru | Sri Lanka | Naval vessel | 4 | 5 | N | Boat bomb | 3 | Dvora gunboat | Pape/UPI |
| 18-Dec-99 | LTTE | Columbo | Sri Lanka | Govt/Police | 8 | 70 | N | Belt bomb | 3 | UNP Election meeting | SATP/IPCS |
| 18-Dec-99 | LTTE | Columbo | Sri Lanka | Govt/Police** | 24 | 110 | N | Bag bomb | 3 | President of Sri Lanka Kumaratunga | Pape/SATP |
| 29-Dec-99 | Hezbollah | Qlaia | Lebanon | Military | 1 | 13 | N | Car bomb | 2 | 4 vehicle IDF convoy | Pape/ICT |
| 30-Dec-99 | LTTE | Jaffna | Sri Lanka | Naval vessel | 2 | 2 | N | Boat bomb | 3 | Sri Lankan Navy boats in harbor | Pape/TN |
| 1-Jan-00 | LeT | Surankote | Kashmir/India | Military | 11 | 23 | N | Grenades | 9 | Attack on Army BDE HQ | ST/TOI |
| 5-Jan-00 | LTTE | Columbo | Sri Lanka | Govt/Police | 11 | 30 | N | Belt bomb | 3 | PM's residence | Pape/SATP |
| 7-Jan-00 | LTTE | Ratmalana | Sri Lanka | Govt/Police* | 20 | 60 | N | Belt bomb | 3 | Cabinet Minister Gooneratne | MIPT/TN |
| 12-Jan-00 | LeT | Anantang | Kashmir/India | Military | 0 | 1 | N | Grenades | 9 | Rashtriya Rifles camp | ST/THI |
| 4-Feb-00 | LTTE | Trincomalee | Sri Lanka | Military | 0 | 0 | N | Boat bomb | 3 | Naval Command HQ/killed by guards | ST/UPI |
| 16-Feb-00 | Unknown | Beijing | China | Civilian | 0 | 1 | N | Belt bomb | x | Dissident in Tianamen Square | ST/TOL |
| 2-Mar-00 | LTTE | Rajagiriya | Sri Lanka | Hospital | 25 | 0+ | N | Mines | 3 | 3 man suicide team/Ayurveda | IPCS |
| 2-Mar-00 | LTTE | Trincomalee | Sri Lanka | Military** | 3 | 0 | N | Belt bomb | 3 | Female/Army COL Abeysekera | Pape/SATP |
| 10-Mar-00 | LTTE | Columbo | Sri Lanka | Govt/Police** | 20 | 46 | N | Belt bomb | 3 | Government convoy/early detonation | Pape/SATP |
| 31-Mar-00 | None | Shajian | China | Civilian | 36 | 30 | N | Cart bomb | x | Disgruntled miner/wedding | BBC/CYD |
| 19-Apr-00 | JeM | Srinagar | Kashmir/India | Military | 0 | 7 | N | Car bomb | 9 | Partially foiled/Indian Army HQ | ST/SATP |
| 17-May-00 | LTTE | Batticaloa | Sri Lanka | Religious site | 29 | 78 | N | Belt bomb | 3 | Buddhist temple/Vasek holiday | ST/TOL |

| Date | Group | Location | Country | Target | Killed | Wounded | ? | Weapon | Code | Notes | Source |
|---|---|---|---|---|---|---|---|---|---|---|---|
| 22-May-00 | LTTE | Kantalai | Sri Lanka | Govt/Police** | 0 | 1 | N | Belt bomb | 3 | Political leader | Pape/ST |
| 5-Jun-00 | LTTE | Northeast coast | Sri Lanka | Naval vessel | 34 | 0 | N | Boat bomb | 3 | Ammo ship | Pape/SATP |
| 7-Jun-00 | LTTE | Columbo | Sri Lanka | Govt/Police* | 20 | 50 | N | Belt bomb | 3 | Industries Minister C.V. Gunaratne | Pape/SATP |
| 7-Jun-00 | Chechen sep | Alkhan-Yurt | Russia | Govt/Police | 2 | 5 | N | Truck bomb | 6 | Police Station | Pape/ST |
| 9-Jun-00 | Chechen sep | Alkhan-Kala | Russia | Military | 27 | 53 | N | Truck bomb | 6 | Russian SF base/2 bombers in truck | ICT/ST |
| 11-Jun-00 | Chechen sep | Khankala | Russia | Govt/Police | 2 | 0 | N | Car bomb | 6 | Russian convert/police checkpoint | Pape/ST |
| 14-Jun-00 | LTTE | Wattala | Sri Lanka | Military | 2 | 7 | N | Bike bomb | 3 | Air force bus | Pape/SATP |
| 25-Jun-00 | LTTE | Northern coast | Sri Lanka | Naval vessel | 10 | 7 | N | Boat bomb | 3 | Merchant Vessel *Uhana* | Pape/SATP |
| 3-Jul-00 | Chechen sep | Argun | Russia | Military | 30 | 81 | N | Truck bomb | 6 | Military/police barracks | Pape/ICT |
| 3-Jul-00 | Chechen sep | Gudermes | Russia | Military | 1 | 3 | N | Truck bomb | 6 | Stopped at bridge | Pape/ST |
| 3-Jul-00 | Chechen sep | Gudermes | Russia | Military | 7 | 12 | N | Truck bomb | 6 | Second bomb in Gudermes | TI/TG |
| 3-Jul-00 | Chechen sep | Novogrozny | Russia | Military | 3 | 20 | N | Truck bomb | 6 | 3-5 tons of explosives in truck | Pape/ST |
| 3-Jul-00 | Chechen sep | Urua-Martan | Russia | Military | 2 | 0 | N | Truck bomb | 6 | Tried to assault military building | Pape/ST |
| 10-Jul-00 | LTTE | Trincomalee | Sri Lanka | Religious site | 4 | 1 | N | Belt bomb | 3 | Buddhist temple | ST/DN |
| 4-Aug-00 | LTTE | Jaffna | Sri Lanka | Military | 0 | 0+ | N | Belt bomb | 3 | Police checkpoint | ST |
| 16-Aug-00 | LTTE | Columbo | Sri Lanka | Military | 1 | 5 | N | Belt bomb | 3 | Military vehicle | Pape/SATP |
| 15-Sep-00 | LTTE | Columbo | Sri Lanka | Hospital | 7 | 28 | N | Belt bomb | 3 | Detonated after checkpoint discovery | Pape/SATP |
| 20-Sep-00 | Unknown | Zamboanga | Philippines | Naval vessel | 0 | 5 | N | Belt bomb | x | Probable suicide attack on ferry | MIPT/AFP |
| 2-Oct-00 | LTTE | Trincomalee | Sri Lanka | Govt/Police* | 24 | 50 | N | Belt bomb | 3 | Political leader Baithullah | Pape/SATP |
| 5-Oct-00 | LTTE | Columbo | Sri Lanka | Govt/Police | 9 | 25 | N | Belt bomb | 3 | People's Alliance political rally | Pape/SATP |
| 12-Oct-00 | al-Qaeda | Aden | Yemen | Naval vessel | 17 | 39 | Y | Boat bomb | 7 | *USS Cole* | Pape/ICT |
| 19-Oct-00 | LTTE | Columbo | Sri Lanka | Govt/Police | 5 | 21 | N | Belt bomb | 3 | Columbo town hall/police challenge | Pape/SATP |
| 23-Oct-00 | LTTE | Trincomalee | Sri Lanka | Naval vessel | 2 | 87 | N | Boat bomb | 3 | Gunboat | Pape/ST |
| 23-Oct-00 | LTTE | Trincomalee | Sri Lanka | Naval vessel | 0 | 0 | N | Boat bomb | 3 | Troop carrier | UPI/MH |
| 26-Oct-00 | PIJ | Kissufim | Gaza | Military | 0 | 1 | N | Bike bomb | 4 | Detonated after police challenge | CSS/MEJ |
| 28-Oct-00 | Unknown | Mergui | Burma | Airplane | 0 | 0 | N | Belt bomb | x | Detonated after arrest at airport | MIPT/DVB |
| 31-Oct-00 | Chechen sep | Gudermes | Russia | Govt/Police | 0 | 0 | N | Belt bomb | 6 | Govt building/security alerted of plot | ITAR/PW |
| 6-Nov-00 | Hamas | Rafah | Gaza | Naval vessel | 0 | 0 | N | Boat bomb | 4 | First Hamas boat bomb | CSS/ST |
| 6-Nov-00 | Unknown | Karachi | Pakistan | Civilian | 2 | 5 | N | Belt bomb | 10 | Newspaper office/female bomber | MIPT/XNA |
| 8-Dec-00 | Chechen sep | Gudermes | Russia | Market | 1 | 10 | N | Truck bomb | 6 | Pyatigorsk market | Pape/MIPT |
| 15-Dec-00 | Hamas | Erez crossing | Gaza | Military | 0 | 0 | N | Belt bomb | 4 | Detonated after police stop | CSS/ST |
| 22-Dec-00 | PIJ | Mehola | West Bank | Restaurant | 0 | 5 | N | Car bomb | 4 | Near roadside café | CSS/ICT |
| 22-Dec-00 | LeT | New Delhi | India | Military | 3 | 4 | N | Belt bomb | 9 | Indian Army at Red Fort | UPI/TNL |
| 25-Dec-00 | JeM | Srinagar | Kashmir/India | Military | 9 | 14 | N | Car bomb | 9 | Indian Army HQ Badami Bagh | Pape/ST |
| 25-Dec-00 | Unknown | Cotabato | Philippines | Civilian | 0 | 3 | N | Belt bomb | x | Cinema | MIPT/GMA |
| 1-Jan-01 | Hamas | Netanya | Israel | Civilian | 0 | 35 | N | Car bomb | 4 | Partially failed bomb | CSS/ICT |
| 3-Jan-01 | DHKP-C | Istanbul | Turkey | Govt/Police | 1 | 7 | N | Belt bomb | 8 | Sisli District police station | MIPT/TI |
| 1-Mar-01 | Hamas | Mei Ami junction | Israel | Military | 1 | 10 | N | Belt bomb | 4 | Bomber survived/arrested | CSS/ST |
| 4-Mar-01 | Hamas | Netanya | Israel | Civilian | 3 | 53 | N | Belt bomb | 4 | Near bus station | CSS/ICT |
| 24-Mar-01 | Chechen sep | Mineralnye Vody | Russia | Military | 20 | 142 | N | Belt bomb | 6 | 3 explosions/Chechen border | ICT/ST |
| 27-Mar-01 | Hamas | Jerusalem | Israel | Bus | 0 | 21 | N | Belt bomb | 4 | French Hill area near No. 6 bus | CSS/ICT |
| 28-Mar-01 | Hamas | Neve Yamin | Israel | Bus | 2 | 4 | N | Belt bomb | 4 | Bus stop near gas station | CSS/ICT |
| 9-Apr-01 | None | Guangdong | China | Bus | 25 | 0 | N | Belt bomb | x | Police officer transporting detainees | SCMP/CNN |

| Date | Group | Location | Country | Target | Killed | Wounded | ? | Weapon | # | Notes | Source |
|---|---|---|---|---|---|---|---|---|---|---|---|
| 14-Apr-01 | Unknown | Dhaka | Bangladesh | Civilian | 9 | 24 | N | Belt bomb | 15 | Probable suicide attack at concert | MIPT/SCMP |
| 22-Apr-01 | Hamas | Kfar Saba | Israel | Bus | 1 | 60 | N | Belt bomb | 4 | Bus stop/No. 29 bus line | CSS/ICT |
| 29-Apr-01 | Hamas | Shavei Shomron | West Bank | Bus | 0 | 0 | N | Car bomb | 4 | Near school bus | CSS/ICT |
| 9-May-01 | LeT | Srinagar | Kashmir/India | Military | 7 | 6 | N | Cart bomb | 9 | Ice cream cart/paramilitary camp | AP/CNN |
| 18-May-01 | Hamas | Netanya | Israel | Mall | 5 | 86 | N | Belt bomb | 4 | Stopped by security at entrance | CSS/ICT |
| 25-May-01 | PIJ | Hadera | Israel | Bus | 0 | 66 | N | Car bomb | 4 | 2 bombers in car | CSS/MEJ |
| 25-May-01 | Hamas | Netsarim | Gaza | Govt/Police | 0 | 0 | N | Truck bomb | 4 | Detonated after police gunfire | CSS/MIPT |
| 29-May-01 | Hamas | Tofah checkpoint | Gaza | Military | 0 | 2 | N | Grenades | 4 | Stopped at police checkpoint | CSS/ST |
| 1-Jun-01 | Hamas | Tel Aviv | Israel | Nightclub | 21 | 120 | N | Belt bomb | 4 | Dolphinarium nightclub | CSS/ICT |
| 16-Jun-01 | ICS | Narayanganj | Bangladesh | Govt/Police | 20 | 110 | N | Belt bomb | 15 | Possible 3 female bombers | MIPT/SATP |
| 17-Jun-01 | PIJ | Dahaniya | Gaza | Military | 0 | 0 | N | Barrel | 4 | Low-order bomb/arrested | CSS/ST |
| 21-Jun-01 | Hamas | Gush Katif | Gaza | Military | 2 | 1 | N | Car bomb | 4 | Jeep on side on road | CSS/ICT |
| 9-Jul-01 | Hamas | Gush Katif | Gaza | Military | 0 | 1 | N | Car bomb | 4 | Kissufim crossing south Gaza | CSS/ICT |
| 11-Jul-01 | Unknown | Afula | Israel | Unknown | 0 | 0 | N | Bag bomb | 4 | Bomber tackled by police | MIPT/NYP |
| 16-Jul-01 | PIJ | Binyamina | Israel | Bus | 2 | 8 | N | Belt bomb | 4 | Bus stop near train station | CSS/ICT |
| 22-Jul-01 | PIJ | Haifa | Israel | Military | 0 | 0 | N | Belt bomb | 4 | Arrested before detonation | CSS/MIPT |
| 24-Jul-01 | LTTE | Columbo | Sri Lanka | Airport | 12 | 17 | N | Truck bomb | 3 | 14 man suicide team | Pape/SATP |
| 28-Jul-01 | LTTE | Mannar | Sri Lanka | Unknown | 1 | 1 | N | Belt bomb | 3 | Premature detonation | REUT/CNN |
| 2-Aug-01 | PIJ | Jerusalem | Israel | Bus | 0 | 0 | N | Bag bomb | 4 | Arrested before detonation | CSS/MIPT |
| 4-Aug-01 | Hamas | Jordan Valley | West Bank | Bus | 0 | 0 | N | Bag bomb | 4 | Foiled by bus driver | CSS/ICT |
| 8-Aug-01 | Hamas | Bekaot checkpoint | West Bank | Military | 0 | 1 | N | Car bomb | 4 | Premature detonation/roadblock | CSS/ICT |
| 9-Aug-01 | Hamas | Jerusalem | Israel | Restaurant | 15 | 132 | N | Belt bomb | 4 | Sbarro pizzeria | CSS/ICT |
| 12-Aug-01 | PIJ | Kiryat Mozkin | Israel | Restaurant | 0 | 20 | N | Belt bomb | 4 | Wall Street café | CSS/ICT |
| 15-Aug-01 | Unknown | Ambon | Indonesia | Market | 0 | 8 | N | Motorcycle | x | 2 bombers killed on motorcycle | MIPT/JAP |
| 18-Aug-01 | PIJ | Jenin | West Bank | Nightclub | 0 | 0 | N | Bag bomb | 4 | Arrested/Haifa City Hall club target | TEL/JP |
| 25-Aug-01 | Chechen sep | Gudermes | Russia | Govt/Police | 1 | 11 | N | Bag bomb | 6 | Probable premature detonation | MIPT/AP |
| 3-Sep-01 | Chechen sep | Grozny | Russia | Unknown | 0 | 0 | N | Car bomb | 6 | Probable premature detonation | MIPT/ITAR |
| 4-Sep-01 | Hamas | Jerusalem | Israel | Bus | 0 | 13 | N | Belt bomb | 4 | Detonated after police approach | CSS/ICT |
| 6-Sep-01 | JeM | Magam | Kashmir/India | Military | 2 | 6 | N | Truck bomb | 9 | Special Operations Group camp | ST/SATP |
| 9-Sep-01 | PIJ | Beit Lid junction | Israel | Military | 0 | 12 | N | Car bomb | 4 | Former Fatah member | ICT/HAA |
| 9-Sep-01 | Hamas | Nahariya | Israel | Train | 3 | 46 | N | Belt bomb | 4 | First Israeli Arab | CSS/ICT |
| 9-Sep-01 | al-Qaeda | Afghanistan | Afghanistan | Govt/Police* | 2 | 2 | N | Camera | 7 | Northern Alliance head Mashood | Pape/ICT |
| 10-Sep-01 | PKK | Istanbul | Turkey | Govt/Police | 3 | 20 | N | Belt bomb | 8 | Riot police near German consulate | MIPT/ST |
| 11-Sep-01 | al-Qaeda | New York | United States | Civilian | 1811 | 1559 | Y | Airplane | 7 | 1 World Trade Center | Pape/MIPT |
| 11-Sep-01 | al-Qaeda | New York | United States | Civilian | 815 | 702 | Y | Airplane | 7 | 2 World Trade Center | Pape/MIPT |
| 11-Sep-01 | al-Qaeda | Pennsylvania | United States | Govt/Police | 40 | 0 | Y | Airplane | 7 | Capitol probable target | Pape/MIPT |
| 11-Sep-01 | al-Qaeda | Washington DC | United States | Govt/Police | 184 | 76 | Y | Airplane | 7 | Pentagon | Pape/MIPT |
| 15-Sep-01 | LTTE | Columbo | Sri Lanka | Naval vessel | 15 | 43 | N | Boat bomb | 3 | Naval troop transport (1,200 pax) | Pape/SFC |
| 17-Sep-01 | Chechen sep | Argun | Russia | Govt/Police** | 1 | 0 | N | Truck bomb | 6 | Pro-Russian official Movsar Timerbayev | MIPT/INT |
| 26-Sep-01 | Unknown | Ankara | Turkey | Unknown | 0 | 0 | N | Belt bomb | 8 | Early detonation/asst wounded | MIPT/SPI |
| 1-Oct-01 | JeM | Srinagar | Kashmir/India | Govt/Police | 22 | 60 | N | Car bomb | 9 | Car bomb hit gate/gunmen ran in | Pape/IPCS |
| 2-Oct-01 | Unknown | Howrah | India | Bus | 0 | 3 | N | Bag bomb | 9 | Possible premature detonation | MIPT/TST |
| 6-Oct-01 | Unknown | Khobar | Saudi Arabia | Civilian | 1 | 5 | Y | Car bomb | x | Probable suicide attack | MIPT/ST |

| Date | Group | Location | Country | Target | Killed | Wounded | ? | Weapon | Sec | Notes | Source |
|---|---|---|---|---|---|---|---|---|---|---|---|
| 7-Oct-01 | PIJ | Kibbutz Shluhot | Israel | Civilian | 1 | 0 | N | Belt bomb | 4 | Kibbutz entrance | CSS/ICT |
| 17-Oct-01 | PFLP | Kibbutz Be'eri | Israel | Military | 0 | 2 | N | Belt bomb | 4 | IDF disguise/target IDF jeep | CSS/ST |
| 22-Oct-01 | LeT | Awantipora base | India | Military | 2 | 2 | N | Grenades | 9 | Indian Air Force base | ST/SATP |
| 29-Oct-01 | LTTE | Columbo | Sri Lanka | Govt/Police** | 2 | 13 | N | Belt bomb | 3 | Possible attempt on PM | Pape/SAT |
| 30-Oct-01 | LTTE | Jaffna | Sri Lanka | Military | 7 | 0 | N | Boat bomb | 3 | Attack on *MV Silk Pride* | Pape/SAT |
| 6-Nov-01 | Unknown | Abu Dis | West Bank | Unknown | 0 | 0 | N | Belt bomb | 4 | Arrested before detonation | MIPT/NYF |
| 6-Nov-01 | Hamas | Erez crossing | Gaza | Govt/Police | 0 | 2 | N | Belt bomb | 4 | Border checkpoint | CSS/MIPT |
| 8-Nov-01 | Hamas | Baka al-Sharkiya | West Bank | Military | 0 | 2 | N | Belt bomb | 4 | Detonated after police challenge | CSS/MEJ |
| 9-Nov-01 | LTTE | Batticaloa | Sri Lanka | Govt/Police** | 0 | 1 | N | Belt bomb | 3 | Police chief | Pape/ST |
| 14-Nov-01 | None | Chongqing | China | Hospital | 4 | 35 | N | Bag bomb | x | Ophthalmology ward/botched operation | SCMP/CD |
| 15-Nov-01 | LTTE | Batticaloa | Sri Lanka | Civilian | 3 | 8 | N | Belt bomb | 3 | Crowd | Pape/SAT |
| 25-Nov-01 | Taliban | Mazar-e-Sharif | Afghanistan | Military | 3 | 2 | N | Grenades | 12 | Kala-i-Jangi prison uprising | ST/TP |
| 26-Nov-01 | Hamas | Erez crossing | Gaza | Military | 0 | 2 | N | Car bomb | 4 | Targeted border post | JA/MIPT |
| 29-Nov-01 | PIJ | Hadera | Israel | Bus | 3 | 10 | N | Belt bomb | 4 | No. 823 bus | CSS/ICT |
| 29-Nov-01 | Chechen sep | Urus-Martan | Russia | Military** | 3 | 1 | N | Belt bomb | 6 | Military commander | Pape/ICT |
| 1-Dec-01 | Hamas | Jerusalem | Israel | Civilian^ | 5 | 85 | N | Belt bomb | 4 | 2 bombers/Zion Square | CSS/ICT |
| 1-Dec-01 | Hamas | Jerusalem | Israel | Civilian^ | 6 | 85 | N | Belt bomb | 4 | 2 bombers/Ben Yehuda mall | CSS/ICT |
| 2-Dec-01 | Hamas | Haifa | Israel | Bus | 15 | 35 | N | Belt bomb | 4 | No. 16 bus/Halissa neighborhood | CSS/ICT |
| 5-Dec-01 | PIJ | Jerusalem | Israel | Bus | 0 | 5 | N | Belt bomb | 4 | Near Hilton/unable to board bus | CSS/ICT |
| 8-Dec-01 | LeT | Baramulla | Kashmir/India | Military | 2 | 7 | N | Belt bomb | 9 | Police convoy | ST/SATP |
| 9-Dec-01 | PIJ | Haifa | Israel | Bus | 0 | 30 | N | Belt bomb | 4 | Bus stop/police approach | CSS/ICT |
| 12-Dec-01 | Hamas | Gush Katif | Gaza | Civilian | 0 | 3 | N | Bag bomb | 4 | 2 bombers/Ganei Tal | CSS/HAA |
| 13-Dec-01 | JeM | New Delhi | India | Govt/Police | 10 | 18 | N | Car bomb | 9 | Bomb led assault/Indian Parliament | IPCS/ST |
| 15-Dec-01 | PIJ | Tulkarm | West Bank | Mall | 0 | 0 | N | Belt bomb | 4 | Premature detonation | CSS/MIPT |
| 22-Dec-01 | al-Qaeda | North Atlantic | Atlantic | Airplane | 0 | 0 | Y | Shoe bomb | 7 | Reid/foiled by passengers flight 63 | AP/CNN |
| 28-Dec-01 | PIJ | Netzarim | Gaza | Military | 0 | 0 | N | Belt bomb | 4 | Killed by police before detonation | TI/TES |
| 30-Dec-01 | Unknown | Sederot | Gaza | Unknown | 0 | 0 | N | Belt bomb | 4 | 3 bombers killed by security | MIPT/HAA |
| 18-Jan-02 | Fatah | Hadera | Israel | Civilian | 5 | 30 | N | Belt bomb failed/use grenades/wedding | 4 | | DR/DP |
| 24-Jan-02 | PFLP | Kfar Darom | Gaza | Civilian | 0 | 0 | N | Car bomb | 4 | Premature detonation | MIPT/QP |
| 25-Jan-02 | PIJ | Tel Aviv | Israel | Civilian | 0 | 26 | N | Belt bomb | 4 | Crowd near Central Bus Station | CSS/ICT |
| 27-Jan-02 | Fatah | Jerusalem | Israel | Mall | 1 | 150 | N | Bag bomb | 4 | First Palestinian female bomber | CSS/ICT |
| 30-Jan-02 | Fatah | Taibe | West Bank | Govt/Police | 0 | 2 | N | Belt bomb | 4 | At meeting with Shin Bet agents | CSS/MEJ |
| 1-Feb-02 | None | Urumqi | China | Govt/Police | 1 | 2 | N | Belt bomb | x | Ethnic Han/near Tiashan Dept store | XNA/TNL |
| 6-Feb-02 | Hamas | Jerusalem | Israel | Bus | 0 | 0 | N | Belt bomb | 4 | Arrested on bus/failed bomb | CSS/ST |
| 7-Feb-02 | Unknown | Bethlehem | West Bank | Unknown | 0 | 0 | N | Belt bomb | 4 | Premature detonation | SLPD/UPI |
| 16-Feb-02 | PFLP | Karnei Shomron | West Bank | Mall | 3 | 29 | N | Belt bomb | 4 | Outdoor food court | CSS/ICT |
| 17-Feb-02 | Fatah | Hadera | Israel | Military | 0 | 2 | N | Belt bomb | 4 | 2 bombers killed in car by police | CSS/ST |
| 18-Feb-02 | Fatah | Jerusalem | Israel | Military | 1 | 2 | N | Car bomb | 4 | Car stopped by police | CSS/ICT |
| 19-Feb-02 | Fatah | Mehola junction | West Bank | Bus | 0 | 0 | N | Belt bomb | 4 | Bomber foiled by bus driver | CSS/ST |
| 22-Feb-02 | Fatah | Efrat | West Bank | Market | 0 | 3 | N | Belt bomb | 4 | Bomber killed/ low-order bomb | CSS/ST |
| 27-Feb-02 | Fatah | Maccabim | West Bank | Military | 0 | 2 | N | Belt bomb | 4 | Bomber/two drivers killed checkpoint | CSS/ICT |
| 2-Mar-02 | Fatah | Jerusalem | Israel | Religious site | 10 | 46 | N | Belt bomb | 4 | Near a Yhiva | CSS/ICT |
| 5-Mar-02 | PIJ | Afula | Israel | Bus | 1 | 20 | N | Belt bomb | 4 | No. 823 bus | CSS/MEJ |

| Date | Group | Location | Country | Target | Killed | Wounded | Sui | Weapon | Col9 | Notes | Source |
|---|---|---|---|---|---|---|---|---|---|---|---|
| 7-Mar-02 | PFLP | Ariel | West Bank | Hotel | 0 | 9 | N | Belt bomb | 4 | Supermarket/partially foiled | CSS/ICT |
| 7-Mar-02 | Hamas | Jerusalem | Israel | Restaurant | 0 | 0 | N | Bag bomb | 4 | Bomber foiled by café Kapit waiter | CSS/MEJ |
| 7-Mar-02 | PIJ | Karkur | Israel | Military | 0 | 0 | N | Belt bomb | 4 | Bomber spotted, fled, arrested | CSS/ST |
| 8-Mar-02 | Unknown | Jerusalem | Israel | Unknown | 0 | 0 | N | Bag bomb | 4 | Killed by police before detonation | MIPT/XNA |
| 9-Mar-02 | Hamas | Jerusalem | Israel | Restaurant | 11 | 58 | N | Belt bomb | 4 | Moment café | CSS/ICT |
| 17-Mar-02 | Fatah/PIJ | Jerusalem | Israel | Bus | 0 | 25 | N | Belt bomb | 4 | Tried to board bus | CSS/HAA |
| 20-Mar-02 | PIJ | Vadi Ara | Israel | Bus | 7 | 28 | N | Belt bomb | 4 | No. 823 bus | CSS/ICT |
| 21-Mar-02 | Fatah | Jerusalem | Israel | Restaurant | 3 | 86 | N | Belt bomb | 4 | Aroma café | CSS/ICT |
| 22-Mar-02 | Fatah/PIJ | Salem checkpoint | West Bank | Military | 0 | 1 | N | Belt bomb | 4 | Detonated after police stop | CSS/ICT |
| 26-Mar-02 | PFLP | Ariel | West Bank | Govt/Police | 0 | 0 | N | Belt bomb | 4 | Bomber fled after police stop | CSS/ITV |
| 26-Mar-02 | Fatah | Jerusalem | Israel | Govt/Police | 0 | 0 | N | Belt bomb | 4 | Premature detonation/police stop | ICT/ST |
| 27-Mar-02 | Hamas | Netanya | Israel | Hotel | 30 | 144 | N | Bag bomb | 4 | Restaurant inside hotel/Passover meal | CSS/ICT |
| 29-Mar-02 | Fatah | Jerusalem | Israel | Market | 2 | 30 | N | Belt bomb | 4 | Supermarket/female bomber | CSS/ICT |
| 30-Mar-02 | Fatah | Baka al-Gharbia | Israel | Govt/Police | 1 | 1 | N | Belt bomb | 4 | Detonated under fire | CSS/TEL |
| 30-Mar-02 | Fatah | Tel Aviv | Israel | Restaurant | 1 | 30 | N | Belt bomb | 4 | My Coffee Shop | CSS/ICT |
| 31-Mar-02 | Fatah | Efrat | West Bank | Civilian | 0 | 6 | N | Belt bomb | 4 | Near ambulance station | CSS/ICT |
| 31-Mar-02 | Hamas | Haifa | Israel | Restaurant | 15 | 40 | N | Belt bomb | 4 | Matza restaurant | CSS/ICT |
| 1-Apr-02 | Fatah | Jerusalem | Israel | Govt/Police | 1 | 0 | N | Car bomb | 4 | Premature detonation/police stop | CSS/ICT |
| 2-Apr-02 | Fatah | Bakka al-Sharkiya | West Bank | Unknown | 0 | 0 | | Belt bomb | 4 | Detonated/soldiers opened fire | ICT/MEJ |
| 9-Apr-02 | Unknown | Jenin | West Bank | Military | 13 | 9 | N | Belt bomb | 4 | IDF lured to alley | HC/TNL |
| 10-Apr-02 | Hamas/PIJ | Yagur junction | Israel | Bus | 8 | 22 | N | Belt bomb | 4 | Express bus/IDF disguise | CSS/MEJ |
| 11-Apr-02 | Hamas | Hebron | West Bank | Unknown | 0 | 0 | N | Car bomb | 4 | Premature detonation/4 bombers | MIPT/VOI |
| 11-Apr-02 | al-Qaeda | Djerba | Tunisia | Religious site | 19 | 26 | N | Car bomb | 7 | Synagogue | Pape/ICT |
| 12-Apr-02 | Fatah | Jerusalem | Israel | Market | 6 | 64 | | Belt bomb | 4 | Market because of bus security | CSS/ICT |
| 19-Apr-02 | PIJ | Gush Katif | Gaza | Military | 0 | 2 | N | Car bomb | 4 | Military checkpoint | CSS/MEJ |
| 20-Apr-02 | Hamas | Kalkilya | West Bank | Military | 0 | 0 | | Belt bomb | 4 | Detonated after police challenge | CSS/ST |
| 7-May-02 | Hamas | Rishon Lezion | Israel | Nightclub | 15 | 51 | N | Suitcase | 4 | Sheffield Hall pool hall | CSS/ICT |
| 8-May-02 | PIJ | Megiddo junction | Israel | Bus | 0 | 3 | N | Suitcase | 4 | Probable premature detonation | CSS/ICT |
| 8-May-02 | al-Qaeda | Karachi | Pakistan | Bus | 13 | 25 | N | Car bomb | 7 | French contractors at Sheraton hotel | Pape/ST |
| 19-May-02 | PFLP | Netanya | Israel | Market | 3 | 60 | N | Belt bomb | 4 | Open-air market | CSS/ICT |
| 20-May-02 | PIJ | Ta'anakhim junc | Israel | Unknown | 0 | 3 | N | Belt bomb | 4 | Detonated after challenge | CSS/HAA |
| 22-May-02 | PIJ | Jenin | West Bank | Govt/Police | 0 | 0 | N | Belt bomb | 4 | Approached by police | MIPT/TES |
| 22-May-02 | Fatah | Rishon LeZion | Israel | Civilian | 2 | 36 | N | Belt bomb | 4 | Semi-open park area | CSS/ICT |
| 24-May-02 | Fatah | Tel Aviv | Israel | Military | 0 | 7 | N | Car bomb | 4 | Shot by guard in front of Studio 49 | CSS/ICT |
| 27-May-02 | Fatah | Petah Tikva | Israel | Restaurant | 2 | 37 | N | Belt bomb | 4 | Ice cream parlor/Bravissimo café | CSS/ICT |
| 31-May-02 | Chechen sep | Grozny | Russia | | 4 | 0+ | N | Bag bomb | 6 | | Pape |
| 5-Jun-02 | PIJ | Megiddo junction | Israel | Bus | 17 | 42 | N | Car bomb | 4 | No. 830 bus | CSS/ICT |
| 11-Jun-02 | Fatah | Herzliya | Israel | Restaurant | 1 | 12 | N | Belt bomb | 4 | Schwarma stand | CSS/ICT |
| 14-Jun-02 | al-Qaeda | Karachi | Pakistan | Embassy | 12 | 40 | Y | Car bomb | 7 | U.S. consulate | Pape/ST |
| 17-Jun-02 | Fatah | Tulkarm | West Bank | Military | 0 | 0 | N | Belt bomb | 4 | Detonated as police approached | CSS/MEJ |
| 18-Jun-02 | Hamas | Jerusalem | Israel | Bus | 19 | 50 | N | Belt bomb | 4 | No. 32 bus near Patt intersection | CSS/ICT |
| 19-Jun-02 | Fatah | Jerusalem | Israel | Bus | 7 | 43 | N | Belt bomb | 4 | Bus stop near French Hill | CSS/ICT |
| 17-Jul-02 | Fatah | Tel Aviv | Israel | Mall^ | 2 | 16 | N | Belt bomb | 4 | 2 bombers/Neve Sha'anan Quarter | CSS/ICT |

| Date | Group | Location | Country | Target | Killed | Wounded | ? | Type | # | Notes | Source |
|---|---|---|---|---|---|---|---|---|---|---|---|
| 17-Jul-02 | Fatah | Tel Aviv | Israel | Mall^ | 3 | 17 | N | Belt bomb | 4 | 2 bombers/Neve Sha'anan Quarter | CSS/ICT |
| 30-Jul-02 | Fatah | Jerusalem | Israel | Mall | 0 | 5 | N | Bag bomb | 4 | Detonated after police challenge | CSS/ICT |
| 30-Jul-02 | Unknown | Kabul | Afghanistan | Unknown | 0 | 0 | N | Car bomb | 12 | Arrested after traffic accident | MIPT/TS |
| 4-Aug-02 | Hamas | Miron junction | Israel | Bus | 9 | 52 | N | Belt bomb | 4 | No. 361 bus | CSS/ICT |
| 6-Aug-02 | Fatah | Umm al Fahm | Israel | Civilian | 0 | 1 | N | Belt bomb | 4 | Early detonation in car transit | CSS/ST |
| 18-Sep-02 | PIJ | Umm al Fahm | Israel | Govt/Police | 1 | 4 | N | Belt bomb | 4 | Detonated as police approached | CSS/ICT |
| 19-Sep-02 | Hamas | Tel Aviv | Israel | Bus | 6 | 7 | N | Belt bomb | 4 | No. 4 bus | CSS/ICT |
| 2-Oct-02 | Unknown | Guilin | China | Civilian | 1 | 18 | N | Belt bomb | x | Central Square | ICT/ST |
| 6-Oct-02 | al-Qaeda | Yemen coast | Yemen | Naval vessel | 0 | 12 | N | Boat bomb | 7 | French oil tanker | Pape/ST |
| 10-Oct-02 | Hamas | Ramat Gan | Israel | Bus | 1 | 48 | N | Belt bomb | 4 | Bomber partially foiled | CSS/ICT |
| 10-Oct-02 | Chechen sep | Grozny | Russia | Govt/Police | 25 | 9 | N | Belt bomb | 6 | Zvodskoi district police station | ST/AFP |
| 11-Oct-02 | Hamas | Tel Aviv | Israel | Restaurant | 0 | 0 | N | Belt bomb | 4 | Arrested before detonation/Tayelet café | CSS/ST |
| 12-Oct-02 | JI | Bali | Indonesia | Nightclub | 202 | 300 | N | Car bomb | 7 | Sari Club Discotheque | Pape/ST |
| 21-Oct-02 | PIJ | Pardes Hannah | Israel | Bus | 14 | 48 | N | Car bomb | 4 | 2 bombers in car | CSS/HAA |
| 24-Oct-02 | Chechen sep | Moscow | Russia | Civilian | 0 | 0 | N | Belt bomb | 6 | 18 theater bombers/killed by security | ICT/TM |
| 27-Oct-02 | Hamas | Ariel | West Bank | Civilian | 3 | 17 | N | Belt bomb | 4 | Security tried to subdue bomber | CSS/ICT |
| 4-Nov-02 | Fatah | Kfar Saba | Israel | Mall | 2 | 37 | N | Belt bomb | 4 | Partially foiled by security | CSS/HAA |
| 7-Nov-02 | Unknown | Jif junction | West Bank | Unknown | 2 | 1 | N | Belt bomb | 4 | Detonated after police gunfire/Nablus | MIPT/TOL |
| 11-Nov-02 | PIJ | Erez crossing | Gaza | Military | 0 | 0 | N | Belt bomb | 4 | Premature detonation | CSS/ICT |
| 11-Nov-02 | Unknown | Kibbutz Metzer | West Bank | Unknown | 0 | 0 | N | Car bomb | 4 | Detonated after police challenge | MIPT/CNN |
| 21-Nov-02 | Hamas | Jerusalem | Israel | Bus | 11 | 50 | N | Bag bomb | 4 | Mexico Street/No. 20 bus | CSS/ICT |
| 22-Nov-02 | PIJ | Gaza | Gaza | Naval vessel | 0 | 4 | N | Boat bomb | 4 | Gunboat stopped fishing vessel | CSS/ICT |
| 22-Nov-02 | Unknown | Kabul | Afghanistan | Govt/Police** | 0 | 0 | N | Belt bomb | 12 | Arrested/failed bomb/VP Fahim | MIPT/TH |
| 27-Nov-02 | PFLP | Erez crossing | Gaza | Military | 0 | 0 | N | Car bomb | 4 | IDF checkpoint | CSS/ST |
| 28-Nov-02 | al-Qaeda | Mombassa | Kenya | Hotel | 16 | 40 | N | Car bomb | 7 | 3 bombers in car/Paradise Hotel | Pape/ST |
| 8-Dec-02 | Unknown | Atil | West Bank | Unknown | 0 | 0 | N | Grenades | 4 | Arrested wearing 33 lb bomb | NYT/JP |
| 20-Dec-02 | Unknown | Kabul | Afghanistan | Military | 2 | 3 | N | Belt bomb | 12 | German ISAF HQ entrance | NYT/DN |
| 27-Dec-02 | RaS | Grozny | Russia | Govt/Police^ | 41 | 105 | N | Truck bomb | 6 | 2 trucks bombs/Chechen Govt HQ | Pape/ST |
| 27-Dec-02 | RaS | Grozny | Russia | Govt/Police^ | 42 | 105 | N | Truck bomb | 6 | 2 trucks bombs/Chechen Govt HQ | Pape/ST |
| 28-Dec-02 | None | Jerusalem | Israel | Govt/Police | 0 | 0 | N | Car bomb | 4 | Police station/bomb failed/arrested | CSS/ST |
| 5-Jan-03 | Fatah | Tel Aviv | Israel | Market^ | 11 | 53 | N | Belt bomb | 4 | Coordinated attack | CSS/MEJ |
| 5-Jan-03 | Fatah | Tel Aviv | Israel | Bus^ | 12 | 53 | N | Belt bomb | 4 | Coordinated attack | CSS/MEJ |
| 17-Jan-03 | Hamas | Gaza | Gaza | Naval vessel | 0 | 0 | N | Raft bomb | 4 | Detonated by gunfire at distance | CSS/ST |
| 25-Jan-03 | FARC | Araquita | Columbia | Govt/Police | 6 | 5 | N | Car bomb | x | Possible unwitting hostage driver | MIPT/EFE |
| 8-Feb-03 | LTTE | Sea | Sri Lanka | Naval vessel | 0 | 0 | N | Boat bomb | 3 | LTTE smuggling boat/stopped by Navy | ST/WP |
| 9-Feb-03 | PIJ | Gush Katif | Gaza | Military | 0 | 4 | N | Car bomb | 4 | 3 bombers in car/IDF post | CSS/ST |
| 10-Feb-03 | Hamas | Ramallah | West Bank | Unknown | 0 | 0 | N | Bag bomb | 4 | Arrested before detonation/44 lb bomb | JP/NYT |
| 19-Feb-03 | Hamas | Gaza | Gaza | Military | 0 | 0 | N | Belt bomb | 4 | IDF tank | MEJ/TES |
| 26-Feb-03 | Ansar al-Islam | Zamaqi | Iraq | Govt/Police | 3 | 0 | N | Belt bomb | 13 | Kurd HQ/Detonated after police stop | SBO/MIPT |
| 5-Mar-03 | Hamas | Haifa | Israel | Bus | 17 | 42 | N | Belt bomb | 4 | Near Carmel Center | CSS/MEJ |
| 13-Mar-03 | Ansar al-Islam | Northern Iraq | Iraq | Govt/Police | 0 | 0 | N | Belt bomb | 13 | Kurdish political leaders | SBO/VBPJ |
| 22-Mar-03 | Ansar al-Islam | Khurmal | Iraq | Media | 4 | 24 | N | Car bomb | 13 | Kurd checkpoint/journalist | Pape/SBO |
| 29-Mar-03 | Iraq military | Najaf | Iraq | Military | 5 | 2 | Y | Car bomb | 13 | Taxi at US military checkpoint | ST/SBO |

| Date | Group | Location | Country | Target | Killed | Wounded | ? | Weapon | ? | Notes | Source |
|---|---|---|---|---|---|---|---|---|---|---|---|
| 30-Mar-03 | PIJ | Netanya | Israel | Restaurant | 0 | 54 | N | Belt bomb | 4 | Security partly foiled/Café London | CSS/MEJ |
| 3-Apr-03 | Unknown | Haditha | Iraq | Military | 3 | 2 | Y | Car bomb | 13 | Haditha dam/2 female bombers | Pape/CSM |
| 4-Apr-03 | Iraq military | Baghdad | Iraq | Military | 3 | 2 | Y | Car bomb | 13 | US military convoy | ICT/SBO |
| 10-Apr-03 | Unknown | Baghdad | Iraq | Military | 1 | 4 | Y | Belt bomb | 13 | US military checkpoint/Saddam City | Pape/SBO |
| 12-Apr-03 | Unknown | Baghdad | Iraq | Military | 0 | 5 | Y | Belt bomb | 13 | US military checkpoint | SBO/SB |
| 15-Apr-03 | Hamas | Karni crossing | Gaza | Military | 2 | 3 | N | Belt bomb | 4 | Killed by police before detonation | CSS/MIPT |
| 24-Apr-03 | Fatah | Kfar Saba | Israel | Bus | 1 | 15 | N | Belt bomb | 4 | Partially foiled by security | CSS/MEJ |
| 26-Apr-03 | Unknown | Srinagar | Kashmir/India | Civilian | 2 | 7 | N | Car bomb | 9 | Radio Kashmir | Pape/SATP |
| 30-Apr-03 | Hamas | Tel Aviv | Israel | Restaurant | 0 | 0 | N | Book bomb | 4 | British citizen bomber/failed | CSS/MEJ |
| 30-Apr-03 | Hamas | Tel Aviv | Israel | Restaurant | 3 | 62 | N | Belt bomb | 4 | British citizen bomber/Mike's Place | CSS/MEJ |
| 8-May-03 | Fatah | Gaza | Gaza | Military | 0 | 0 | N | Car bomb | 4 | Targeted IDF tank after gunfire | CSS/ST |
| 12-May-03 | RaS | Znamenskaya | Russia | Military | 59 | 300 | N | Truck bomb | 6 | 3 x bombers in truck/FSB HQ | Pape/ICT |
| 12-May-03 | al-Qaeda | Riyadh | Saudi Arabia | Hotel^ | 6 | 40 | Y | Car bomb | 7 | Al Hamra western housing compound | AP/CNN |
| 12-May-03 | al-Qaeda | Riyadh | Saudi Arabia | Hotel^ | 6 | 40 | Y | Car bomb | 7 | Jedawal western housing compound | AP/CNN |
| 12-May-03 | al-Qaeda | Riyadh | Saudi Arabia | Hotel^ | 7 | 40 | Y | Car bomb | 7 | Siyanco HQ | AP/CNN |
| 12-May-03 | al-Qaeda | Riyadh | Saudi Arabia | Military^ | 6 | 40 | Y | Car bomb | 7 | Vinnell compound | AP/CNN |
| 14-May-03 | RaS | Iliskhan-Yurt | Russia | Religious site | 16 | 145 | N | Belt bomb | 6 | Coordinated attack/2 bombers | Pape/ICT |
| 14-May-03 | RaS | Iliskhan-Yurt | Russia | Religious site | 0 | 0 | N | Belt bomb | 6 | Coordinated attack/2 bombers | Pape/ICT |
| 16-May-03 | Assirat al-M | Casablanca | Morocco | Hotel | 2 | 10 | N | Car bomb | 7 | Hotel Farah/western customers | AP/CNN |
| 16-May-03 | Assirat al-M | Casablanca | Morocco | Religious site | 3 | 0 | N | Belt bomb | 7 | Near Jewish cemetery/wrong target | AP/CNN |
| 16-May-03 | Assirat al-M | Casablanca | Morocco | Restaurant | 20 | 20 | N | Belt bomb | 7 | Casa de Espana Spanish restaurant | AP/CNN |
| 16-May-03 | Assirat al-M | Casablanca | Morocco | Civilian | 4 | 0 | N | Car bomb | 7 | Jewish community center | AP/CNN |
| 16-May-03 | Assirat al-M | Casablanca | Morocco | Embassy | 2 | 1 | N | Car bomb | 7 | Belgian consulate/Italian restaurant | AP/CNN |
| 17-May-03 | Hamas | Hebron | West Bank | Civilian | 2 | 0 | N | Belt bomb | 4 | Detonated after security alerted | CSS/ST |
| 18-May-03 | Hamas | al-Aram CP | Israel | Unknown | 0 | 0 | N | Belt bomb | 4 | Stopped by police at checkpoint | CSS/ST |
| 18-May-03 | Hamas | Jerusalem | Israel | Bus | 7 | 20 | N | Belt bomb | 4 | French Hill area | MEJ/SBC |
| 19-May-03 | Fatah/PIJ | Afula | Israel | Mall | 3 | 50 | N | Bag bomb | 4 | Female bomber/Amaqim mall | CSS/ICT |
| 19-May-03 | Hamas | Kfar Darom | Gaza | Military | 0 | 3 | N | Bike bomb | 4 | IDF jeep in Gaza | CSS/MEJ |
| 20-May-03 | DHKP-C | Ankara | Turkey | Restaurant | 0 | 1 | N | Belt bomb | 8 | Early bomb/Crocodile coffee shop | ICT/MIPT |
| 27-May-03 | Ansar Allah | Baquba | Iraq | Military | 0 | 0 | Y | Grenades | 13 | Female/US military base/grenades | ST/WP |
| 5-Jun-03 | RaS | Mozdok | Russia | Bus | 18 | 15 | N | Belt bomb | 6 | Air force/civilian bus/female bomber | Pape/ICT |
| 7-Jun-03 | Unknown | Kabul | Afghanistan | Military | 5 | 29 | N | Car bomb | 12 | German ISAF bus | Pape/TCF |
| 11-Jun-03 | Hamas | Jerusalem | Israel | Bus | 17 | 104 | N | Belt bomb | 4 | No 14 bus/Revenge for Rantisi death | CSS/SBC |
| 19-Jun-03 | PIJ | Sdei Trumot | Israel | Market | 1 | 0 | N | Belt bomb | 4 | Early detonation/suspicious worker | CSS/MEJ |
| 20-Jun-03 | Chechen sep | Grozny | Russia | Govt/Police | 8 | 36 | N | Truck bomb | 6 | Early detonation/govt buildings | Pape/ICT |
| 22-Jun-03 | Chechen sep | Grozny | Russia | Unknown | 0 | 0 | N | Belt bomb | 6 | 3 bombers killed/police ambush | MIPT/ITAR |
| 24-Jun-03 | al-Tawhid | Baghdad | Iraq | Govt/Police | 4 | 6 | N | Car bomb | 13 | Police checkpoint | MIPT/AP |
| 26-Jun-03 | Unknown | Baquba | Iraq | Religious site | 0 | 0 | N | Belt bomb | 13 | 4 attackers/ 1 bomber killed by police | MIPT/AP |
| 4-Jul-03 | LeJ | Quetta | Pakistan | Religious site | 41 | 100 | N | Belt bomb | 10 | Shiite mosque/2 armed attackers | ST/MIPT |
| 5-Jul-03 | RaS | Moscow | Russia | Civilian | 0 | 0 | N | Belt bomb | 6 | 2 female bombers/rock concert | ICT/ST |
| 5-Jul-03 | RaS | Moscow | Russia | Civilian | 17 | 50 | N | Belt bomb | 6 | 2 female bombers/rock concert | Pape/ICT |
| 7-Jul-03 | PIJ | Kfar Yaavez | Israel | Civilian | 1 | 6 | N | Belt bomb | 4 | Premature detonation | CSS/SBC |

| Date | Group | City | Country | Target | Killed | Wounded | ? | Weapon | # | Notes | Source |
|---|---|---|---|---|---|---|---|---|---|---|---|
| 10-Jul-03 | Chechen sep | Moscow | Russia | Restaurant | 1 | 0 | N | Bag bomb | 6 | Bomber got lost/arrested at Mon café | TG/ICT |
| 22-Jul-03 | Chechen sep | Ingushetia | Russia | Govt/Police | 0 | 1 | N | Belt bomb | 6 | Detonated after police stop | Pape/MIP |
| 27-Jul-03 | Chechen sep | Tstasan-Turt | Russia | Govt/Police** | 1 | 0 | N | Belt bomb | 6 | Future Chechen President's son | Pape/ICT |
| 1-Aug-03 | RaS | Mozdok | Russia | Hospital | 51 | 72 | N | Truck bomb | 6 | Military hospital | Pape/ST |
| 1-Aug-03 | al-Qaeda | Mombassa | Kenya | Govt/Police | 1 | 3 | N | Grenades | 7 | Detonated in police car after arrest | AAIW/AFP |
| 5-Aug-03 | al-Qaeda | Jakarta | Indonesia | Hotel | 15 | 150 | N | Car bomb | 7 | Marriott hotel | Pape/ST |
| 7-Aug-03 | Unknown | Baghdad | Iraq | Embassy | 18 | 50 | N | Truck bomb | 13 | Jordanian Embassy | Pape/SBC |
| 12-Aug-03 | Hamas | Ariel | West Bank | Civilian | 2 | 2 | N | Belt bomb | 4 | Bus stop/noticed security | CSS/HAA |
| 12-Aug-03 | Fatah | Rosh Haayin | Israel | Market | 1 | 9 | N | Bag bomb | 4 | Supermarket | CSS/SBC |
| 19-Aug-03 | PIJ | Jenin | West Bank | Unknown | 0 | 0 | N | Belt bomb | 4 | Arrested before detonation/10kg bomb | HAA/MIPT |
| 19-Aug-03 | Hamas/PIJ | Jerusalem | Israel | Bus | 23 | 115 | N | Belt bomb | 4 | Near Shmuel HaNavi | CSS/ST |
| 19-Aug-03 | al-Tawhid | Baghdad | Iraq | Hotel | 22 | 100 | N | Truck bomb | 13 | U.N. headquarters | Pape/SBC |
| 29-Aug-03 | Unknown | Najaf | Iraq | Religious site | 80 | 140 | N | Car bomb | 13 | Near Imam Ali Mosque | Pape/SBC |
| 2-Sep-03 | Unknown | Baghdad | Iraq | Govt/Police | 1 | 10 | N | Car bomb | 13 | Police station | Pape/MIP |
| 3-Sep-03 | Unknown | Ramadi | Iraq | Military | 1 | 2 | Y | Belt bomb | 13 | US military base entrance | SBO/ST |
| 6-Sep-03 | Chechen sep | Moscow | Russia | Civilian | 0 | 0 | N | Belt bomb | 6 | Arrested before detonation | MIPT/MK |
| 9-Sep-03 | Hamas | Jerusalem | Israel | Restaurant | 7 | 70 | N | Belt bomb | 4 | Café Hillel | CSS/MEJ |
| 9-Sep-03 | Hamas | Tel Aviv | Israel | Bus | 9 | 14 | N | Belt bomb | 4 | Bus stop | CSS/MEJ |
| 9-Sep-03 | Sunna | Irbil | Iraq | Military | 3 | 17 | Y | Car bomb | 13 | U.S. intelligence compound | Pape/SBC |
| 15-Sep-03 | Chechen sep | Magas | Russia | Govt/Police | 3 | 40 | N | Truck bomb | 6 | Russian HQ/2 bombers in truck | Pape/MIP |
| 22-Sep-03 | al-Qaeda | Baghdad | Iraq | Govt/Police | 1 | 19 | N | Car bomb | 13 | U.N. HQ | SBO/MIPT |
| 4-Oct-03 | PIJ | Haifa | Israel | Restaurant | 19 | 48 | N | Belt bomb | 4 | Female bomber/Maxims' | CSS/ICT |
| 9-Oct-03 | PIJ | Tulkarm | West Bank | Military | 0 | 4 | N | Belt bomb | 4 | IDF office | CSS/BBC |
| 9-Oct-03 | al-Tawhid | Baghdad | Iraq | Govt/Police | 9 | 40 | N | Car bomb | 13 | Police Station/Sadr City | Pape/SBC |
| 12-Oct-03 | al-Tawhid | Baghdad | Iraq | Hotel^ | 3 | 20 | Y | Car bomb | 13 | 2 car bombs/Baghdad Hotel | Pape/SBC |
| 12-Oct-03 | al-Tawhid | Baghdad | Iraq | Hotel^ | 4 | 20 | Y | Car bomb | 13 | 2 car bombs/Baghdad Hotel | Pape/SBC |
| 14-Oct-03 | Sunna | Baghdad | Iraq | Embassy | 0 | 13 | N | Car bomb | 13 | Turkish Embassy | Pape/SBC |
| 16-Oct-03 | Unknown | Irbil | Iraq | Govt/Police | 0 | 0 | N | Car bomb | 13 | Interior Ministry/killed by police | MIPT/AFP |
| 24-Oct-03 | Unknown | Baghdad | Iraq | Govt/Police | 4 | 0+ | N | Car bomb | 13 | Police Station | Pape/SBC |
| 27-Oct-03 | Ansar Allah | Baghdad | Iraq | Govt/Police | 0 | 8 | N | Car bomb | 13 | Police Station | Pape/SBC |
| 27-Oct-03 | Ansar Allah | Baghdad | Iraq | Govt/Police | 4 | 4 | N | Car bomb | 13 | Police Station/al-Khadra | Pape/SBC |
| 27-Oct-03 | Ansar Allah | Baghdad | Iraq | Govt/Police | 15 | 39 | N | Car bomb | 13 | Police Station/al-Dora | Pape/SBC |
| 27-Oct-03 | Ansar Allah | Baghdad | Iraq | Govt/Police | 13 | 10 | N | Car bomb | 13 | Police Station/al-Hadrah | Pape/SBC |
| 27-Oct-03 | Ansar Allah | Baghdad | Iraq | Hospital | 12 | 224 | N | Car bomb | 13 | Red Cross | Pape/SBC |
| 27-Oct-03 | Ansar Allah | Baghdad | Iraq | Govt/Police | 0 | 0 | N | Car bomb | 13 | Foiled attack/Syrian bomber | Pape/ET |
| 28-Oct-03 | Unknown | Falluja | Iraq | Govt/Police | 4 | 7 | N | Truck bomb | 13 | Police Station | AP/Pape |
| 31-Oct-03 | Unknown | Baghdad | Iraq | Civilian | 1 | | | | 13 | | ST |
| 3-Nov-03 | Fatah | Kalkilya | West Bank | Military | 0 | 2 | N | Belt bomb | 4 | Near IDF patrol | CSS/HAA |
| 8-Nov-03 | al-Qaeda | Riyadh | Saudi Arabia | Civilian | 17 | 122 | N | Car bomb | 7 | Wealthy/Western housing | Pape/MIP |
| 12-Nov-03 | Unknown | Baghdad | Iraq | Military | 2 | 4 | | | 13 | | ST |
| 12-Nov-03 | al-Tawhid | Nasiriya | Iraq | Military | 29 | 100 | N | Car bomb | 13 | Italian military compound | Pape/SBC |
| 15-Nov-03 | al-Qaeda | Istanbul | Turkey | Religious site^ | 15 | 300 | N | Truck bomb | 7 | Neve Shalom Synagogue | Pape/MIP |
| 15-Nov-03 | al-Qaeda | Istanbul | Turkey | Religious site^ | 15 | 300 | N | Truck bomb | 7 | Beit Israel Synagogue | Pape/MIP |
| 20-Nov-03 | al-Qaeda | Istanbul | Turkey | Bank^ | 13 | 225 | N | Truck bomb | 7 | HSBC Bank | Pape/ST |

| Date | Group | City | Country | Target | Killed | Wounded | F | Weapon | Region | Notes | Source |
|---|---|---|---|---|---|---|---|---|---|---|---|
| 20-Nov-03 | al-Qaeda | Istanbul | Turkey | Embassy^ | 13 | 225 | N | Truck bomb | 7 | U.K. Embassy | Pape/ST |
| 20-Nov-03 | Sunna | Kirkuk | Iraq | Military | 2 | 37 | N | Truck bomb | 13 | PUK HQ | SBO/MIPT |
| 22-Nov-03 | Unknown | Baquba | Iraq | Govt/Police | 9 | 25 | N | Car bomb | 13 | Police station | SBO/MIPT |
| 22-Nov-03 | al-Tawhid | Khan Bani Saad | Iraq | Govt/Police | 9 | 10 | N | Car bomb | 13 | Police station | SBO/MIPT |
| 23-Nov-03 | Unknown | Baghdad | Iraq | Military | 0 | 2 | Y | Grenades | 13 | Female/US military vehicle | ST |
| 3-Dec-03 | PIJ | Bardale | West Bank | School^ | 0 | 0 | N | Belt bomb | 4 | Arrested before detonation | MIPT/AAIW |
| 5-Dec-03 | RaS | Stavropol | Russia | Train | 42 | 160 | N | Bag bomb | 6 | 2 bombers and 2 accomplices | Pape/ICT |
| 9-Dec-03 | Fatah | Rosh Haayin | Israel | Unknown | 0 | 0 | N | Belt bomb | 4 | Arrested before detonation | MIPT/AFP |
| 9-Dec-03 | RaS | Moscow | Russia | Hotel | 5 | 14 | N | Belt bomb | 6 | National Hotel, looking for Duma | Pape/ICT |
| 9-Dec-03 | Unknown | Baghdad | Iraq | Religious site | 3 | 2 | N | Car bomb | 13 | Sunni mosque/premature detonation | BBC/AFP |
| 9-Dec-03 | Unknown | Husseiniya | Iraq | Military | 0 | 2 | Y | Bag bomb | 13 | BFV at US military base | SBO/LAT |
| 9-Dec-03 | Unknown | Talafar | Iraq | Military | 0 | 59 | Y | Car bomb | 13 | US military base/101st ABN | AFP/SLPD |
| 10-Dec-03 | Unknown | Baghdad | Iraq | Military | 0 | 0+ | Y | Car bomb | 13 | US military base | Pape |
| 11-Dec-03 | Unknown | Ramadi | Iraq | Military | 1 | 14 | Y | Truck bomb | 13 | 82nd Airborne HQ/Furniture truck | CC/ST |
| 11-Dec-03 | None | Beirut | Lebanon | Embassy | 0 | 0 | Y | Belt bomb | x | Arrested 500 yards from US Embassy | BP/MIPT |
| 12-Dec-03 | Unknown | Baghdad | Iraq | Govt/Police | 7 | 40 | | | 13 | | ST |
| 14-Dec-03 | al-Tawhid | Khalidiya | Iraq | Govt/Police | 17 | 33 | N | Car bomb | 13 | Police station | Pape/SBO |
| 15-Dec-03 | Unknown | Ameriyah | Iraq | Civilian | 0 | 12 | N | Car bomb | 13 | Police station | SBO/MIPT |
| 15-Dec-03 | Unknown | Ameriyah | Iraq | Civilian | 0 | 0 | N | Car bomb | 13 | Police station/2nd bomber foiled | SBO/MIPT |
| 15-Dec-03 | Unknown | Husainiyah | Iraq | Govt/Police | 8 | 20 | N | Car bomb | 13 | Police Station | SBO/MIPT |
| 16-Dec-03 | Unknown | Baghdad | Iraq | Govt/Police | 9 | 20 | N | Truck bomb | 13 | Hit bus heading for police station | Pape/SBO |
| 16-Dec-03 | Unknown | Tikrit | Iraq | Govt/Police | 0 | 2 | N | Unknown | 13 | Iraqi police | SBO/KNT |
| 24-Dec-03 | Sunna | Irbil | Iraq | Govt/Police** | 4 | 101 | N | Truck bomb | 13 | Kurdish Interior Ministry | SBO/RFE |
| 25-Dec-03 | PFLP | Petah Tikva | Israel | Civilian | 4 | 26 | N | Belt bomb | 4 | Bus stop at Geha interchange | CSS/JP |
| 25-Dec-03 | JeM | Karachi | Pakistan | Govt/Police**^ | 7 | 25 | N | Car bomb | 10 | President Musharraf | Pape/MIPT |
| 25-Dec-03 | JeM | Karachi | Pakistan | Govt/Police**^ | 7 | 25 | N | Car bomb | 10 | President Musharraf | Pape/MIPT |
| 27-Dec-03 | Unknown | Karbala | Iraq | Govt/Police^ | 4 | 29 | N | Car bomb | 13 | 4 bombers/city hall | AFP/XNA |
| 27-Dec-03 | Unknown | Karbala | Iraq | Govt/Police^ | 4 | 29 | N | Car bomb | 13 | 4 bombers/city hall | AFP/XNA |
| 27-Dec-03 | Unknown | Karbala | Iraq | Govt/Police^ | 4 | 29 | N | Car bomb | 13 | 4 bombers/Coalition military base | AFP/XNA |
| 27-Dec-03 | Unknown | Karbala | Iraq | Govt/Police^ | 4 | 29 | N | Truck bomb | 13 | 4 bombers/Coalition military base | SBO/ST |
| 28-Dec-03 | Taliban | Kabul | Afghanistan | Govt/Police | 5 | 0 | N | Belt bomb | 12 | Bomber detained, then detonated | Pape/TCF |
| 31-Dec-03 | Unknown | Baghdad | Iraq | Restaurant | 8 | 30 | N | Car bomb | 13 | Nabil's restaurant/Christian-friendly | SBO/ST |
| 31-Dec-03 | GAM | Peureulak | Indonesia | Civilian | 9 | 30 | N | Belt bomb | x | New Year's Eve concert | XNA/AIW |
| 9-Jan-04 | Unknown | Baghdad | Iraq | Govt/Police | 0 | 7 | N | Car bomb | 13 | Iraq police station/Ameriyah area | CNN |
| 9-Jan-04 | Unknown | Baquba | Iraq | Religious site | 5 | 37 | N | Bike bomb | 13 | Sadeq Shiite Mosque | Pape/SBO |
| 11-Jan-04 | Fatah/PIJ | Qedumin | West Bank | Unknown | 0 | 0 | N | Belt bomb | 4 | Probable premature detonation | CSS/NCTC |
| 14-Jan-04 | Hamas | Erez crossing | Gaza | Govt/Police | 4 | 12 | N | Belt bomb | 4 | First Hamas female bomber | CSS/NCTC |
| 14-Jan-04 | al-Tawhid | Baquba | Iraq | Govt/Police | 3 | 28 | N | Car bomb | 13 | Police station/police opened fire | Pape/NCTC |
| 18-Jan-04 | al-Tawhid | Baghdad | Iraq | Military | 30 | 130 | N | Truck bomb | 13 | Green zone CP/Assassin's Gate | Pape/NCTC |
| 24-Jan-04 | Unknown | Khalidiya | Iraq | Military | 3 | 14 | Y | Car bomb | 13 | US military checkpoint | SBO/ST |
| 27-Jan-04 | Taliban | Kabul | Afghanistan | Military | 2 | 11 | N | Belt bomb | 12 | Canadian military vehicle | RFE/TCF |
| 28-Jan-04 | Taliban | Kabul | Afghanistan | Military | 1 | 4 | N | Car bomb | 12 | Drove taxi bomb into UK Land Rover | LE/ET |
| 28-Jan-04 | al-Tawhid | Baghdad | Iraq | Hotel | 3 | 15 | N | Car bomb | 13 | Ambulance at Shahine hotel | Pape/NCTC |

| Date | Group | City | Country | Target | Killed | Wounded | ? | Weapon | Region | Notes | Source |
|---|---|---|---|---|---|---|---|---|---|---|---|
| 29-Jan-04 | Hamas/Fatah | Jerusalem | Israel | Bus | 11 | 44 | N | Belt bomb | 4 | No.19 bus near PM's residence | CSS/NCTC |
| 31-Jan-04 | Sunna | Mosul | Iraq | Govt/Police | 9 | 45 | N | Belt bomb | 13 | Iraqi police collecting pay | Pape/NCTC |
| 1-Feb-04 | Sunna | Irbil | Iraq | Govt/Police^ | 39 | 73 | N | Belt bomb | 13 | Multiple bombers v. Kurd leaders | Pape/NCTC |
| 1-Feb-04 | Sunna | Irbil | Iraq | Govt/Police^ | 39 | 74 | N | Belt bomb | 13 | Multiple bombers v. Kurd leaders | Pape/NCTC |
| 1-Feb-04 | Sunna | Irbil | Iraq | Govt/Police^ | 39 | 74 | N | Belt bomb | 13 | Multiple bombers v. Kurd leaders | Pape/NCTC |
| 2-Feb-04 | Chechen sep | Shelkovsky | Russia | Unknown | 0 | 0 | N | Belt bomb | 6 | Female arrested before detonation | MIPT/CNN |
| 6-Feb-04 | RaS | Moscow | Russia | Train | 39 | 130 | N | Briefcase | 6 | Up to 3 bombers together | NCTC/MIPT |
| 9-Feb-04 | Unknown | Ramadi | Iraq | Govt/Police | 0 | 4 | N | Belt bomb | 13 | Tribal leaders | NCTC/SBO |
| 10-Feb-04 | Ansar Allah | Iskandariyah | Iraq | Govt/Police | 55 | 67 | N | Truck bomb | 13 | Police station/recruits/250 kg bomb | SBO/MIPT |
| 11-Feb-04 | al-Tawhid | Baghdad | Iraq | Military | 47 | 55 | N | Car bomb | 13 | Army recruiting center | Pape/SBO |
| 18-Feb-04 | al-Tawhid | Hillah | Iraq | Military | 11 | 106 | N | Car bomb | 13 | Polish military base | Pape/SBO |
| 18-Feb-04 | al-Tawhid | Hillah | Iraq | Military | 0 | 0 | N | Car bomb | 13 | Polish base/2nd bomb/killed by troops | AFP/AP |
| 22-Feb-04 | Fatah | Jerusalem | Israel | Bus | 8 | 68 | N | Bag bomb | 4 | No. 14 bus | CSS/NCTC |
| 23-Feb-04 | Sunna | Kirkuk | Iraq | Govt/Police | 10 | 45 | N | Car bomb | 13 | Rahimawa Police station/shift change | Pape/NCTC |
| 27-Feb-04 | PIJ | Kfar Darom | Gaza | Unknown | 0 | 0 | N | Belt bomb | 4 | Premature detonation | JP/NCTC |
| 28-Feb-04 | Unknown | Rawalpindi | Pakistan | Religious site | 0 | 4 | N | Belt bomb | 10 | Early detonation/Shiite mosque | NCTC/ST |
| 29-Feb-04 | PIJ | Jenin | West Bank | Unknown | 0 | 0 | N | Pipe bomb | 4 | 3 arrested before detonation | MIPT/TOL |
| 2-Mar-04 | Ansar Allah | Baghdad | Iraq | Religious site^ | 31 | 106 | N | Belt bomb | 13 | Coordinated attack/Shiite shrine | Pape/NCTC |
| 2-Mar-04 | Ansar Allah | Baghdad | Iraq | Religious site^ | 31 | 107 | N | Belt bomb | 13 | Coordinated attack/Shiite shrine | Pape/NCTC |
| 2-Mar-04 | Ansar Allah | Baghdad | Iraq | Religious site^ | 32 | 107 | N | Belt bomb | 13 | Coordinated attack/Shiite shrine | Pape/NCTC |
| 2-Mar-04 | al-Qaeda | Karbala | Iraq | Religious site | 101 | 230 | N | Belt bomb | 13 | Shiite pilgrims/combo assault | NCTC/SBO |
| 3-Mar-04 | LeJ | Quetta | Pakistan | Civilian | 44 | 154 | N | Belt bomb | 10 | Shiite Ashura procession | MIPT/ST |
| 6-Mar-04 | Fatah | Erez crossing | Gaza | Military | 2 | 20 | N | Car bomb | 4 | Bombers foiled by security | CSS/NCTC |
| 6-Mar-04 | Unknown | Khalidiya | Iraq | Military | 0 | 3 | Y | Truck bomb | 13 | US military patrol at bridge/opened fire | CNN |
| 9-Mar-04 | Abu Hafs | Istanbul | Turkey | Civilian^ | 0 | 2 | N | Car bomb | 7 | 2 bombers/one survived/masonic lodge | NCTC/MIPT |
| 9-Mar-04 | Abu Hafs | Istanbul | Turkey | Civilian^ | 1 | 3 | N | Car bomb | 7 | 2 bombers/one lived/masonic lodge | NCTC/MIPT |
| 14-Mar-04 | Fatah/Hamas | Ashdod | Israel | Civilian^ | 5 | 9 | N | Belt bomb | 4 | 2 bombers at port in container | CSS/NCTC |
| 14-Mar-04 | Fatah/Hamas | Ashdod | Israel | Civilian^ | 5 | 9 | N | Belt bomb | 4 | 2 bombers at port in container | CSS/NCTC |
| 16-Mar-04 | Unknown | Turkey | Turkey | Civilian | 0 | 0 | N | Belt bomb | 8 | Arrested before detonating/Jewish TV | MIPT/NTV |
| 17-Mar-04 | al-Tawhid | Baghdad | Iraq | Hotel | 17 | 35 | N | Car bomb | 13 | Mount Lebanon Hotel/Karrada area | NCTC/SBO |
| 18-Mar-04 | al-Tawhid | Basra | Iraq | Hotel | 3 | 15 | N | Car bomb | 13 | Hotel/UK military patrol nearby | Pape/SBO |
| 21-Mar-04 | Unknown | Balad | Iraq | Military | 1 | 8 | Y | Car bomb | 13 | US military at LSA Anaconda | AFP/CNN |
| 25-Mar-04 | Fatah | Hawara CP | West Bank | Military | 0 | 0 | N | Belt bomb | 4 | Arrested before detonation | JP/AP |
| 28-Mar-04 | Taliban | Khost | Afghanistan | Military | 0 | 0 | N | Belt bomb | 12 | Premature detonation | AIP/DTL |
| 28-Mar-04 | Unknown | Bukhara | Uzbekistan | Civilian | 5 | 4 | N | Belt bomb | 14 | Apartments in Romitan district | MIPT/CSM |
| 28-Mar-04 | None | Brescia | Italy | Restaurant | 0 | 0 | N | Car bomb | x | Bomber's note said acting alone | NCTC/MIPT |
| 29-Mar-04 | Hizb-ub-Tahir | Tashkent | Uzbekistan | Market | 3 | 26 | N | Belt bomb | 14 | Chorsu market/Children's World | NCTC/MIPT |
| 29-Mar-04 | IJU | Tashkent | Uzbekistan | Govt/Police | 1 | 0 | N | Belt bomb | 14 | Female/bus stop near Chorsu market | NCTC/CSM |
| 30-Mar-04 | Unknown | Hillah | Iraq | Govt/Police** | 0 | 7 | N | Car bomb | 13 | Hillah police chief | NCTC/MIPT |
| 30-Mar-04 | Unknown | Tashkent | Uzbekistan | Govt/Police | 6 | 5 | N | Belt bomb | 14 | Police checkpoint | NCTC/ITAR |
| 30-Mar-04 | None | La Paz | Bolivia | Govt/Police | 2 | 10 | N | Belt bomb | x | Disgruntled miner/National Congress | MIPT/EIU |
| 31-Mar-04 | Unknown | Ramadi | Iraq | Market | 4 | 6 | N | Car bomb | 13 | Ramadi market | XNA/AJ |

| Date | Group | City | Country | Target | Killed | Wounded | Suicide | Type | Region | Notes | Source |
|---|---|---|---|---|---|---|---|---|---|---|---|
| 31-Mar-04 | Unknown | Tashkent | Uzbekistan | Govt/Police | 0 | 2 | N | Belt bomb | 14 | Bukhara Region | NCTC/DP |
| 1-Apr-04 | Unknown | Baquba | Iraq | Civilian | 0 | 7 | N | Car bomb | 13 | Iraq government convoy | NCTC/EC |
| 2-Apr-04 | Unknown | Ar Riyad | Iraq | Govt/Police | 2 | 0 | N | Belt bomb | 13 | Stopped by security at city hall | NCTC/AJ |
| 3-Apr-04 | Unknown | Madrid | Spain | Govt/Police | 1 | 15 | N | Bag bomb | 7 | Detonated during arrest attempt | NCTC/EIW |
| 4-Apr-04 | Unknown | Abu Ghurayb | Iraq | Govt/Police | 3 | 3 | N | Car bomb | 13 | Police checkpoint | Pape |
| 6-Apr-04 | RaS | Nazran | Russia | Govt/Police** | 2 | 7 | N | Car bomb | 6 | Ingush President Murat Zyazikov | NCTC/MIPT |
| 11-Apr-04 | Unknown | Karachi | Pakistan | Civilian | 1 | 8 | N | Car bomb | x | Indo-Pak peace concert near Golf Club | PTI/AAIW |
| 13-Apr-04 | Unknown | Falluja | Iraq | Military | 0 | 0 | Y | Belt bomb | 13 | 2 bombers killed nearing US patrol | AP/DT |
| 15-Apr-04 | Tanzim | Ariel | West Bank | Unknown | 0 | 0 | N | Bag bomb | 4 | Arrested before detonation/female | MIPT/AAIW |
| 17-Apr-04 | Hamas/Fatah | Erez crossing | Gaza | Military | 1 | 3 | N | Belt bomb | 4 | Israeli Border Police checkpoint | CSS/HAA |
| 21-Apr-04 | al-Qaeda | Riyadh | Saudi Arabia | Govt/Police | 4 | 148 | N | Car bomb | 7 | Saudi national police | NCTC/MIPT |
| 21-Apr-04 | al-Tawhid | Basra | Iraq | Govt/Police^ | 14 | 40 | N | Car bomb | 13 | 1 of 5 police stations attacked | NCTC/MIPT |
| 21-Apr-04 | al-Tawhid | Basra | Iraq | Govt/Police^ | 14 | 40 | N | Car bomb | 13 | 1 of 5 police stations attacked | NCTC/MIPT |
| 21-Apr-04 | al-Tawhid | Basra | Iraq | Govt/Police^ | 15 | 40 | N | Car bomb | 13 | 1 of 5 police stations attacked | NCTC/MIPT |
| 21-Apr-04 | al-Tawhid | Basra | Iraq | Govt/Police^ | 15 | 40 | N | Car bomb | 13 | 1 of 5 police stations attacked | NCTC/MIPT |
| 21-Apr-04 | al-Tawhid | Basra | Iraq | Govt/Police^ | 15 | 40 | N | Car bomb | 13 | 1 of 5 police stations attacked | NCTC/MIPT |
| 24-Apr-04 | al-Tawhid | Basra | Iraq | Naval vessel | 0 | 0 | N | Boat bomb | 13 | 3 boat attack on oil terminal | Pape/NCTC |
| 24-Apr-04 | al-Tawhid | Basra | Iraq | Naval vessel | 0 | 0 | N | Boat bomb | 13 | 3 boat attack on oil terminal | Pape/NCTC |
| 24-Apr-04 | al-Tawhid | Basra | Iraq | Naval vessel | 3 | 4 | Y | Boat bomb | 13 | 3 boat attack/boarded by US Navy | Pape/NCTC |
| 24-Apr-04 | Unknown | Tikrit | Iraq | Govt/Police | 4 | 16 | N | Car bomb | 13 | Iraq government convoy | AP/NOW |
| 28-Apr-04 | Hamas | Kfar Darom | Gaza | Military | 0 | 4 | N | Car bomb | 4 | Early detonation under police fire | CSS/MIPT |
| 29-Apr-04 | al-Tawhid | Mahmudiyah | Iraq | Military | 8 | 4 | Y | Car bomb | 13 | US military patrol | DMN/WP |
| 30-Apr-04 | Unknown | Falluja | Iraq | Military | 2 | 6 | Y | Car bomb | 13 | US Marine base | CNN/XNA |
| 2-May-04 | Unknown | Vientiane | Laos | Govt/Police | 0 | 0 | N | Belt bomb | x | Early detonation/Women's group | NCTC |
| 6-May-04 | al-Tawhid | Baghdad | Iraq | Military | 6 | 26 | N | Belt bomb | 13 | Green Zone checkpoint | Pape/NCTC |
| 6-May-04 | Unknown | Baghdad | Iraq | Hotel | 0 | 2 | N | Belt bomb | 13 | 2 hotels damaged | NCTC |
| 7-May-04 | LeJ | Karachi | Pakistan | Religious site | 23 | 200 | N | Belt bomb | 10 | Hyderi Shiite mosque | IPCS/NCTC |
| 10-May-04 | PIJ | Jenin | West Bank | Unknown | 0 | 0 | N | Belt bomb | 4 | Arrested before detonation | MIPT/SEA |
| 14-May-04 | Unknown | Balad | Iraq | Military | 1 | 2 | Y | Car bomb | 13 | 1 x US mil/LSA Anaconda | IC/LHL |
| 17-May-04 | Unknown | Baghdad | Iraq | Military | 0 | 2 | Y | Car bomb | 13 | US military truck carrying paper plates | NYT |
| 17-May-04 | Arab Resistance | Baghdad | Iraq | Govt/Police* | 7 | 17 | N | Car bomb | 13 | Iraqi Governing Council head | Pape/NCTC |
| 22-May-04 | PIJ | West Bank | West Bank | Govt/Police | 0 | 4 | N | Belt bomb | 4 | Army checkpoint | CSS/NCTC |
| 22-May-04 | al-Tawhid | Baghdad | Iraq | Govt/Police** | 5 | 13 | N | Car bomb | 13 | Deputy Interior Minister Jabbar Yousef | Pape/NCTC |
| 22-May-04 | Unknown | Mahmudiyah | Iraq | Military | 1 | 3 | Y | Car bomb | 13 | US tank | UPI/SL |
| 23-May-04 | Unknown | Falluja | Iraq | Military | 2 | 5 | Y | Car bomb | 13 | US military convoy | UPI |
| 28-May-04 | Fatah/PIJ | Rafah | Gaza | Govt/Police | 0 | 2 | N | Car bomb | 4 | Jeep bomb got stuck/bus target | CSS/UPI |
| 1-Jun-04 | Unknown | Baghdad | Iraq | Govt/Police | 3 | 20 | N | Car bomb | 13 | Sunni Leader Ghazi Yanar speech | TM |
| 1-Jun-04 | Unknown | Bayji | Iraq | Govt/Police | 11 | 18 | N | Car bomb | 13 | Police checkpoint near U.S. base | MIPT/ST |
| 3-Jun-04 | Unknown | Waziristan | Pakistan | Govt/Police | 1 | 2 | N | Belt bomb | 10 | Likely Uzbek/border checkpoint | SATP |
| 4-Jun-04 | Tanzim | Jerusalem | Israel | Civilian | 0 | 0 | N | Bag bomb | 4 | Arrested at CP after bomb failed | MIPT/UPI |
| 4-Jun-04 | Unknown | Baquba | Iraq | Military | 0 | 1 | N | Car bomb | 13 | 2 bombers/killed by Iraqi Army | MNFI/NCTC |
| 6-Jun-04 | al-Tawhid | Taji | Iraq | Govt/Police | 0 | 18 | N | Car bomb | 13 | Iraqi police station | CNN |
| 6-Jun-04 | al-Tawhid | Taji | Iraq | Military | 9 | 30 | Y | Car bomb | 13 | US military base | Pape/ST |

| Date | Group | City | Country | Target | Killed | Wounded | S | Weapon | W | Notes | Source |
|---|---|---|---|---|---|---|---|---|---|---|---|
| 8-Jun-04 | Unknown | Baquba | Iraq | Military | 5 | 26 | Y | Car bomb | 13 | FOB War Horse | EG/DR |
| 8-Jun-04 | Unknown | Mosul | Iraq | Govt/Police | 9 | 25 | N | Car bomb | 13 | 3 bombers in taxi near mayor's office | NCTC/MIP |
| 12-Jun-04 | Unknown | Balad | Iraq | Govt/Police | 6 | 4 | N | Car bomb | 13 | Iraqi Army post by govt building | NYT/SEA |
| 13-Jun-04 | Unknown | Orangi | Pakistan | Govt/Police | 0 | 0 | N | Bag bomb | 10 | Arrested at police station | PPI/AP |
| 13-Jun-04 | Unknown | Baghdad | Iraq | Govt/Police | 12 | 13 | Y | Car bomb | 13 | Camp Cuervo/Partly foiled by security | Pape/NCT |
| 14-Jun-04 | al-Tawhid | Baghdad | Iraq | Civilian | 13 | 60 | N | Car bomb | 13 | GE contractor convoy/Tahrir Square | Pape/NCT |
| 14-Jun-04 | al-Tawhid | Baghdad | Iraq | Govt/Police | 4 | 4 | N | Car bomb | 13 | Iraq police patrol/Salman Pak area | NCTC/ST |
| 17-Jun-04 | al-Tawhid | Baghdad | Iraq | Govt/Police | 41 | 141 | N | Car bomb | 13 | Recruiting center/al-Muthana airfield | Pape/NCT |
| 17-Jun-04 | al-Tawhid | Balad | Iraq | Govt/Police | 6 | 4 | N | Car bomb | 13 | Iraq Army checkpoint | TOL/KNT |
| 24-Jun-04 | al-Tawhid | Baghdad | Iraq | Military | 5 | 5 | N | Car bomb | 13 | Iraq Army checkpoint/Abu Dasheer | ST/CNN |
| 24-Jun-04 | al-Tawhid | Mosul | Iraq | Govt/Police^ | 21 | 73 | N | Car bomb | 13 | Police stations | Pape/NCT |
| 24-Jun-04 | al-Tawhid | Mosul | Iraq | Govt/Police^ | 21 | 73 | N | Car bomb | 13 | Police stations | Pape/NCT |
| 24-Jun-04 | al-Tawhid | Mosul | Iraq | Govt/Police^ | 21 | 73 | N | Car bomb | 13 | Police stations | Pape/NCT |
| 4-Jul-04 | Unknown | Baquba | Iraq | Govt/Police | 2 | 1 | N | Car bomb | 13 | Iraq National Guard HQ | NCTC/ST |
| 6-Jul-04 | Sunna | Khalis | Iraq | Civilian | 13 | 37 | N | Car bomb | 13 | Funeral | Pape/NCT |
| 7-Jul-04 | LTTE | Columbo | Sri Lanka | Govt/Police** | 4 | 11 | N | Belt bomb | 3 | Tamil government minister | SATP/IPC |
| 8-Jul-04 | Unknown | Samarra | Iraq | Military | 6 | 6 | Y | Car bomb | 13 | Attack on US/Iraqi patrol base | SEA/FOX |
| 11-Jul-04 | Fatah | Tel Aviv | Israel | Bus | 1 | 20 | N | Belt bomb | 4 | Bus stop | NCTC/CN |
| 14-Jul-04 | Unknown | Baghdad | Iraq | Govt/Police | 10 | 40 | N | Car bomb | 13 | Checkpoint near U.K. Embassy | Pape/NCT |
| 15-Jul-04 | Unknown | Haditha | Iraq | Govt/Police | 10 | 27 | N | Car bomb | 13 | Iraqi police station | DT/AP |
| 16-Jul-04 | Unknown | Syrian border | Iraq | Military | 11 | 4 | N | Belt bomb | 13 | Iraq National Guard office | CT/KRT |
| 17-Jul-04 | al-Tawhid | Baghdad | Iraq | Govt/Police** | 5 | 8 | N | Car bomb | 13 | Justice Minister Malek Dohan Hassan | Pape/MIP |
| 17-Jul-04 | al-Tawhid | Mahmudiyah | Iraq | Govt/Police | 2 | 47 | N | Car bomb | 13 | Iraq National Guard station | ST/CBS |
| 19-Jul-04 | Unknown | Baghdad | Iraq | Govt/Police | 9 | 62 | N | Truck bomb | 13 | Police station/Seidiyeh area | Pape/MIP |
| 24-Jul-04 | Chechen sep | Nazran | Russia | Govt/Police | 0 | 2 | N | Belt bomb | 6 | At police station during questioning | SPT/AIW |
| 24-Jul-04 | al-Mansoorain | Srinagar | Kashmir/India | Govt/Police | 4 | 2 | N | Belt bomb | 9 | Police station/56th Battalion CRPF | MIPT/PTI |
| 26-Jul-04 | Unknown | Mosul | Iraq | Military | 3 | 6 | Y | Car bomb | 13 | US military base near Mosul airfield | Pape/ST |
| 27-Jul-04 | Unknown | Baquba | Iraq | Military | 0 | 0 | N | Car bomb | 13 | Premature detonation | ST/AP |
| 28-Jul-04 | Unknown | Jhang | Pakistan | Civilian | 0 | 5 | N | Bike bomb | 10 | Mohallah Khakshah Road shops | XNA/ST |
| 28-Jul-04 | al-Qaeda in Iraq | Baquba | Iraq | Govt/Police | 68 | 56 | N | Car bomb | 13 | Police recruiting line/al-Najda | Pape/NCT |
| 29-Jul-04 | IMU | Tashkent | Uzbekistan | Govt/Police | 1 | 4 | N | Belt bomb | 14 | Prosecutor's office | NCTC/MI |
| 29-Jul-04 | IMU | Tashkent | Uzbekistan | Embassy | 2 | 1 | Y | Belt bomb | 14 | U.S. Embassy | NCTC/MI |
| 29-Jul-04 | IMU | Tashkent | Uzbekistan | Embassy | 2 | 2 | N | Belt bomb | 14 | Israeli Embassy | NCTC/MI |
| 30-Jul-04 | al-Islambouli | Jaffar | Pakistan | Govt/Police** | 6 | 50 | N | Belt bomb | 10 | PM designate Shaukut Aziz | NCTC/MI |
| 1-Aug-04 | Unknown | Baghdad | Iraq | Civilian^ | 1 | 6 | N | Car bomb | 13 | 2 bombs/Christian Armenian church | TM/EIW |
| 1-Aug-04 | Unknown | Baghdad | Iraq | Civilian^ | 2 | 6 | N | Car bomb | 13 | 2 bombs/Catholic Syriac church | TM/EIW |
| 1-Aug-04 | Unknown | Mosul | Iraq | Govt/Police | 4 | 53 | N | Truck bomb | 13 | Summar Police station | Pape/IPC |
| 3-Aug-04 | Unknown | Baquba | Iraq | Govt/Police | 4 | 6 | N | Car bomb | 13 | Police checkpoint | IPCS/CNN |
| 4-Aug-04 | Unknown | Ramadi | Iraq | Military | 0 | 0 | Y | Car bomb | 13 | US military checkpoint | AJ |
| 5-Aug-04 | Unknown | Mahaweel | Iraq | Govt/Police | 4 | 24 | N | Car bomb | 13 | Police station south of Baghdad | IPCS/NC |
| 9-Aug-04 | Tanzim | Baquba | Iraq | Govt/Police* | 5 | 16 | N | Car bomb | 13 | Deputy Gov Agil Hamid al-Adili | IPCS/AP |
| 11-Aug-04 | Fatah | Jerusalem | Israel | Govt/Police | 1 | 13 | N | Bag bomb | 4 | Police checkpoint | IPCS/JP |
| 22-Aug-04 | Unknown | Khalis | Iraq | Govt/Police** | 2 | 8 | N | Car bomb | 13 | Governor Chassan Abbas al-Khadran | EIW/KST |

| Date | Group | City | Country | Target | Killed | Wounded | ? | Weapon | Code | Notes | Source |
|---|---|---|---|---|---|---|---|---|---|---|---|
| 24-Aug-04 | RaS | Rostov-on-Don | Russia | Airplane | 43 | 0 | N | Bag bomb | 6 | Volga-AviaExpress flight 1303 | IPCS/NCTC |
| 24-Aug-04 | RaS | Rostov-on-Don | Russia | Airplane | 45 | 0 | N | Bag bomb | 6 | Siberia Airlines flight 1047 | IPCS/NCTC |
| 24-Aug-04 | Tanzim | Baghdad | Iraq | Govt/Police** | 4 | 4 | N | Car bomb | 13 | Environment Minister al-Moumin | Pape/EIW |
| 28-Aug-04 | Unknown | Mosul | Iraq | Govt/Police | 0 | 0 | N | Car bomb | 13 | Kurdish media team | MIPT/ST |
| 29-Aug-04 | Chechen sep | Grozny | Russia | Govt/Police | 0 | 0 | N | Belt bomb | 6 | Polling center | NCTC/LAT |
| 31-Aug-04 | Hamas | Beer Sheba | Israel | Bus^ | 8 | 50 | N | Belt bomb | 4 | Coordinated attack on 2 buses | CSS/IPCS |
| 31-Aug-04 | Hamas | Beer Sheba | Israel | Bus^ | 8 | 50 | N | Belt bomb | 4 | Coordinated attack on 2 buses | CSS/IPCS |
| 31-Aug-04 | Unknown | Erez crossing | Gaza | Unknown | 0 | 0 | N | Belt bomb | 4 | Bomber arrested by police | UPI/TES |
| 31-Aug-04 | RaS | Moscow | Russia | Market | 9 | 51 | N | Belt bomb | 6 | Car park near Moscow market/metro | IPCS/NCTC |
| 1-Sep-04 | Chechen sep | Beslan | Russia | School^ | 23 | 47 | N | Belt bomb | 6 | Bombers/gunmen seized school No 1 | GRP/AIW |
| 4-Sep-04 | Unknown | Kirkuk | Iraq | Govt/Police | 20 | 30 | N | Car bomb | 13 | Police Academy | Pape/NCTC |
| 6-Sep-04 | Unknown | Siirt | Turkey | Unknown | 0 | 0 | N | Grenades | 8 | Killed herself instead of arrest | MIPT/ST |
| 6-Sep-04 | Unknown | Falluja | Iraq | Military | 10 | 8 | Y | Car bomb | 13 | US Marine convoy | SEA/UPI |
| 8-Sep-04 | Fatah | Qarni | Gaza | Unknown | 0 | 0 | N | Belt bomb | 4 | Bomber killed by police | IMFA/JA |
| 9-Sep-04 | JI | Jakarta | Indonesia | Embassy | 9 | 182 | N | Car bomb | 7 | Australian Embassy | MIPT/ST |
| 12-Sep-04 | Unknown | Abu Ghurayb | Iraq | Military | 0 | 8 | Y | Car bomb | 13 | US military at Abu Ghraib prison | AAIW/CAP |
| 12-Sep-04 | Unknown | Baghdad | Iraq | Military | 0 | 6 | Y | Car bomb | 13 | BFV near Iraqi Ministry | CT/SDU |
| 12-Sep-04 | Unknown | Baghdad | Iraq | Military | 2 | 3 | Y | Car bomb | 13 | US military convoy near BIAP | AAIW |
| 12-Sep-04 | Unknown | Baghdad | Iraq | Govt/Police | 2 | 4 | N | Car bomb | 13 | Iraqi police patrol | RFE/DTL |
| 12-Sep-04 | Unknown | Baghdad | Iraq | Govt/Police | 0 | 0 | N | Belt bomb | 13 | Council bldg/Killed by police | MIPT/CNN |
| 14-Sep-04 | Fatah | Qalqilya | West Bank | Govt/Police | 0 | 2 | N | Bike bomb | 4 | Border checkpoint | CSS/JP |
| 14-Sep-04 | al-Tawhid | Baghdad | Iraq | Govt/Police | 46 | 114 | N | Car bomb | 13 | Police recruits/Hayfa Street | Pape/MIPT |
| 14-Sep-04 | Unknown | Baghdad | Iraq | Civilian | 0 | 0 | N | Car bomb | 13 | Civilian contractor convoy targeted | MIPT/NYT |
| 15-Sep-04 | Unknown | Suwaira | Iraq | Military | 2 | 10 | N | Car bomb | 13 | Iraq Army checkpoint | NYT/IHT |
| 17-Sep-04 | Unknown | Baghdad | Iraq | Military | 0 | 1 | Y | Car bomb | 13 | US/Iraqi CP/Haifa street/troops fired | AP/SL |
| 17-Sep-04 | Unknown | Baghdad | Iraq | Govt/Police | 8 | 20 | N | Car bomb | 13 | Iraq police convoy/Rasheed Street | MB/LE |
| 17-Sep-04 | Unknown | Kirkuk | Iraq | Govt/Police | 4 | 20 | N | Car bomb | 13 | Army recruiting center/National Guard | NCTC/MIPT |
| 18-Sep-04 | Unknown | Baghdad | Iraq | Military | 0 | 0 | N | Car bomb | 13 | 2 bombers killed/bomb defused | CC |
| 18-Sep-04 | Unknown | Baghdad | Iraq | Military | 2 | 8 | Y | Car bomb | 13 | US military convoy | NYT/BBC |
| 18-Sep-04 | Unknown | Kirkuk | Iraq | Military | 20 | 67 | N | Car bomb | 13 | Army recruiting center | Pape/MIPT |
| 19-Sep-04 | Unknown | Samarra | Iraq | Military | 3 | 7 | Y | Car bomb | 13 | US/Iraqi patrol approached car | EIW/AP |
| 20-Sep-04 | Unknown | Mosul | Iraq | Unknown | 1 | 0 | N | Car bomb | 13 | Premature detonation, 3 in car | MIPT/ST |
| 21-Sep-04 | Chechen sep | Urus-Martan | Russia | Unknown | 0 | 0 | N | Belt bomb | 6 | Female arrested wearing bomb | MOS/AAIW |
| 21-Sep-04 | Unknown | Baghdad | Iraq | Military | 1 | 19 | Y | Car bomb | 13 | US military convoy/near airport | NCTC/EIW |
| 21-Sep-04 | Unknown | Baghdad | Iraq | Military | 0 | 0 | N | Car bomb | 13 | Hit kiosk/target recruiting center | EIW/TI |
| 22-Sep-04 | Fatah | Jerusalem | Israel | Civilian | 2 | 15 | N | Belt bomb | 4 | Crowd vice soldiers' pickup spot | CSS/NCTC |
| 22-Sep-04 | Unknown | Baghdad | Iraq | Military | 11 | 54 | N | Car bomb | 13 | Temporary Army recruiting center | Pape/MIPT |
| 27-Sep-04 | Unknown | Falluja | Iraq | Military | 3 | 3 | N | Car bomb | 13 | Iraq Army CP on Falluja/Ramadi road | AJ/AP |
| 30-Sep-04 | Unknown | Baghdad | Iraq | Civilian | 42 | 140 | Y | Car bomb | 13 | Sewage plant opening/U.S. troops | MIPT/WP |
| 30-Sep-04 | Unknown | Baghdad | Iraq | Govt/Police | 9 | 60 | N | Car bomb | 13 | Govt buildings near Abu Ghraib | MIPT/ST |
| 1-Oct-04 | Unknown | Sialkot | Pakistan | Religious site | 31 | 75 | N | Car bomb | 10 | Shiite mosque at Friday prayers | SATP/REUT |
| 1-Oct-04 | Unknown | Mosul | Iraq | Military | 4 | 30 | Y | Car bomb | 13 | US military convoy | CBS/CNN |

| Date | Group | Location | Country | Target | Killed | Wounded | Arr | Weapon | Grp | Notes | Source |
|---|---|---|---|---|---|---|---|---|---|---|---|
| 2-Oct-04 | Unknown | Hasaybah | Iraq | Military | 6 | 20 | N | Car bomb | 13 | US military convoy | NCTC |
| 4-Oct-04 | Unknown | Baghdad | Iraq | Military | 4 | 20 | Y | Car bomb | 13 | US military convoy/Al-Sa'dun Street | AJ/NCTC |
| 4-Oct-04 | Unknown | Baghdad | Iraq | Govt/Police | 9 | 76 | N | Truck bomb | 13 | Police compound | NCTC/MIPT |
| 5-Oct-04 | Hamas | Jebaliya | Gaza | Military | 0 | 0 | N | Belt bomb | 4 | Near IDF patrol | CSS/AFP |
| 6-Oct-04 | Unknown | Anah | Iraq | Military | 16 | 24 | N | Car bomb | 13 | Iraq National Guard Camp | Pape/NCTC |
| 7-Oct-04 | Unknown | Taba | Egypt | Civilian^ | 17 | 79 | N | Car bomb | 5 | Hilton Hotel/Israeli tourists | NCTC/HC |
| 7-Oct-04 | Unknown | Taba | Egypt | Civilian^ | 17 | 80 | N | Belt bomb | 5 | Hilton Hotel//by swimming pool | NCTC/HC |
| 7-Oct-04 | Unknown | Kirkuk | Iraq | Military | 0 | 5 | Y | Car bomb | 13 | US military convoy/troops fired | AAIW |
| 9-Oct-04 | Unknown | Singapora | Kashmir/India | Military | 5 | 25 | N | Car bomb | 9 | Hit bus carrying Indian troops | XNA/SATP |
| 10-Oct-04 | Unknown | Lahore | Pakistan | Religious site | 5 | 6 | N | Bag bomb | 10 | Mochi Gate/Shiite mosque | MIPT/SATP |
| 10-Oct-04 | al-Tawhid | Baghdad | Iraq | Govt/Police | 17 | 30 | N | Car bomb | 13 | Police recruits | NCTC/MIPT |
| 10-Oct-04 | Unknown | Baghdad | Iraq | Religious site | 4 | 16 | N | Bag bomb | 13 | Killed by police at mosque gate | ST |
| 10-Oct-04 | Unknown | Baghdad | Iraq | Military | 3 | 0 | Y | Car bomb | 13 | US military convoy | TM |
| 11-Oct-04 | Unknown | Mosul | Iraq | Military | 3 | 27 | N | Car bomb | 13 | Combined with armed attack | NCTC/AP |
| 12-Oct-04 | Unknown | Youssifiyah | Iraq | Military | 0 | 0 | Y | Car bomb | 13 | US Marines fired/early detonation | AP |
| 13-Oct-04 | Unknown | Mosul | Iraq | Military | 2 | 5 | Y | Car bomb | 13 | US military convoy | CC/Pape |
| 14-Oct-04 | Tanzim | Baghdad | Iraq | Govt/Police | 8 | 4 | N | Car bomb | 13 | Green Zone checkpoint | UPI/BBC |
| 14-Oct-04 | Unknown | Najaf | Iraq | Religious site | 0 | 0 | N | Belt bomb | 13 | Arrested before reaching mosque | MIPT/AAIW |
| 15-Oct-04 | Unknown | al-Qaim | Iraq | Military | 4 | 1 | Y | Car bomb | 13 | US military patrol | LVRJ/SM |
| 15-Oct-04 | al-Tawhid | Baghdad | Iraq | Restaurant | 2 | 2 | N | Belt bomb | 13 | In Green Zone | MIPT/ST |
| 15-Oct-04 | al-Tawhid | Baghdad | Iraq | Restaurant | 6 | 18 | N | Belt bomb | 13 | In Green Zone | MIPT/ST |
| 15-Oct-04 | Unknown | Baghdad | Iraq | Govt/Police | 5 | 10 | N | Car bomb | 13 | Police patrol/al-Dora area | MIPT/AAIW |
| 16-Oct-04 | Unknown | Khalidiya | Iraq | Military | 0 | 1 | Y | Car bomb | 13 | US tank | AP |
| 17-Oct-04 | Unknown | Baghdad | Iraq | Govt/Police | 4 | 0+ | N | Car bomb | 13 | Tadiriyah area/near embassies | AP |
| 17-Oct-04 | Unknown | Baghdad | Iraq | Govt/Police** | 8 | 27 | N | Belt bomb | 13 | Iraqi police general | NCTC |
| 18-Oct-04 | Unknown | Mosul | Iraq | Civilian | 5 | 15 | N | Car bomb | 13 | Target Iraqi civilians | NCTC |
| 19-Oct-04 | Unknown | Habaniyah | Iraq | Military | 0 | 2 | Y | Car bomb | 13 | US military patrol | BBC |
| 20-Oct-04 | Unknown | Baghdad | Iraq | Military | 0 | 4 | Y | Car bomb | 13 | US/Iraqi patrol near BIAP | AJ/AP |
| 20-Oct-04 | Unknown | Samarra | Iraq | Govt/Police^ | 5 | 6 | N | Car bomb | 13 | 2 bombs/City council meeting | AP/AIW |
| 20-Oct-04 | Unknown | Samarra | Iraq | Govt/Police^ | 5 | 6 | N | Car bomb | 13 | 2 bombs/City council meeting | AP/AIW |
| 23-Oct-04 | Taliban | Kabul | Afghanistan | Market | 2 | 8 | N | Belt bomb | 12 | Chicken Street/posed as beggar | NCTC/RFE |
| 23-Oct-04 | Unknown | khan al-Baghdadi | Iraq | Govt/Police | 16 | 30 | N | Car bomb | 13 | Police station near US Marine base | Pape/MIPT |
| 23-Oct-04 | Unknown | Samarra | Iraq | Military | 3 | 2 | N | Car bomb | 13 | Iraq Army camp | UPI/SOS |
| 24-Oct-04 | Unknown | Baghdad | Iraq | Military | 2 | 6 | Y | Car bomb | 13 | US military convoy | USA |
| 25-Oct-04 | Tanzim | Baghdad | Iraq | Military | 0 | 3 | N | Car bomb | 13 | Australian convoy | AAIW |
| 25-Oct-04 | Unknown | Khalidiya | Iraq | Military | 0 | 4 | Y | Car bomb | 13 | US military convoy | AP/BP |
| 25-Oct-04 | Unknown | Mosul | Iraq | Govt/Police | 3 | 9 | N | Car bomb | 13 | Ninevah govt compound | MIPT/ST |
| 25-Oct-04 | Unknown | Mosul | Iraq | Govt/Police | 1 | 0 | N | Car bomb | 13 | Ninevah govt compound | MIPT/ST |
| 27-Oct-04 | Unknown | Baquba | Iraq | Military | 1 | 2 | Y | Car bomb | 13 | US military convoy | CNN/SEA |
| 29-Oct-04 | Unknown | Ramadi | Iraq | Military | 1 | 1 | Y | Car bomb | 13 | US Army convoy | REUT/SEA |
| 30-Oct-04 | Unknown | Abu Ghurayb | Iraq | Military | 8 | 9 | Y | Car bomb | 13 | US Marine convoy | NYT/IHT |
| 30-Oct-04 | IAI | Baghdad | Iraq | Civilian | 6 | 19 | N | Car bomb | 13 | al-Arabiya TV station | NYT/IHT |
| 1-Nov-04 | PFLP | Tel Aviv | Israel | Market | 3 | 32 | N | Belt bomb | 4 | Carmel market | CSS/NCTC |
| 2-Nov-04 | Unknown | Baghdad | Iraq | Govt/Police | 8 | 29 | N | Car bomb | 13 | Education Ministry/Ameriyah area | NBC/MIPT |

| Date | Group | City | Country | Target | Killed | Wounded | Suicide | Weapon | Code | Notes | Source |
|---|---|---|---|---|---|---|---|---|---|---|---|
| 3-Nov-04 | Unknown | Baghdad | Iraq | Govt/Police | 0 | 9 | N | Car bomb | 13 | Prematurely detonated near BIAP | NCTC/MIPT |
| 4-Nov-04 | Unknown | Dujail | Iraq | Govt/Police | 3 | 9 | N | Car bomb | 13 | Government offices | AP |
| 4-Nov-04 | Unknown | Iskandariyah | Iraq | Military | 7 | 13 | N | Car bomb | 13 | Iraq Army checkpoint | AAIW |
| 4-Nov-04 | Unknown | Ramadi | Iraq | Military | 0 | 0 | Y | Car bomb | 13 | US Marine convoy | AP/TR |
| 4-Nov-04 | Unknown | Tikrit | Iraq | Govt/Police | 4 | 18 | N | Car bomb | 13 | Govt building, partially foiled | NCTC/MIPT |
| 5-Nov-04 | Tanzim | Falluja | Iraq | Military | 4 | 8 | N | Car bomb | 13 | UK military patrol | TOL/SL |
| 6-Nov-04 | Unknown | Baghdad | Iraq | Military | 0 | 3 | Y | Car bomb | 13 | US military convoy near BIAP | AJ |
| 6-Nov-04 | Unknown | Ramadi | Iraq | Military | 0 | 18 | Y | Car bomb | 13 | US mil convoy/bomber in police car | AP/UPI |
| 6-Nov-04 | Tanzim | Samarra | Iraq | Govt/Police | 6 | 23 | N | Car bomb | 13 | Police station - 3 bombs | NCTC/MIPT |
| 6-Nov-04 | Tanzim | Samarra | Iraq | Govt/Police | 13 | 16 | N | Car bomb | 13 | Police station - 3 bombs | NCTC/MIPT |
| 6-Nov-04 | Tanzim | Samarra | Iraq | Govt/Police | 4 | 22 | N | Car bomb | 13 | Police station - 3 bombs | NCTC/MIPT |
| 7-Nov-04 | Unknown | Baghdad | Iraq | Military | 3 | 2 | N | Car bomb | 13 | UK base | Pape/TOL |
| 8-Nov-04 | Unknown | Kashmir | Kashmir/India | Military | 0 | 9 | N | Belt bomb | 9 | Sundervani Village army camp | SATP/FWN |
| 8-Nov-04 | Unknown | Baghdad | Iraq | Religious site^ | 1 | 20 | N | Car bomb | 13 | St. George's Catholic Church | MIPT/ST |
| 8-Nov-04 | Unknown | Baghdad | Iraq | Religious site^ | 2 | 20 | N | Car bomb | 13 | St. Mathew's Catholic church | MIPT/ST |
| 8-Nov-04 | Unknown | Baghdad | Iraq | Military** | 2 | 2 | Y | Belt bomb | 13 | US weapons inspector | NCTC/NBC |
| 8-Nov-04 | Unknown | Mosul | Iraq | Civilian | 0 | 13 | N | Car bomb | 13 | US military convoy | NCTC |
| 9-Nov-04 | Unknown | Kirkuk | Iraq | Civilian | 3 | 2 | N | Car bomb | 13 | Iraqi Army base | NCTC/REUT |
| 11-Nov-04 | Chechen sep | Khasavyurt | Russia | Govt/Police | 0 | 0 | N | Car bomb | 6 | Police checkpoint | NCTC |
| 11-Nov-04 | Unknown | Baghdad | Iraq | Market | 18 | 15 | N | Car bomb | 13 | Saddoun Street/US vehicle nearby | MIPT/ST |
| 13-Nov-04 | Unknown | Hillah | Iraq | Govt/Police** | 0 | 4 | N | Car bomb | 13 | Hillah police chief | MIPT/ST |
| 17-Nov-04 | Unknown | Bayji | Iraq | Military | 0 | 0 | N | Car bomb | 13 | UK military (Queen's Dragoon Guards) | TM/TI |
| 17-Nov-04 | Unknown | Bayji | Iraq | Military | 10 | 20 | Y | Car bomb | 13 | US military convoy | Pape/NCTC |
| 18-Nov-04 | Unknown | Baghdad | Iraq | Market | 2 | 4 | N | Car bomb | 13 | Yarmouk police station/US mil convoy | Pape/NCTC |
| 18-Nov-04 | Unknown | Xima | China | Civilian | 13 | 18 | N | Belt bomb | x | Tea house | NCTC/KWN |
| 19-Nov-04 | Unknown | Baghdad | Iraq | Govt/Police | 5 | 10 | N | Car bomb | 13 | Police patrol/Zayouna area | MIPT/ST |
| 19-Nov-04 | Unknown | Hillah | Iraq | Govt/Police | 0 | 0 | N | Car bomb | 13 | Jabal police station | AP |
| 20-Nov-04 | Unknown | Baghdad | Iraq | Military | 1 | 1 | Y | Car bomb | 13 | US convoy near Al-A'zamiyah police | AAIW |
| 20-Nov-04 | Unknown | Baghdad | Iraq | Civilian | 0 | 1 | N | Car bomb | 13 | Missed convoy of 5 jeeps | NCTC/AAIW |
| 21-Nov-04 | Unknown | Hillah | Iraq | Govt/Police** | 0 | 0 | N | Car bomb | 13 | Hillah police chief Gen. Abdullah | AP |
| 24-Nov-04 | Unknown | Baghdad | Iraq | Civilian | 3 | 2 | N | Car bomb | 13 | Western convoy near BIAP | AP/WP |
| 25-Nov-04 | Unknown | Samarra | Iraq | Govt/Police | 0 | 0 | N | Car bomb | 13 | Main police station/Al-Jisr area | AP/AJ |
| 25-Nov-04 | Unknown | Tallinn | Estonia | Unknown | 0 | 4 | N | Belt bomb | x | Detonated while in police car | MIPT/ITAR |
| 26-Nov-04 | Unknown | Baghdad | Iraq | Govt/Police | 2 | 5 | N | Car bomb | 13 | 14 July Bridge | MIPT/ST |
| 27-Nov-04 | Chechen sep | Grozny | Russia | Govt/Police | 1 | 3 | N | Belt bomb | 6 | Café after arrest attempt/Zavodskoy | NCTC |
| 27-Nov-04 | Unknown | Baghdad | Iraq | Military | 0 | 0 | Y | Car bomb | 13 | US military convoy/near BIAP | AP/CT |
| 28-Nov-04 | Unknown | Baghdad | Iraq | Military | 0 | 3 | Y | Car bomb | 13 | US military convoy/near BIAP | CNN |
| 28-Nov-04 | Unknown | Karbala | Iraq | Prison | 0 | 0 | N | Bag bomb | 13 | Arrested smuggling bomb into prison | RFE |
| 29-Nov-04 | Unknown | Ramadi | Iraq | Govt/Police | 11 | 10 | N | Car bomb | 13 | Police station in West Ramadi | Pape/RFE |
| 30-Nov-04 | Unknown | Baghdad | Iraq | Military | 0 | 5 | Y | Car bomb | 13 | US military convoy/near BIAP | XNA/UPI |
| 30-Nov-04 | Unknown | Bayji | Iraq | Military | 4 | 19 | Y | Car bomb | 13 | US Army convoy | UPI/AP |
| 1-Dec-04 | Unknown | Baghdad | Iraq | Military | 1 | 4 | Y | Car bomb | 13 | US military convoy | XNA/IPCS |
| 1-Dec-04 | Unknown | Haditha | Iraq | Military | 1 | 1 | Y | Car bomb | 13 | US military convoy | XNA/AP |

| Date | Group | Location | Country | Target | Killed | Wounded | Suicide | Weapon | Code | Notes | Source |
|---|---|---|---|---|---|---|---|---|---|---|---|
| 1-Dec-04 | Unknown | Iskandariyah | Iraq | Civilian | 1 | 7 | N | Car bomb | 13 | Iraq Army checkpoint near bridge | NCTC/UP |
| 2-Dec-04 | Unknown | Bayji | Iraq | Military | 1 | 4 | Y | Car bomb | 13 | US BFV at Iraqi Army checkpoint | IHT/RFE |
| 3-Dec-04 | Unknown | Anbar province | Iraq | Military | 2 | 5 | Y | Car bomb | 13 | US military base/Jordan border | Pape/AIW |
| 3-Dec-04 | Tanzim | Baghdad | Iraq | Govt/Police | 0 | 5 | N | Car bomb | 13 | Police station at Housing Ministry | MIPT/NYT |
| 3-Dec-04 | Unknown | Baghdad | Iraq | Religious site | 14 | 19 | N | Truck bomb | 13 | Shiite mosque, 4 bombers in van | Pape/MIP |
| 4-Dec-04 | Unknown | Baghdad | Iraq | Govt/Police | 8 | 38 | N | Bus bomb | 13 | Shalhiya police station/by Green Zone | Pape/MIP |
| 4-Dec-04 | Unknown | Mosul | Iraq | Govt/Police | 15 | 25 | N | Car bomb | 13 | Bus carrying Kurdish forces | Pape/NCT |
| 5-Dec-04 | Unknown | Bayji | Iraq | Military | 3 | 18 | N | Car bomb | 13 | Iraq Army checkpoint | SUN/BBC |
| 8-Dec-04 | Unknown | Samarra | Iraq | Military | 0 | 0 | Y | Car bomb | 13 | US military patrol | CNN/AJ |
| 11-Dec-04 | Unknown | Mosul | Iraq | Military | 0 | 7 | Y | Car bomb | 13 | US military patrol | CC |
| 12-Dec-04 | Unknown | Haditha | Iraq | Military | 0 | 0 | Y | Car bomb | 13 | US Marine convoy | AP/AIW |
| 13-Dec-04 | Tanzim | Baghdad | Iraq | Military | 13 | 15 | N | Car bomb | 13 | Green Zone Western Gate/Harthiya | Pape/MIP |
| 14-Dec-04 | Tanzim | Baghdad | Iraq | Govt/Police | 6 | 13 | N | Car bomb | 13 | Green Zone Western Gate/2nd day | NCTC/MIP |
| 18-Dec-04 | Unknown | Bayji | Iraq | Bus | 0 | 4 | Y | Car bomb | 13 | U.S. employees of Cochise Security | WP/NYT |
| 19-Dec-04 | Unknown | Karbala | Iraq | Civilian | 13 | 50 | N | Car bomb | 13 | Main bus station | Pape/MIP |
| 19-Dec-04 | Unknown | Najaf | Iraq | Civilian | 54 | 142 | N | Car bomb | 13 | Funeral near Imam Ali shrine | MIPT/XN |
| 21-Dec-04 | Sunna | Mosul | Iraq | Military | 23 | 64 | Y | Belt bomb | 13 | FOB Marez dining facility | Pape/AIW |
| 22-Dec-04 | Unknown | al-Latifiyah | Iraq | Govt/Police | 8 | 13 | N | Car bomb | 13 | Police checkpoint | NCTC/MIP |
| 24-Dec-04 | Unknown | Baghdad | Iraq | Embassy | 8 | 19 | N | Truck bomb | 13 | Near Libya/Jordan Embassies | NCTC/MIP |
| 25-Dec-04 | Unknown | Bayji | Iraq | Military | 0 | 6 | Y | Car bomb | 13 | US military convoy | UPI |
| 27-Dec-04 | Tanzim | Baghdad | Iraq | Govt/Police** | 12 | 50 | N | Car bomb | 13 | SCIRI leader Abdul Aziz al-Hakim | Pape/MIP |
| 28-Dec-04 | Unknown | Baghdad | Iraq | Military** | 0 | 8 | N | Car bomb | 13 | Iraq Army General Mudher al-Mula | NCTC/XN |
| 28-Dec-04 | Unknown | Baquba | Iraq | Military | 8 | 12 | N | Car bomb | 13 | Iraq Army patrol/Al-Mu'allimin area | AAIW/BBC |
| 28-Dec-04 | Unknown | Samarra | Iraq | Military | 6 | 7 | Y | Car bomb | 13 | US/Iraqi military patrol | BBC |
| 29-Dec-04 | al-Qaeda | Riyadh | Saudi Arabia | Govt/Police | 1 | 6 | N | Car bomb | 7 | Interior Ministry | MIPT/ST |
| 29-Dec-04 | al-Qaeda | Riyadh | Saudi Arabia | Govt/Police | 0 | 4 | N | Car bomb | 7 | Recruiting center | MIPT/ST |
| 29-Dec-04 | Unknown | Mosul | Iraq | Military^ | 0 | 7 | Y | Truck bomb | 13 | US military base | AS/TH |
| 29-Dec-04 | Unknown | Mosul | Iraq | Military^ | 1 | 7 | Y | Car bomb | 13 | Hit US military response to 1st bomb | TH |
| 29-Dec-04 | Unknown | Muradiya | Iraq | Unknown | 5 | 20 | N | Car bomb | 13 | Iraqi Civilians casualties | MIPT/AP |
| 29-Dec-04 | Unknown | Samarra | Iraq | Unknown | 1 | 10 | N | Belt bomb | 13 | Center of city/possible premature bomb | MIPT/ST |
| 31-Dec-04 | Unknown | Bayji | Iraq | Military | 2 | 5 | N | Car bomb | 13 | Iraqi Army patrol | SPI/NYT |
| 2-Jan-05 | Unknown | Baghdad | Iraq | Military | 1 | 2 | Y | Car bomb | 13 | US military patrol/southwest Baghdad | SEA/AS |
| 2-Jan-05 | Tanzim | Balad | Iraq | Military | 19 | 6 | N | Car bomb | 13 | Iraqi Army bus near US base | EIW/BBC |
| 3-Jan-05 | Sunna | Baghdad | Iraq | Govt/Police | 3 | 25 | N | Car bomb | 13 | National Accord Party HQ | Pape/MIP |
| 3-Jan-05 | Unknown | Baghdad | Iraq | Civilian | 4 | 0 | N | Car bomb | 13 | Western convoy (Kroll security) | Pape/MIP |
| 3-Jan-05 | Unknown | Balad | Iraq | Military | 4 | 14 | N | Car bomb | 13 | Iraq Army | DR/DM |
| 4-Jan-05 | Tanzim | Baghdad | Iraq | Govt/Police | 10 | 60 | N | Truck bomb | 13 | Police commando base/al-Qadisiya | Pape/MIP |
| 5-Jan-05 | Unknown | Baghdad | Iraq | Civilian | 2 | 10 | N | Car bomb | 13 | Funeral procession for governor | TNL/EIW |
| 5-Jan-05 | Tanzim | Baquba | Iraq | Govt/Police | 6 | 13 | N | Car bomb | 13 | Police checkpoint | Pape/MIP |
| 5-Jan-05 | Unknown | Haditha | Iraq | Military | 0 | 0 | Y | Car bomb | 13 | US military convoy | DR |
| 5-Jan-05 | Tanzim | Hillah | Iraq | Govt/Police | 19 | 25 | N | Truck bomb | 13 | Police graduation | Pape/MIP |
| 5-Jan-05 | Unknown | Qayyarah | Iraq | Military | 0 | 3 | N | Car bomb | 13 | Iraq Army checkpoint | DTL/PT |
| 6-Jan-05 | Hamas | Gush Katif | Gaza | Civilian | 0 | 0 | N | Belt bomb | 4 | Bomber killed by IDF | MIPT/ST |

| Date | Group | Location | Country | Target | Killed | Wounded | ? | Weapon | ? | Notes | Source |
|---|---|---|---|---|---|---|---|---|---|---|---|
| 8-Jan-05 | Unknown | Baghdad | Iraq | Civilian | 4 | 19 | N | Car bomb | 13 | Gas station | NCTC/MIPT |
| 9-Jan-05 | Unknown | Youssifiyah | Iraq | Govt/Police | 3 | 0 | N | Belt bomb | 13 | Police checkpoint | NCTC/BBC |
| 10-Jan-05 | Unknown | Baghdad | Iraq | Govt/Police | 6 | 19 | N | Car bomb | 13 | Police station/Zaafarania area | Pape/MIPT |
| 10-Jan-05 | Unknown | Rubai'a | Iraq | Military | 4 | 0 | N | Car bomb | 13 | Border police station | MIPT/ST |
| 11-Jan-05 | Unknown | Basra | Iraq | Govt/Police** | 1 | 7 | N | Car bomb | 13 | Interior Ministry | NCTC/MIPT |
| 11-Jan-05 | Unknown | Basra | Iraq | Govt/Police | 0 | 0 | N | Car bomb | 13 | Election commission | MIPT/ST |
| 11-Jan-05 | Tanzim | Tikrit | Iraq | Govt/Police | 7 | 12 | N | Car bomb | 13 | Police station | Pape/MIPT |
| 12-Jan-05 | Unknown | Mosul | Iraq | Military | 2 | 2 | Y | Car bomb | 13 | US/Iraqi military patrol | WP/MST |
| 13-Jan-05 | Fatah | Karni crossing | Gaza | Military | 6 | 15 | N | Car bomb | 4 | 1 bomber and 2 gunmen | MIPT/ST |
| 16-Jan-05 | Unknown | Kut | Iraq | Civilian | 7 | 13 | N | Car bomb | 13 | Funeral procession for police officer | MIPT/ST |
| 17-Jan-05 | Unknown | Bayji | Iraq | Govt/Police | 9 | 20 | N | Car bomb | 13 | Bayji police HQ | MIPT/ST |
| 17-Jan-05 | Unknown | Ramadi | Iraq | Military | 3 | 9 | Y | Car bomb | 13 | US Marines investigate suspicious car | TM/DR |
| 18-Jan-05 | Hamas | Gush Katif | Gaza | Military | 1 | 6 | N | Belt bomb | 4 | Detonated at security interview | CSS/NCTC |
| 18-Jan-05 | Tanzim | Baghdad | Iraq | Govt/Police | 4 | 8 | N | Car bomb | 13 | SCIRI building | Pape/NCTC |
| 19-Jan-05 | Tanzim | Baghdad | Iraq | Embassy | 1 | 8 | N | Car bomb | 13 | Australian Embassy | MIPT/XNA |
| 19-Jan-05 | Tanzim | Baghdad | Iraq | Govt/Police | 17 | 21 | N | Car bomb | 13 | Checkpoint near Al Alahi hospital | NCTC/MIPT |
| 19-Jan-05 | Tanzim | Baghdad | Iraq | Govt/Police | 2 | 3 | N | Car bomb | 13 | Army/police checkpoint near BIAP | NCTC/MIPT |
| 19-Jan-05 | Tanzim | Baghdad | Iraq | Govt/Police | 2 | 7 | N | Car bomb | 13 | Army/police checkpoint near bank | NCTC/MIPT |
| 19-Jan-05 | Tanzim | Baghdad | Iraq | Military | 0 | 7 | N | Car bomb | 13 | Military base/al-Muthana air base | ST/MIPT |
| 20-Jan-05 | Unknown | Sherberghan | Afghanistan | Civilian** | 0 | 21 | N | Belt bomb | 12 | Alhaj Abdorrashid Dostum | NCTC/MIPT |
| 20-Jan-05 | Tanzim | Basra | Iraq | Military | 0 | 9 | N | Car bomb | 13 | UK base at Shaibah airfield | TS/DT |
| 20-Jan-05 | None | Xinjiang | China | Bus | 11 | 7 | N | Bag bomb | x | Disgruntled miner/work dispute | UPI/XNA |
| 21-Jan-05 | Unknown | Baghdad | Iraq | Religious site | 15 | 42 | N | Car bomb | 13 | Shuhada al-Taf Shiite mosque | MIPT/ST |
| 21-Jan-05 | Unknown | Youssifiyah | Iraq | Civilian | 21 | 16 | N | Car bomb | 13 | Shiite wedding/ambulance used | Pape/NCTC |
| 23-Jan-05 | Sunna | Hillah | Iraq | Civilian | 0 | 9 | N | Car bomb | 13 | Polling center | MIPT/ST |
| 24-Jan-05 | Tanzim | Baghdad | Iraq | Govt/Police | 0 | 10 | N | Car bomb | 13 | Checkpoint/National Accord Party | NCTC/MIPT |
| 26-Jan-05 | Unknown | Baghdad | Iraq | Military | 0 | 3 | Y | Car bomb | 13 | US Military convoy | MIPT/AP |
| 26-Jan-05 | Unknown | Riyadh | Iraq | Govt/Police | 7 | 2 | N | Car bomb | 13 | Police station | NCTC/MIPT |
| 26-Jan-05 | Unknown | Riyadh | Iraq | Govt/Police | 2 | 1 | N | Car bomb | 13 | Riyadh mayor's office | NCTC/MIPT |
| 26-Jan-05 | Tanzim | Sinjar | Iraq | Govt/Police | 14 | 30 | N | Tractor | 13 | KDP office | MIPT/ST |
| 27-Jan-05 | Tanzim | Baquba | Iraq | Govt/Police | 5 | 9 | N | Car bomb | 13 | Diyala governor's office | NCTC/MIPT |
| 27-Jan-05 | Unknown | Samarra | Iraq | Govt/Police | 11 | 7 | N | Car bomb | 13 | Polling center | MIPT/REUT |
| 28-Jan-05 | Unknown | Baghdad | Iraq | Govt/Police | 6 | 4 | N | Car bomb | 13 | al-Dora Police station | MIPT/ST |
| 29-Jan-05 | Tanzim | Khananqin | Iraq | Govt/Police | 8 | 5 | Y | Belt bomb | 13 | US/Iraqi center | NCTC/MIPT |
| 30-Jan-05 | Tanzim | Baghdad | Iraq | Civilian | 1 | 10 | N | Belt bomb | 13 | Polling center/Ishkan area | MIPT/ST |
| 30-Jan-05 | Tanzim | Baghdad | Iraq | Civilian | 1 | 5 | N | Belt bomb | 13 | Polling center at al-Zahawi school | NCTC/MIPT |
| 30-Jan-05 | Tanzim | Baghdad | Iraq | Civilian | 2 | 9 | N | Belt bomb | 13 | Polling center at Maysalon | NCTC/MIPT |
| 30-Jan-05 | Tanzim | Baghdad | Iraq | Civilian | 1 | 4 | N | Belt bomb | 13 | Polling center at al-Shouhada | NCTC/MIPT |
| 30-Jan-05 | Tanzim | Baghdad | Iraq | Civilian | 1 | 16 | N | Belt bomb | 13 | Polling center at al-Jawahiri | NCTC/MIPT |
| 30-Jan-05 | Tanzim | Baghdad | Iraq | Civilian | 1 | 5 | N | Belt bomb | 13 | Polling center at Badar | NCTC/MIPT |
| 30-Jan-05 | Tanzim | Baghdad | Iraq | Civilian | 2 | 5 | N | Belt bomb | 13 | 0800/Polling center at al-Assil | NCTC/MIPT |
| 30-Jan-05 | Tanzim | Baghdad | Iraq | Govt/Police** | 1 | 4 | N | Car bomb | 13 | Justice Minister Malik al-Hasan | NCTC/MIPT |
| 30-Jan-05 | Tanzim | Baghdad | Iraq | Civilian | 5 | 13 | N | Belt bomb | 13 | Polling center/Abu Alwan | NCTC/MIPT |

| | | | | | | | | | | | |
|---|---|---|---|---|---|---|---|---|---|---|---|
| 30-Jan-05 | Tanzim | Baghdad | Iraq | Civilian | 3 | 9 | N | Belt bomb | 13 | Polling center | NCTC/IPCS |
| 30-Jan-05 | Tanzim | Baghdad | Iraq | Civilian | 3 | 6 | N | Belt bomb | 13 | Polling center | NCTC/THI |
| 31-Jan-05 | Tanzim | Baghdad | Iraq | Civilian | 0 | 10 | N | Belt bomb | 13 | 0900/Iskan area | NCTC/THI |
| 31-Jan-05 | Tanzim | Baghdad | Iraq | Civilian | 8 | 0 | N | Belt bomb | 13 | Polling center | NCTC/THI |
| 31-Jan-05 | Tanzim | Baghdad | Iraq | Civilian | 1 | 0 | N | Belt bomb | 13 | Polling center/stopped by voter | NCTC/THI |
| 31-Jan-05 | Tanzim | Baghdad | Iraq | Civilian^ | 7 | 2 | N | Belt bomb | 13 | 6 bombers/Polling center | NCTC |
| 31-Jan-05 | Tanzim | Baghdad | Iraq | Civilian^ | 8 | 2 | N | Belt bomb | 13 | 6 bombers/Polling center | NCTC |
| 31-Jan-05 | Tanzim | Baghdad | Iraq | Civilian^ | 8 | 2 | N | Belt bomb | 13 | 6 bombers/Polling center | NCTC |
| 2-Feb-05 | Unknown | Musayyib | Iraq | Hospital | 18 | 26 | N | Car bomb | 13 | Police nearby/near govt bldg | MIPT/ST |
| 3-Feb-05 | Tanzim | Baghdad | Iraq | Military | 0 | 4 | Y | Car bomb | 13 | Attacked convoy on airport road | MIPT/ST |
| 5-Feb-05 | Unknown | Basra | Iraq | Military | 4 | 2 | N | Motorcycle | 13 | Iraqi Army | SM/AJ |
| 7-Feb-05 | Tanzim | Baquba | Iraq | Govt/Police | 14 | 17 | N | Car bomb | 13 | Police recruits at police station | Pape/RFE |
| 7-Feb-05 | Tanzim | Mosul | Iraq | Govt/Police | 12 | 6 | N | Car bomb | 13 | Police at Jumhouri hospital | NCTC/RFE |
| 8-Feb-05 | Tanzim | Baghdad | Iraq | Military | 21 | 27 | N | Belt bomb | 13 | Army recruit center/Muthana airfield | NCTC/MIPT |
| 10-Feb-05 | Unknown | Baghdad | Iraq | Military | 3 | 5 | Y | Car bomb | 13 | Missed US mil convoy/Tahrir Square | NCTC/BBC |
| 10-Feb-05 | Unknown | Baghdad | Iraq | Govt/Police | 14 | 60 | N | Car bomb | 13 | Salman Pak police station | BBC |
| 10-Feb-05 | Tanzim | Baquba | Iraq | Govt/Police | 11 | 14 | N | Car bomb | 13 | Diyala police station | SITE |
| 11-Feb-05 | Tanzim | Balad Ruz | Iraq | Religious site | 13 | 40 | N | Truck bomb | 13 | Shiite mosque at evening prayers | Pape/MIPT |
| 11-Feb-05 | Unknown | Dhuluiyah | Iraq | Military | 0 | 11 | Y | Car bomb | 13 | US military patrol | PDO |
| 12-Feb-05 | Unknown | Al Musayyib | Iraq | Hospital | 18 | 21 | N | Car bomb | 13 | Damaged hospital | NCTC/CNN |
| 14-Feb-05 | Unknown | Beirut | Lebanon | Govt/Police* | 23 | 220 | N | Car bomb | x | Former PM Hariri/1,800 kg bomb | NYT/UN |
| 15-Feb-05 | Unknown | Baquba | Iraq | Govt/Police** | 0 | 0 | N | Car bomb | 13 | Iraq government official | NCTC |
| 16-Feb-05 | Unknown | Quetta | Pakistan | Religious site | 0 | 0 | N | Grenades | 10 | Bomber arrested at mosque | MIPT/NAW |
| 16-Feb-05 | Unknown | Baghdad | Iraq | Unknown | 0 | 0 | N | Belt bomb | 13 | Killed by police before detonation | MIPT/AP |
| 18-Feb-05 | Unknown | Baghdad | Iraq | Govt/Police | 5 | 4 | N | Car bomb | 13 | Police checkpoint in Sunni area | NCTC/MIPT |
| 18-Feb-05 | Unknown | Baghdad | Iraq | Religious site | 16 | 23 | N | Belt bomb | 13 | al-Khadimain Shiite mosque | Pape/NCTC |
| 18-Feb-05 | Unknown | Baghdad | Iraq | Religious site | 10 | 31 | N | Belt bomb | 13 | Ali Baiya Shiite mosque | NCTC/MIPT |
| 18-Feb-05 | Unknown | Baghdad | Iraq | Religious site | 0 | 0 | N | Belt bomb | 13 | Ali Baiya Mosque/Killed by police | MIPT/CNN |
| 18-Feb-05 | Unknown | Iskandariyah | Iraq | Religious site | 8 | 13 | N | Car bomb | 13 | Also small arms fire/Al-Hadi mosque | NCTC/ST |
| 19-Feb-05 | Unknown | Baghdad | Iraq | Civilian | 5 | 55 | N | Motorcycle | 13 | Funeral tent of Sunnis | NCTC/MIPT |
| 19-Feb-05 | Unknown | Baghdad | Iraq | Religious site | 3 | 40 | N | Belt bomb | 13 | Shiite mosque/Ashura procession | NCTC/MIPT |
| 19-Feb-05 | Unknown | Baghdad | Iraq | Bus | 16 | 41 | N | Belt bomb | 13 | Mostly Shiites/Khadimiya square | NCTC/MIPT |
| 19-Feb-05 | Unknown | Baghdad | Iraq | Religious site | 7 | 55 | N | Belt bomb | 13 | Shiite Ashura parade/Nada Mosque | NCTC/MIPT |
| 19-Feb-05 | Unknown | Baghdad | Iraq | Govt/Police | 2 | 0 | N | Belt bomb | 13 | Police patrol | AP/IPCS |
| 19-Feb-05 | Unknown | Baghdad | Iraq | Unknown | 0 | 0 | N | Belt bomb | 13 | Arrested before detonation | MIPT/AP |
| 19-Feb-05 | Unknown | Baghdad | Iraq | Civilian | 0 | 0 | N | Belt bomb | 13 | Killed by U.S. military before attack | MIPT/AP |
| 19-Feb-05 | Unknown | Baghdad | Iraq | School | 0 | 0 | N | Belt bomb | 13 | Legal education building | NCTC/MIPT |
| 19-Feb-05 | Unknown | Baquba | Iraq | Military | 3 | 2 | N | Car bomb | 13 | Iraqi Army base | NCTC/AP |
| 22-Feb-05 | Unknown | Baghdad | Iraq | Hospital | 0 | 0 | N | Belt bomb | 13 | Arrested before detonating | MIPT/AP |
| 22-Feb-05 | Unknown | Baghdad | Iraq | Govt/Police | 4 | 30 | N | Car bomb | 13 | Police commando convoy | MIPT/ST |
| 23-Feb-05 | Unknown | Mosul | Iraq | Unknown | 1 | 14 | Y | Car bomb | 13 | Premature detonation | AJ/USA |
| 24-Feb-05 | Unknown | Iskandariyah | Iraq | Govt/Police | 5 | 8 | N | Car bomb | 13 | SCIRI headquarters | NCTC/MIPT |
| 24-Feb-05 | Unknown | Kirkuk | Iraq | Govt/Police | 2 | 1 | N | Car bomb | 13 | Iraqi police patrol | AAIW/IHT |

| Date | Group | City | Country | Target | Killed | Wounded | S | Weapon | Region | Notes | Source |
|---|---|---|---|---|---|---|---|---|---|---|---|
| 24-Feb-05 | Unknown | Tikrit | Iraq | Govt/Police | 15 | 22 | N | Car bomb | 13 | Police station at shift change | NCTC/MIPT |
| 25-Feb-05 | PIJ | Tel Aviv | Israel | Nightclub | 5 | 52 | N | Belt bomb | 4 | Stage nightclub entrance | CSS/NCTC |
| 26-Feb-05 | Unknown | Baghdad | Iraq | Military | 2 | 2 | Y | Car bomb | 13 | US military convoy (Tank)/Al Adl area | NCTC/UPI |
| 28-Feb-05 | Tanzim | Hillah | Iraq | Hospital | 125 | 140 | N | Car bomb | 13 | Clinic screening Army recruits | NCTC/MIPT |
| 28-Feb-05 | Tanzim | Mosul | Iraq | Military | 0 | 2 | Y | Car bomb | 13 | US military patrol | WP |
| 28-Feb-05 | Unknown | Musayyib | Iraq | Govt/Police | 1 | 3 | N | Car bomb | 13 | Police checkpoint | MIPT/ST |
| 2-Mar-05 | Tanzim | Baghdad | Iraq | Military | 7 | 28 | N | Car bomb | 13 | Army recruiting center/Al-Muthanna | NCTC/MIPT |
| 3-Mar-05 | Tanzim | Baghdad | Iraq | Govt/Police^ | 2 | 7 | N | Car bomb | 13 | 2 car bombs/Interior Ministry | MIPT/ST |
| 3-Mar-05 | Tanzim | Baghdad | Iraq | Govt/Police^ | 3 | 8 | N | Car bomb | 13 | 2 car bombs/Interior Ministry | MIPT/ST |
| 3-Mar-05 | Tanzim | Baquba | Iraq | Govt/Police | 1 | 18 | N | Car bomb | 13 | Police station | NCTC/MIPT |
| 7-Mar-05 | Unknown | Balad | Iraq | School | 15 | 23 | N | Car bomb | 13 | Elementary school/ING officer's house | NCTC/XNA |
| 7-Mar-05 | Tanzim | Baquba | Iraq | Govt/Police | 10 | 20 | N | Car bomb | 13 | Police convoy near police station | MIPT/ST |
| 8-Mar-05 | IAI | Baghdad | Iraq | Govt/Police | 0 | 0 | N | Belt bomb | 13 | 2 arrested before attack/courthouse | MIPT/AS |
| 8-Mar-05 | IAI | Baghdad | Iraq | Govt/Police | 0 | 0 | N | Belt bomb | 13 | 2 arrested before attack/courthouse | MIPT/AS |
| 9-Mar-05 | Tanzim | Baghdad | Iraq | Hotel | 4 | 40 | Y | Truck bomb | 13 | Al-Sadir Hotel used by Westerners | Pape/NCTC |
| 9-Mar-05 | Unknown | Habaniyah | Iraq | Military | 0 | 0 | Y | Car bomb | 13 | US military base checkpoint | AP/HC |
| 10-Mar-05 | Prophet's C | Mosul | Iraq | Civilian | 53 | 100 | N | Belt bomb | 13 | Funeral at Shahedayein mosque | Pape/NCTC |
| 13-Mar-05 | Tanzim | Kirkuk | Iraq | Military | 0 | 0 | N | Car bomb | 13 | Arrested/target Kiwan Army base | AS |
| 13-Mar-05 | Unknown | Yusufiyah | Iraq | Govt/Police | 4 | 2 | N | Car bomb | 13 | Iraqi police checkpoint | NCTC/AS |
| 14-Mar-05 | Unknown | Baghdad | Iraq | Military | 4 | 0 | N | Car bomb | 13 | Army/police checkpoint | MIPT/ST |
| 15-Mar-05 | Tanzim | Baghdad | Iraq | Military | 4 | 7 | Y | Car bomb | 13 | US military convoy near BIAP | AAIW/SITE |
| 15-Mar-05 | Tanzim | Baghdad | Iraq | Govt/Police | 1 | 4 | N | Car bomb | 13 | Police patrol near Bab al-Muadhim | MIPT/ST |
| 16-Mar-05 | Tanzim | Baquba | Iraq | Military | 3 | 8 | N | Car bomb | 13 | Iraqi Army patrol | NCTC/AS |
| 17-Mar-05 | Tanzim | Mosul | Iraq | Military | 2 | 15 | Y | Car bomb | 13 | US military patrol | MST/BJ |
| 18-Mar-05 | Unknown | Haditha | Iraq | Military | 0 | 0 | N | Car bomb | 13 | Iraqi Army CP/partial detonation | IPCS/DT |
| 19-Mar-05 | Levant Army | Doha | Qatar | Theater | 0 | 16 | N | Car bomb | 7 | Targeted Western theater | NCTC/MIPT |
| 19-Mar-05 | Unknown | Fatehpur | Pakistan | Religious site | 50 | 100 | N | Belt bomb | 10 | Shrine of Shia saint | PTI/AAIW |
| 19-Mar-05 | Tanzim | Ramadi | Iraq | Military | 0 | 1 | Y | Car bomb | 13 | US military patrol/early detonation | XNA/IPCS |
| 20-Mar-05 | Unknown | Falluja | Iraq | Govt/Police | 2 | 0 | N | Car bomb | 13 | Western convoy | NCTC/MIPT |
| 20-Mar-05 | Unknown | Mosul | Iraq | Military | 0 | 3 | Y | Car bomb | 13 | US military patrol | AAIW |
| 20-Mar-05 | Tanzim | Mosul | Iraq | Govt/Police* | 3 | 2 | N | Car bomb | 13 | Iraq police leader Walid Kashmoula | NCTC/MIPT |
| 21-Mar-05 | Unknown | Samarra | Iraq | Hospital | 0 | 14 | N | Truck bomb | 13 | Detonated early | NCTC/MIPT |
| 23-Mar-05 | Unknown | Baghdad | Iraq | Civilian | 0 | 0 | N | Car bomb | 13 | Premature detonation/Kazamiyah area | NCTC |
| 23-Mar-05 | Tanzim | Mosul | Iraq | Military | 0 | 4 | Y | Car bomb | 13 | US military patrol | FOX/SITE |
| 24-Mar-05 | IAI | Ramadi | Iraq | Govt/Police | 11 | 14 | N | Car bomb | 13 | Iraq police commando checkpoint | Pape/MIPT |
| 25-Mar-05 | Unknown | al Haswah | Iraq | Civilian | 3 | 19 | N | Belt bomb | 13 | Iraqi police barracks | NCTC/TG |
| 25-Mar-05 | Unknown | Iskandariyah | Iraq | Military | 4 | 9 | N | Car bomb | 13 | Iraq Army convoy | AAIW/TG |
| 26-Mar-05 | Unknown | Baghdad | Iraq | Military | 2 | 2 | Y | Car bomb | 13 | US military patrol | AP/HC |
| 27-Mar-05 | Unknown | Mosul | Iraq | Military | 0 | 2 | Y | Car bomb | 13 | US military patrol | AJ |
| 28-Mar-05 | Unknown | Karbala | Iraq | Civilian | 6 | 9 | N | Car bomb | 13 | Shiite pilgrims | Pape/NCTC |
| 28-Mar-05 | Unknown | Musayyib | Iraq | Military | 5 | 10 | N | Motorcycle | 13 | Police checkpoint protecting pilgrims | NCTC/MIPT |
| 30-Mar-05 | Taliban | Jalalabad | Afghanistan | Govt/Police | 1 | 1 | N | Car bomb | 12 | Near governor's office | NCTC/ST |
| 30-Mar-05 | Unknown | Baghdad | Iraq | Military | 1 | 5 | Y | Car bomb | 13 | US military patrol | AS |

| 30-Mar-05 | Unknown | Mosul | Iraq | Military | 0 | 2 | Y | Car bomb | 13 | US military patrol | SITE |
|---|---|---|---|---|---|---|---|---|---|---|---|
| 31-Mar-05 | Tanzim | Samarra | Iraq | Military | 2 | 12 | Y | Car bomb | 13 | US military convoy | Pape/SL |
| 31-Mar-05 | Unknown | Tuz Khormato | Iraq | Govt/Police | 5 | 16 | N | Car bomb | 13 | Police checkpoint protecting pilgrims | NCTC/ST |
| 1-Apr-05 | Unknown | Ramadi | Iraq | Military | 0 | 1 | Y | Truck bomb | 13 | US military base/Azud area | AJ |
| 2-Apr-05 | Tanzim | Abu Ghurayb | Iraq | Military | 0 | 57 | Y | Car bomb | 13 | SVBEID/mortar/small arms attack | NCTC/NY |
| 2-Apr-05 | Tanzim | Baghdad | Iraq | Military | 0 | 1 | Y | Car bomb | 13 | US military patrol/al-Taramia area | SITE |
| 3-Apr-05 | Unknown | Baghdad | Iraq | Military | 0 | 0 | Y | Belt bomb | 13 | US military base/arrested/failed bomb | BBC |
| 3-Apr-05 | Unknown | Mosul | Iraq | Military | 1 | 9 | Y | Car bomb | 13 | US military convoy | NCTC/AP |
| 4-Apr-05 | Tanzim | Abu Ghurayb | Iraq | Govt/Police | 3 | 3 | N | Tractor | 13 | Police checkpoint | NCTC/XN |
| 5-Apr-05 | Unknown | Mosul | Iraq | Military | 0 | 5 | Y | Car bomb | 13 | US military patrol | CO |
| 6-Apr-05 | Unknown | Srinagar | Kashmir/India | Govt/Police | 2 | 7 | N | Grenades | 9 | Tourist reception center | IPCS/DE |
| 7-Apr-05 | Islamic Glory | Cairo | Egypt | Civilian | 3 | 18 | N | Belt bomb | 5 | Target tourists in Cairo bazaar | NCTC/MIF |
| 7-Apr-05 | Unknown | Tuz Khormato | Iraq | Military | 4 | 12 | N | Car bomb | 13 | Iraqi Army post | NCTC |
| 8-Apr-05 | Tanzim | Baghdad | Iraq | Military | 0 | 0 | Y | Car bomb | 13 | US military patrol/opened fire | SITE |
| 8-Apr-05 | Unknown | Mosul | Iraq | Military | 0 | 2 | Y | Car bomb | 13 | US military patrol | SLPD/AJ |
| 9-Apr-05 | Unknown | Mosul | Iraq | Govt/Police | 2 | 14 | N | Belt bomb | 13 | Police patrol/near Agriculture Ministry | NCTC/MIF |
| 10-Apr-05 | Unknown | Baghdad | Iraq | Military | 0 | 5 | Y | Car bomb | 13 | Joint US/Iraqi Army patrol | NCTC/MH |
| 10-Apr-05 | Tanzim | Mosul | Iraq | Military | 0 | 3 | Y | Car bomb | 13 | US military patrol | SITE |
| 10-Apr-05 | Tanzim | Mosul | Iraq | Military | 0 | 4 | Y | Car bomb | 13 | US military patrol | SITE |
| 11-Apr-05 | Unknown | al-Qaim | Iraq | Military^ | 0 | 1 | N | Car bomb | 13 | 3 bombs/Camp Gannon | TR/NBC |
| 11-Apr-05 | Unknown | al-Qaim | Iraq | Military^ | 0 | 1 | N | Car bomb | 13 | 3 bombs/Camp Gannon | TR/NBC |
| 11-Apr-05 | Unknown | al-Qaim | Iraq | Military^ | 0 | 1 | N | Truck bomb | 13 | 3 bombs/Camp Gannon/fire truck | TR |
| 11-Apr-05 | Unknown | Samarra | Iraq | Military | 2 | 22 | N | Car bomb | 13 | Iraqi Army patrol/US convoy | Pape/NCT |
| 12-Apr-05 | Tanzim | Baghdad | Iraq | Govt/Police | 4 | 2 | N | Belt bomb | 13 | Contractor convoy/BIAP road | NCTC |
| 12-Apr-05 | Tanzim | Husaybah | Iraq | Civilian | 8 | 0 | Y | Car bomb | 13 | US mil patrol/also small arms fire | NCTC |
| 12-Apr-05 | Unknown | Mosul | Iraq | Military | 5 | 1 | Y | Car bomb | 13 | US military patrol/early detonation | IPCS/KTI |
| 12-Apr-05 | Unknown | Mosul | Iraq | Military | 4 | 2 | Y | Car bomb | 13 | US/Iraqi joint patrol | Pape/NCT |
| 12-Apr-05 | Unknown | Talafar | Iraq | Military | 5 | 8 | N | Car bomb | 13 | Iraqi Army patrol | Pape/NCT |
| 13-Apr-05 | Unknown | Baghdad | Iraq | Military | 0 | 7 | Y | Car bomb | 13 | US mil convoy/BIAP road | NCTC/BB |
| 13-Apr-05 | Unknown | Baghdad | Iraq | Military | 0 | 5 | Y | Car bomb | 13 | US/Iraqi military patrol | NCTC/BB |
| 13-Apr-05 | Tanzim | Mosul | Iraq | Military | 0 | 0 | Y | Car bomb | 13 | US military patrol/early detonation | SITE |
| 13-Apr-05 | Tanzim | Mosul | Iraq | Military | 0 | 1 | Y | Car bomb | 13 | US military patrol/early detonation | SITE |
| 14-Apr-05 | Tanzim | Baghdad | Iraq | Govt/Police^ | 9 | 25 | N | Car bomb | 13 | Police convoy/near Interior Ministry | Pape/NCT |
| 14-Apr-05 | Tanzim | Baghdad | Iraq | Govt/Police^ | 9 | 25 | N | Car bomb | 13 | Police convoy/near Interior Ministry | Pape/NCT |
| 14-Apr-05 | Unknown | Hillah/Mahaweel | Iraq | Market | 4 | 6 | N | Briefcase | 13 | Killed 4 police in market | NCTC/MIF |
| 14-Apr-05 | Unknown | Tikrit | Iraq | Military | 0 | 12 | N | Car bomb | 13 | Iraqi Army patrol | NCTC/BB |
| 15-Apr-05 | Tanzim | Baghdad | Iraq | Military | 0 | 5 | Y | Car bomb | 13 | US military convoy/West Baghdad | NCTC/ST |
| 15-Apr-05 | Unknown | Talafar | Iraq | Military | 0 | 0 | Y | Car bomb | 13 | US/Iraqi military patrol | IHT |
| 16-Apr-05 | Unknown | Baghdad | Iraq | Civilian | 4 | 6 | N | Car bomb | 13 | Western convoy near BIAP | Pape/NCT |
| 16-Apr-05 | Tanzim | Baquba | Iraq | Restaurant | 13 | 5 | N | Belt bomb | 13 | Police-related restaurant | Pape/NCT |
| 16-Apr-05 | Unknown | Mosul | Iraq | Military | 0 | 6 | Y | Car bomb | 13 | US military patrol | AJ/TT |
| 17-Apr-05 | Unknown | Baghdad | Iraq | Civilian | 2 | 5 | N | Car bomb | 13 | Contractor security convoy | NCTC |
| 19-Apr-05 | Tanzim | Baghdad | Iraq | Military | 6 | 44 | N | Car bomb | 13 | Army recruiting center/Adhamiyah | Pape/NCT |

| Date | Group | City | Country | Target | Killed | Wounded | Y/N | Weapon | Code | Notes | Source |
|---|---|---|---|---|---|---|---|---|---|---|---|
| 19-Apr-05 | Unknown | Baghdad | Iraq | Military | 2 | 4 | Y | Car bomb | 13 | US military patrol/Al Amil area | TG/SEA |
| 20-Apr-05 | Tanzim | Baghdad | Iraq | Govt/Police** | 2 | 3 | N | Car bomb | 13 | Prime Minister Allawi | Pape/NCTC |
| 20-Apr-05 | Unknown | Baghdad | Iraq | Govt/Police | 1 | 18 | N | Car bomb | 13 | Iraqi police station/Al Belat | NCTC/BBC |
| 20-Apr-05 | Unknown | Baghdad | Iraq | Govt/Police | 1 | 4 | N | Car bomb | 13 | Iraqi police patrol/Ad Dawrah area | NCTC/BBC |
| 20-Apr-05 | Unknown | Ramadi | Iraq | Military | 0 | 0 | Y | Car bomb | 13 | US military patrol | AJ/SDU |
| 21-Apr-05 | Unknown | Baghdad | Iraq | Govt/Police | 1 | 3 | N | Car bomb | 13 | Western security convoy | NCTC/TJ |
| 22-Apr-05 | Unknown | Baghdad | Iraq | Religious site | 11 | 24 | N | Car bomb | 13 | al-Subaih Shiite mosque | MIPT/ST |
| 23-Apr-05 | Tanzim | Baghdad | Iraq | Military | 1 | 10 | Y | Car bomb | 13 | US military convoy/West Baghdad | NCTC/BBC |
| 23-Apr-05 | Unknown | Basra | Iraq | Religious site | 0 | 8 | N | Car bomb | 13 | 2 bombers in car, Shiite mosque | NCTC/MIPT |
| 23-Apr-05 | Unknown | Mosul | Iraq | Military | 1 | 7 | Y | Car bomb | 13 | US/Iraqi Army patrol | NCTC/AP |
| 24-Apr-05 | Tanzim | Baghdad | Iraq | Market^ | 11 | 28 | N | Car bomb | 13 | Coordinated attack | NCTC/MIPT |
| 24-Apr-05 | Tanzim | Baghdad | Iraq | Religious site^ | 11 | 28 | N | Car bomb | 13 | Coordinated attack/mosque | Pape/NCTC |
| 24-Apr-05 | Prophet's C | Bayji | Iraq | Govt/Police** | 0 | 4 | N | Car bomb | 13 | Political leader Mish'an al-Juburi | MIPT/AS |
| 24-Apr-05 | Tanzim | Tikrit | Iraq | Govt/Police^ | 3 | 13 | N | Car bomb | 13 | Iraq Police Academy | Pape/NCTC |
| 24-Apr-05 | Tanzim | Tikrit | Iraq | Govt/Police^ | 4 | 14 | N | Car bomb | 13 | Iraq Police Academy | Pape/NCTC |
| 25-Apr-05 | Tanzim | Ramadi | Iraq | Military | 1 | 2 | Y | Car bomb | 13 | US military patrol | ST/SITE |
| 28-Apr-05 | Tanzim | Tikrit | Iraq | Military | 0 | 14 | N | Car bomb | 13 | Iraqi Army checkpoint | NCTC/EG |
| 29-Apr-05 | Unknown | Anbar | Iraq | Military^ | 1 | 1 | Y | Car bomb | 13 | US military patrol | NTF/IHT |
| 29-Apr-05 | Tanzim | Baghdad | Iraq | Govt/Police^ | 5 | 13 | N | Car bomb | 13 | Army/police forces Azamiyah area | NCTC/MIPT |
| 29-Apr-05 | Tanzim | Baghdad | Iraq | Govt/Police^ | 5 | 13 | N | Car bomb | 13 | Army/police forces Azamiyah area | NCTC/MIPT |
| 29-Apr-05 | Tanzim | Baghdad | Iraq | Military^ | 5 | 12 | N | Car bomb | 13 | Army/police forces Azamiyah area | NCTC/MIPT |
| 29-Apr-05 | Tanzim | Baghdad | Iraq | Military^ | 5 | 12 | N | Car bomb | 13 | Army/police forces Azamiyah area | NCTC/MIPT |
| 29-Apr-05 | Unknown | Baghdad | Iraq | Military | 1 | 2 | Y | Car bomb | 13 | US military convoy | AP |
| 29-Apr-05 | Tanzim | Baquba | Iraq | Govt/Police | 3 | 20 | N | Car bomb | 13 | Police patrol | NCTC |
| 29-Apr-05 | Unknown | Dujayl | Iraq | Military^ | 1 | 4 | Y | Car bomb | 13 | US military convoy | NTF/IHT |
| 29-Apr-05 | Tanzim | Madeen | Iraq | Govt/Police^ | 3 | 17 | N | Car bomb | 13 | 2 simultaneous bombers | NCTC/MIPT |
| 29-Apr-05 | Tanzim | Madeen | Iraq | Govt/Police^ | 4 | 18 | N | Car bomb | 13 | 2 simultaneous bombers | NCTC/MIPT |
| 29-Apr-05 | Unknown | Taji | Iraq | Unknown | 0 | 0 | N | Car bomb | 13 | Premature detonation | NYT/IHT |
| 30-Apr-05 | Unknown | Cairo | Egypt | Civilian | 0 | 7 | N | Belt bomb | 5 | Detonated police pursuit/Museum | MIPT/ST |
| 30-Apr-05 | Tanzim | Baghdad | Iraq | Govt/Police | 2 | 7 | Y | Car bomb | 13 | US/Iraqi patrol | NCTC/MIPT |
| 30-Apr-05 | Tanzim | Baghdad | Iraq | Govt/Police** | 0 | 10 | N | Car bomb | 13 | Police patrol | NCTC |
| 30-Apr-05 | Tanzim | Baghdad | Iraq | Govt/Police | 1 | 18 | N | Car bomb | 13 | National Dialogue Council/Sunni | NCTC/MIPT |
| 30-Apr-05 | Unknown | Baghdad | Iraq | Govt/Police | 1 | 3 | N | Belt bomb | 13 | Security checkpoint | NCTC |
| 30-Apr-05 | Tanzim | Mosul | Iraq | Govt/Police | 0 | 9 | N | Car bomb | 13 | Police patrol | NCTC/MIPT |
| 30-Apr-05 | Unknown | Mosul | Iraq | Military | 1 | 5 | N | Car bomb | 13 | Iraqi Army patrol | NCTC/AAIW |
| 30-Apr-05 | Unknown | Mosul | Iraq | Govt/Police | 0 | 4 | N | Car bomb | 13 | Police patrol | NCTC/IPCS |
| 1-May-05 | Unknown | Baghdad | Iraq | Military | 5 | 12 | Y | Car bomb | 13 | US military patrol/Zafaraniyya area | ST/SEA |
| 1-May-05 | Unknown | Baghdad | Iraq | Military | 0 | 0 | Y | Car bomb | 13 | US military base/East Baghdad | SEA/STA |
| 1-May-05 | Unknown | Talafar | Iraq | Civilian | 24 | 50 | N | Car bomb | 13 | KDP Funeral procession | Pape/NCTC |
| 2-May-05 | Unknown | Baghdad | Iraq | Military | 0 | 0 | Y | Car bomb | 13 | US military patrol | MEO/HC |
| 2-May-05 | Unknown | Baghdad | Iraq | Military | 0 | 0 | Y | Car bomb | 13 | US military patrol | MEO/HC |
| 2-May-05 | Tanzim | Baghdad | Iraq | Military | 2 | 11 | N | Car bomb | 13 | Iraqi police patrol | NCTC/ST |
| 2-May-05 | Unknown | Mosul | Iraq | Military | 2 | 17 | N | Car bomb | 13 | Iraqi Army patrol | NCTC |
| 3-May-05 | Unknown | Mosul | Iraq | Military | 1 | 4 | Y | Car bomb | 13 | US military patrol | WP/IHT |

| Date | Group | City | Country | Target | Killed | Wounded | S | Weapon | Col | Notes | Source |
|---|---|---|---|---|---|---|---|---|---|---|---|
| 4-May-05 | Unknown | Baghdad | Iraq | Military | 9 | 16 | N | Car bomb | 13 | Iraq Army CP/South Baghdad | NYT/CT |
| 4-May-05 | Sunna | Irbil | Iraq | Govt/Police | 69 | 150 | N | Belt bomb | 13 | Recruiting center/KDP HQ | Pape/NCTC |
| 4-May-05 | Unknown | Mosul | Iraq | Military | 4 | 5 | Y | Car bomb | 13 | US/Iraqi patrol | USA/CBS |
| 5-May-05 | Chechen sep | Grozny | Russia | Govt/Police | 0 | 0 | N | Belt bomb | 6 | Female/killed by police at checkpoint | MIPT/ITAR |
| 5-May-05 | Unknown | Baghdad | Iraq | Govt/Police | 13 | 20 | N | Belt bomb | 13 | Army recruiting center/Al-Muthanna | Pape/NCTC |
| 5-May-05 | Unknown | Baghdad | Iraq | Govt/Police | 1 | 6 | N | Car bomb | 13 | Police patrol/al-Gazaliyah area | MIPT/ST |
| 5-May-05 | Unknown | Baghdad | Iraq | Military | 0 | 0 | Y | Car bomb | 13 | US military convoy/truck destroyed | TR/SL |
| 6-May-05 | Chechen sep | Staropromyslovsky | Russia | Govt/Police | 0 | 0 | N | Belt bomb | 6 | Killed by police before detonation | UPI/ITAR |
| 6-May-05 | Tanzim | Mosul | Iraq | Govt/Police | 5 | 15 | N | Car bomb | 13 | Police patrol | XNA/BP |
| 6-May-05 | Unknown | Suwayra | Iraq | Market | 30 | 45 | N | Car bomb | 13 | Shiite area/vegetable market | Pape/NCTC |
| 6-May-05 | Tanzim | Tikrit | Iraq | Govt/Police | 10 | 13 | N | Car bomb | 13 | Police bus near checkpoint | Pape/NCTC |
| 7-May-05 | Unknown | Kabul | Afghanistan | Civilian | 2 | 6 | N | Belt bomb | 12 | Internet café | NCTC/RFE |
| 7-May-05 | Tanzim | Baghdad | Iraq | Military^ | 11 | 18 | N | Car bomb | 13 | Western security convoy/Tahrir Square | Pape/NCTC |
| 7-May-05 | Tanzim | Baghdad | Iraq | Military^ | 11 | 18 | N | Car bomb | 13 | Western security convoy/Tahrir Square | Pape/NCTC |
| 7-May-05 | Unknown | Haditha | Iraq | Military | 3 | 0 | Y | Car bomb | 13 | Missed US mil convoy/hit hospital | NCTC/IC |
| 8-May-05 | Tanzim | Mosul | Iraq | Military | 0 | 4 | N | Car bomb | 13 | Iraqi Army patrol | KCS/WP |
| 8-May-05 | Unknown | Tikrit | Iraq | Military | 2 | 15 | Y | Car bomb | 13 | US military convoy | WP |
| 9-May-05 | Tanzim | Baghdad | Iraq | Govt/Police | 4 | 9 | N | Car bomb | 13 | Police checkpoint | Pape/NCTC |
| 9-May-05 | Unknown | Husaybah | Iraq | Military^ | 0 | 0 | Y | Car bomb | 13 | US mil patrol/M-1 tank | CC/CNN |
| 9-May-05 | Unknown | Husaybah | Iraq | Military^ | 0 | 5 | Y | Car bomb | 13 | US mil patrol/also small arms fire | CC/CNN |
| 10-May-05 | Unknown | Baghdad | Iraq | Military | 6 | 41 | Y | Car bomb | 13 | US convoy/Al Sa'dun Street | Pape/NCTC |
| 10-May-05 | Unknown | Baghdad | Iraq | Govt/Police | 0 | 3 | N | Car bomb | 13 | Baghdad River Police station | NCTC/MIPT |
| 10-May-05 | Tanzim | Talafar | Iraq | Military | 0 | 0 | Y | Car bomb | 13 | US military patrol | SITE |
| 11-May-05 | Unknown | Baghdad | Iraq | Govt/Police | 3 | 9 | N | Car bomb | 13 | Police station/Dora area | NCTC/MIPT |
| 11-May-05 | Unknown | Baghdad | Iraq | Govt/Police | 2 | 11 | N | Car bomb | 13 | Police patrol/Jordan Square | NCTC/MIPT |
| 11-May-05 | Unknown | Baghdad | Iraq | Govt/Police | 0 | 3 | N | Car bomb | 13 | Police patrol/al-Darweesh bakery | NCTC/MIPT |
| 11-May-05 | Unknown | Baghdad | Iraq | Military | 0 | 3 | Y | Car bomb | 13 | US military patrol | BBC |
| 11-May-05 | Sunna | Hawija | Iraq | Civilian | 32 | 34 | N | Belt bomb | 13 | Recruiting center/Hawija | Pape/NCTC |
| 11-May-05 | Sunna | Tikrit | Iraq | Market | 37 | 84 | N | Car bomb | 13 | Police station/partly foiled | NCTC/MIPT |
| 12-May-05 | Unknown | Baghdad | Iraq | Market | 15 | 84 | N | Car bomb | 13 | Jadida market | NCTC/EIW |
| 13-May-05 | Rasul M. | Makhachkala | Russia | Unknown | 0 | 0 | N | Bag bomb | 6 | Arrested before detonation | MIPT/AP |
| 13-May-05 | Unknown | Baquba | Iraq | Military | 0 | 5 | N | Car bomb | 13 | Iraqi Army convoy | Pape/AS |
| 13-May-05 | Unknown | Bayji | Iraq | Military | 1 | 4 | Y | Car bomb | 13 | US military patrol | SFC/KCS |
| 13-May-05 | Tanzim | Mosul | Iraq | Military | 0 | 0 | Y | Car bomb | 13 | US military patrol | SITE |
| 14-May-05 | Unknown | Baghdad | Iraq | Govt/Police | 4 | 8 | N | Car bomb | 13 | Iraqi police patrol/Al Nidal Street | NCTC/MIPT |
| 14-May-05 | Unknown | Mosul | Iraq | Military | 2 | 3 | Y | Car bomb | 13 | US/Iraqi military patrol | AP/CNN |
| 15-May-05 | Tanzim | Baghdad | Iraq | Military | 0 | 2 | Y | Car bomb | 13 | US military patrol | SITE |
| 15-May-05 | Tanzim | Baquba | Iraq | Govt/Police | 4 | 40 | N | Belt bomb | 13 | Iraqi police patrol | NCTC/KTI |
| 15-May-05 | Tanzim | Baquba | Iraq | Govt/Police** | 0 | 3 | N | Car bomb | 13 | Diyala governor | Pape/NCTC |
| 15-May-05 | Unknown | Mosul | Iraq | Military | 0 | 0 | Y | Car bomb | 13 | US military patrol | CNN |
| 16-May-05 | Unknown | Rabia | Iraq | Govt/Police | 4 | 30 | N | Car bomb | 13 | Border checkpoint | NCTC/MIP |
| 17-May-05 | Unknown | Siirt | Turkey | Govt/Police | 0 | 1 | N | Belt bomb | 8 | Police challenged at Governor's Office | AAIW/ICG |
| 17-May-05 | Unknown | Baghdad | Iraq | Govt/Police | 0 | 0 | N | Car bomb | 13 | Adamiyah Iraqi police station | NCTC |
| 17-May-05 | Unknown | Bayji | Iraq | Military | 0 | 9 | Y | Car bomb | 13 | US/Iraqi military patrol | IPCS/KTI |

| Date | Group | City | Country | Target | Killed | Wounded | Suicide | Weapon | Region | Notes | Source |
|---|---|---|---|---|---|---|---|---|---|---|---|
| 18-May-05 | Tanzim | Mosul | Iraq | Govt/Police | 0 | 0 | N | Car bomb | 13 | PUK compound | NCTC/IPCS |
| 19-May-05 | Unknown | Baquba | Iraq | Civilian | 0 | 0 | N | Car bomb | 13 | Mufrek neighborhood | NCTC |
| 22-May-05 | Unknown | Mosul | Iraq | Civilian | 0 | 8 | Y | Car bomb | 13 | US DOD contractor convoy | NCTC |
| 22-May-05 | Unknown | Tikrit | Iraq | Military | 4 | 4 | Y | Car bomb | 13 | US troops meeting at Iraq police base | GN/PRN |
| 23-May-05 | Unknown | Baghdad | Iraq | Religious site | 9 | 30 | N | Car bomb | 13 | Abul-Fadi Abbas Shiite mosque | Pape/NCTC |
| 23-May-05 | Tanzim | Samarra | Iraq | Military | 4 | 4 | Y | Belt bomb | 13 | 2 bombers/US military base | TDN/SUN |
| 23-May-05 | Tanzim | Samarra | Iraq | Military | 0 | 23 | Y | Car bomb | 13 | 2 bombers/US military base | NCTC/TDN |
| 23-May-05 | Unknown | Talafar | Iraq | Govt/Police** | 15 | 15 | N | Car bomb | 13 | 2 bombs/Shia leader Hassan Baktesh | Pape/NCTC |
| 23-May-05 | Unknown | Talafar | Iraq | Govt/Police** | 5 | 5 | N | Car bomb | 13 | 2 bombs/Shia leader Hassan Baktesh | Pape/NCTC |
| 23-May-05 | Sunna | Tuz Khormato | Iraq | Govt/Police** | 5 | 18 | N | Car bomb | 13 | PUK official Muhammed Jigareti | Pape/NCTC |
| 24-May-05 | Tanzim | Baghdad | Iraq | Govt/Police | 5 | 5 | N | Car bomb | 13 | Iraqi police patrol/Al Wathiq Square | AS/SITE |
| 25-May-05 | Tanzim | Baghdad | Iraq | Civilian | 1 | 7 | Y | Car bomb | 13 | US military convoy/Saidiyah area | NCTC/SITE |
| 25-May-05 | Unknown | Baghdad | Iraq | Govt/Police | 1 | 11 | N | Car bomb | 13 | Police commandos/Dora area | NCTC/DR |
| 25-May-05 | Unknown | Baghdad | Iraq | Govt/Police | 0 | 6 | N | Car bomb | 13 | Police patrol | NCTC |
| 26-May-05 | Sunna | Baghdad | Iraq | Govt/Police | 5 | 17 | N | Car bomb | 13 | Police patrol/Shu'la area | NCTC/MIPT |
| 27-May-05 | Unknown | Nablus | West Bank | Unknown | 0 | 0 | N | Belt bomb | 4 | Arrested before detonation | MIPT/AP |
| 27-May-05 | Unknown | Islamabad | Pakistan | Civilian | 19 | 65 | N | Car bomb | 10 | Bari Imam Shia mosque | MIPT/ST |
| 27-May-05 | Unknown | Bayji | Iraq | Civilian | 0 | 0 | N | Car bomb | 13 | Target commercial security convoy | NCTC/AS |
| 27-May-05 | Unknown | Tikrit | Iraq | Govt/Police^ | 3 | 9 | N | Car bomb | 13 | Police patrol | Pape/NCTC |
| 27-May-05 | Unknown | Tikrit | Iraq | Govt/Police^ | 4 | 10 | N | Car bomb | 13 | Police patrol | Pape/NCTC |
| 28-May-05 | Unknown | Sinjar | Iraq | Military^ | 0 | 6 | N | Car bomb | 13 | 3 simultaneous car bombs | NCTC |
| 28-May-05 | Unknown | Sinjar | Iraq | Military^ | 0 | 6 | N | Car bomb | 13 | 3 simultaneous car bombs | NCTC/TP |
| 28-May-05 | Unknown | Sinjar | Iraq | Military^ | 1 | 6 | N | Car bomb | 13 | 3 simultaneous car bombs | NCTC/TP |
| 29-May-05 | Unknown | Baghdad | Iraq | Govt/Police | 4 | 10 | N | Car bomb | 13 | Police patrol/eastern Baghdad | NCTC/MIPT |
| 29-May-05 | Unknown | Baghdad | Iraq | Govt/Police | 2 | 14 | N | Car bomb | 13 | Oil Ministry, partially foiled | Pape/NCTC |
| 29-May-05 | Unknown | Madain | Iraq | Govt/Police | 2 | 8 | N | Car bomb | 13 | Police commando convoy | NCTC/MIPT |
| 29-May-05 | Unknown | Tuz Khormato | Iraq | Military | 1 | 16 | N | Car bomb | 13 | US logistics convoy | NCTC/SITE |
| 30-May-05 | al-Qaeda | Karachi | Pakistan | Religious site | 5 | 20 | N | Belt bomb | 7 | Shiite mosque/Gulshan-e-Iqbal | NCTC/ST |
| 30-May-05 | Tanzim | Hillah | Iraq | Govt/Police^ | 12 | 59 | N | Belt bomb | 13 | 2 car bombs/Police demonstrators | Pape/NCTC |
| 30-May-05 | Tanzim | Hillah | Iraq | Govt/Police^ | 13 | 59 | N | Belt bomb | 13 | 2 car bombs/Police demonstrators | Pape/NCTC |
| 1-Jun-05 | al-Qaeda | Kandahar | Afghanistan | Religious site | 20 | 52 | N | Belt bomb | 12 | Cleric's funeral at Abdul Raz Mosque | NCTC/RFE |
| 1-Jun-05 | Tanzim | Baghdad | Iraq | Airport | 0 | 15 | N | Car bomb | 13 | BIAP checkpoint one | Pape/NCTC |
| 1-Jun-05 | Tanzim | Taji | Iraq | Military | 1 | 3 | Y | Car bomb | 13 | US military convoy | AS/SITE |
| 2-Jun-05 | Unknown | Baghdad | Iraq | Govt/Police | 0 | 1 | N | Car bomb | 13 | Iraqi police station/Saydiyah | NCTC |
| 2-Jun-05 | Unknown | Baghdad | Iraq | Govt/Police | 0 | 1 | N | Car bomb | 13 | Dora area/detonated after police stop | NCTC/MIPT |
| 2-Jun-05 | Unknown | Balad | Iraq | Religious site | 9 | 12 | N | Car bomb | 13 | Sufi gathering/Saud village | Pape/NCTC |
| 2-Jun-05 | Tanzim | Baquba | Iraq | Military* | 4 | 4 | N | Car bomb | 13 | Diyala council deputy Hussein al-Timini | Pape/NCTC |
| 2-Jun-05 | Sunna | Kirkuk | Iraq | Military | 3 | 11 | N | Car bomb | 13 | National Oil convoy at Arafa complex | Pape/NCTC |
| 2-Jun-05 | Unknown | Mosul | Iraq | Govt/Police | 7 | 10 | N | Motorcycle | 13 | Near Mosul Police HQ | IHT/TES |
| 2-Jun-05 | Sunna | Tuz Khormato | Iraq | Restaurant | 11 | 40 | N | Car bomb | 13 | Prime Minister's bodyguards | Pape/NCTC |
| 3-Jun-05 | Unknown | Mosul | Iraq | Govt/Police | 3 | 5 | N | Car bomb | 13 | Police station | Pape/NCTC |
| 3-Jun-05 | Unknown | Tikrit | Iraq | Govt/Police | 0 | 9 | N | Car bomb | 13 | Iraqi police at US base entrance | NYT/AS |
| 4-Jun-05 | Unknown | Beld | Iraq | Military | 3 | 1 | N | Car bomb | 13 | Iraq Army checkpoint | UPI/IPCS |

| Date | Group | City | Country | Target | Killed | Wounded | S | Weapon | Code | Notes | Source |
|---|---|---|---|---|---|---|---|---|---|---|---|
| 4-Jun-05 | Unknown | Mosul | Iraq | Govt/Police | 0 | 6 | N | Car bomb | 13 | Iraqi police checkpoint | NCTC/IPC |
| 5-Jun-05 | Unknown | Baghdad | Iraq | Military | 1 | 3 | N | Motorcycle | 13 | Iraqi Army patrol/Tulul al-Baji area | AS/KTI |
| 6-Jun-05 | Tanzim | Baghdad | Iraq | Govt/Police | 2 | 4 | N | Car bomb | 13 | Partly foiled/Police commando HQ | NCTC/MIF |
| 6-Jun-05 | Sunna | Baghdad | Iraq | Govt/Police | 0 | 28 | N | Car bomb | 13 | Iraq police convoy/Al-Salm area | NYT/AS |
| 6-Jun-05 | Tanzim | Mosul | Iraq | Military | 0 | 2 | Y | Car bomb | 13 | US military patrol | SITE |
| 6-Jun-05 | Unknown | Tikrit | Iraq | Military | 0 | 4 | N | Car bomb | 13 | Iraqi Army compound | UPI/AS |
| 7-Jun-05 | Unknown | Hawija | Iraq | Govt/Police^ | 6 | 6 | N | Car bomb | 13 | Attacks on Army checkpoints/Dibis | Pape/NCT |
| 7-Jun-05 | Unknown | Hawija | Iraq | Govt/Police^ | 6 | 6 | N | Car bomb | 13 | Attacks on Army checkpoints/Aziziya | Pape/NCT |
| 7-Jun-05 | Unknown | Hawija | Iraq | Govt/Police^ | 6 | 6 | N | Car bomb | 13 | Attacks on Army checkpoints/Baqara | Pape/NCT |
| 7-Jun-05 | Unknown | Hawija | Iraq | Govt/Police | 0 | 0 | N | Car bomb | 13 | Bomb failed/attack on checkpoint | Pape/NCT |
| 7-Jun-05 | Unknown | Mosul | Iraq | Military | 0 | 2 | N | Car bomb | 13 | US mil convoy/failed to detonate | NCTC |
| 8-Jun-05 | Tanzim | Ramadi | Iraq | Military | 0 | 1 | N | Car bomb | 13 | Western convoy | SITE |
| 9-Jun-05 | Tanzim | Abu Ghraib | Iraq | Military | 0 | 1 | Y | Car bomb | 13 | US/Iraqi military patrol | SITE |
| 9-Jun-05 | Tanzim | Bayji | Iraq | Military | 0 | 4 | Y | Car bomb | 13 | US military patrol | AST/SITE |
| 10-Jun-05 | Unknown | Baghdad | Iraq | Restaurant | 10 | 28 | N | Car bomb | 13 | Restaurant in Shiite area | WP/IPCS |
| 10-Jun-05 | Tanzim | Mosul | Iraq | Military | 0 | 7 | Y | Car bomb | 13 | US military patrol | AST/BNS |
| 11-Jun-05 | Tanzim | Baghdad | Iraq | Govt/Police** | 8 | 12 | N | Belt bomb | 13 | Police commando leader Abu Walid | NCTC/MI |
| 11-Jun-05 | Tanzim | Baghdad | Iraq | Embassy | 0 | 4 | N | Car bomb | 13 | Slovakian Embassy | NCTC/MI |
| 13-Jun-05 | Unknown | Pulwama | Kashmir/India | School | 15 | 100 | N | Car bomb | 9 | High school | SATP/TO |
| 13-Jun-05 | Taliban | Kandahar | Afghanistan | Military | 0 | 4 | Y | Car bomb | 12 | US military patrol | AP/CDI |
| 13-Jun-05 | Tanzim | Baghdad | Iraq | Govt/Police** | 2 | 5 | Y | Car bomb | 13 | US Diplomat near Iraq Islamic Party | NCTC/UP |
| 13-Jun-05 | Unknown | Hawija | Iraq | Govt/Police | 0 | 0 | N | Car bomb | 13 | Police checkpoint | CC/NCTC |
| 13-Jun-05 | Unknown | Ramadi | Iraq | Military | 1 | 7 | Y | Car bomb | 13 | US/Iraqi checkpoint | HC/SL |
| 13-Jun-05 | Tanzim | Samarra | Iraq | Govt/Police | 8 | 26 | N | Car bomb | 13 | Joint Army/Police patrol | NCTC/RF |
| 13-Jun-05 | Tanzim | Tikrit | Iraq | Govt/Police | 3 | 16 | N | Car bomb | 13 | Iraq police patrol/Al-Ihtifalat Street | Pape/NCT |
| 14-Jun-05 | Unknown | Baghdad | Iraq | Military | 0 | 4 | N | Car bomb | 13 | Iraqi Army convoy | LE/DTI |
| 14-Jun-05 | Unknown | Baquba/Kan'an | Iraq | Military | 5 | 5 | N | Car bomb | 13 | Iraqi Army patrol | RFE/UPI |
| 14-Jun-05 | Sunna | Khalis | Iraq | Military | 22 | 100 | N | Belt bomb | 13 | In Army uniform/Army mess hall | NCTC/RF |
| 14-Jun-05 | Sunna | Kirkuk | Iraq | Civilian | 22 | 100 | N | Belt bomb | 13 | Crowd in front of Rafdiyan bank | Pape/HC |
| 15-Jun-05 | Unknown | Baghdad | Iraq | Govt/Police | 9 | 30 | N | Car bomb | 13 | Police patrol of 3 cars/Zafaraniya area | Pape/NC |
| 16-Jun-05 | Tanzim | Baghdad | Iraq | Govt/Police | 8 | 25 | N | Car bomb | 13 | Police commando convoy near airport | NCTC/MI |
| 16-Jun-05 | Unknown | Kirkuk | Iraq | Govt/Police | 0 | 5 | N | Car bomb | 13 | Checkpoint at oil facility | NCTC |
| 16-Jun-05 | Tanzim | Mosul | Iraq | Military | 0 | 35 | N | Car bomb | 13 | Truck of Iraq Army recruits | NCTC/SI |
| 17-Jun-05 | Unknown | al Habaniyah | Iraq | Religious site | 3 | 15 | N | Car bomb | 13 | Shiite mosque | NCTC |
| 17-Jun-05 | Unknown | Baghdad | Iraq | Govt/Police | 1 | 4 | N | Car bomb | 13 | Iraq police checkpoint | NCTC |
| 17-Jun-05 | Unknown | Falluja | Iraq | Govt/Police** | 4 | 10 | N | Car bomb | 13 | Falluja mayor MG Mahdi Sabih | NCTC/MI |
| 17-Jun-05 | Sunna | Tuz Khormato | Iraq | Govt/Police | 0 | 6 | N | Car bomb | 13 | Partly foiled/Army commander's house | NCTC/MI |
| 18-Jun-05 | Unknown | Baghdad | Iraq | Military | 2 | 6 | N | Car bomb | 13 | Crowd of Iraqi soldiers/Yarmouk area | XNA/AP |
| 19-Jun-05 | LeT | Mendhar | Kashmir/India | Govt/Police | 1 | 3 | N | Belt bomb | 9 | Commando Group/Police office | NCTC/SAP |
| 19-Jun-05 | Tanzim | Baghdad | Iraq | Govt/Police | 1 | 27 | N | Car bomb | 13 | Iraq police patrol | NCTC/UF |
| 19-Jun-05 | Tanzim | Baghdad | Iraq | Restaurant | 22 | 36 | N | Belt bomb | 13 | Police-related cafe near Green Zone | Pape/NC |
| 19-Jun-05 | Tanzim | Tikrit | Iraq | Govt/Police | 5 | 18 | N | Car bomb | 13 | Security checkpoint at Army base | Pape/NC |
| 20-Jun-05 | Unknown | Erez crossing | Gaza | Unknown | 0 | 0 | N | Belt bomb | 4 | Arrested at checkpoint/bomb failed | MIPT/TM |

| Date | Group | City | Country | Target | Killed | Wounded | ? | Weapon | # | Notes | Source |
|---|---|---|---|---|---|---|---|---|---|---|---|
| 20-Jun-05 | Tanzim | Baghdad | Iraq | Govt/Police | 10 | 23 | N | Car bomb | 13 | 4 bombers/Al-Bayaa police post | NCTC/HC |
| 20-Jun-05 | Unknown | Baghdad | Iraq | Civilian | 2 | 3 | N | Car bomb | 13 | Checkpoint near BIAP | NCTC/EIW |
| 20-Jun-05 | Sunna | Halabja | Iraq | Govt/Police* | 4 | 0 | N | Car bomb | 13 | Halabja security chief Anwar Othman | Pape/NCTC |
| 20-Jun-05 | Unknown | Irbil | Iraq | Govt/Police | 15 | 100 | N | Car bomb | 13 | Police HQ/police recruit roll call | NCTC/RFE |
| 20-Jun-05 | Unknown | Kirkuk | Iraq | Military | 5 | 3 | N | Car bomb | 13 | Iraqi Army checkpoint | EIW/SUN |
| 22-Jun-05 | Sunna | Baghdad | Iraq | Bus stop | 14 | 20 | N | Car bomb | 13 | Shiite bus stop/Shula area | NCTC/MIPT |
| 22-Jun-05 | Sunna | Baghdad | Iraq | Govt/Police** | 0 | 3 | N | Car bomb | 13 | Deputy Interior Minister MG Kamel | NCTC/MIPT |
| 22-Jun-05 | Tanzim | Mosul | Iraq | Military | 1 | 7 | Y | Car bomb | 13 | US military patrol | AP/GRP |
| 22-Jun-05 | Tanzim | Ramadi | Iraq | Civilian | 1 | 3 | N | Car bomb | 13 | Civilian car near US military patrol | AP/GRP |
| 23-Jun-05 | Sunna | Baghdad | Iraq | Govt/Police | 7 | 10 | N | Car bomb | 13 | Police patrol near gas station | NCTC/MIPT |
| 23-Jun-05 | Sunna | Baghdad | Iraq | Mall | 10 | 10 | N | Car bomb | 13 | Karrada commercial area/police near | NCTC/MIPT |
| 23-Jun-05 | Tanzim | Falluja | Iraq | Military | 6 | 13 | Y | Car bomb | 13 | US Marine convoy | AP/CC |
| 23-Jun-05 | Unknown | Tikrit | Iraq | Govt/Police** | 0 | 0 | N | Car bomb | 13 | Bomb failed/Oil Institute convoy | AS |
| 25-Jun-05 | Tanzim | Mosul | Iraq | Govt/Police** | 4 | 0 | N | Car bomb | 13 | Province police chief | Pape/NCTC |
| 25-Jun-05 | Unknown | Samarra | Iraq | Govt/Police** | 9 | 20 | N | Car bomb | 13 | Police LT Muthana al-Shakar | NCTC/MIPT |
| 26-Jun-05 | Unknown | Kirkuk | Iraq | Govt/Police | 0 | 4 | N | Car bomb | 13 | Iraqi police CP/early detonation | NCTC/MIPT |
| 26-Jun-05 | Tanzim | Mosul | Iraq | Govt/Police | 5 | 12 | N | Belt bomb | 13 | Police post at Jumhouri hospital | Pape/NCTC |
| 26-Jun-05 | Tanzim | Mosul | Iraq | Govt/Police | 12 | 14 | N | Truck bomb | 13 | Police headquarters/Bab al-Tob | NCTC/RFE |
| 26-Jun-05 | Tanzim | Mosul | Iraq | Military | 15 | 15 | N | Belt bomb | 13 | Army base parking lot/Al Kasik | Pape/NCTC |
| 27-Jun-05 | Unknown | Talafar | Iraq | Govt/Police | 1 | 3 | N | Car bomb | 13 | Army/police patrol | NCTC |
| 28-Jun-05 | Tanzim | Baghdad | Iraq | Govt/Police* | 5 | 4 | N | Car bomb | 13 | Shia Parliamentarian Dhari al-Fayadh | NCTC/RFE |
| 28-Jun-05 | Unknown | Baghdad | Iraq | Govt/Police | 1 | 17 | N | Car bomb | 13 | Iraqi police checkpoint/Musayyib | NCTC/ADR |
| 28-Jun-05 | Tanzim | Balad | Iraq | Military | 1 | 1 | Y | Car bomb | 13 | MNFI base | CC/RFE |
| 28-Jun-05 | Unknown | Kirkuk | Iraq | Govt/Police** | 2 | 4 | N | Car bomb | 13 | Police chief BG Salar Ahmed | NCTC/MIPT |
| 28-Jun-05 | Unknown | Musayyib | Iraq | Hospital | 2 | 13 | N | Belt bomb | 13 | Dressed as police | NCTC/RFE |
| 29-Jun-05 | Tanzim | Khalidiya | Iraq | Military | 0 | 7 | Y | Car bomb | 13 | US military position | NCTC/AS |
| 1-Jul-05 | DHKP-C | Ankara | Turkey | Govt/Police | 0 | 0 | N | Belt bomb | 8 | Shot by police/PM's office | MIPT/BBC |
| 1-Jul-05 | Tanzim | Baghdad | Iraq | Govt/Police | 1 | 4 | N | Car bomb | 13 | Dawa party office | NCTC/MIPT |
| 2-Jul-05 | Tanzim | Baghdad | Iraq | Govt/Police | 15 | 22 | N | Car bomb | 13 | Police special forces recruiting center | Pape/NCTC |
| 2-Jul-05 | Unknown | Baghdad | Iraq | Govt/Police | 5 | 12 | N | Cart bomb | 13 | Police checkpoint | NCTC/MIPT |
| 2-Jul-05 | Tanzim | Hillah | Iraq | Govt/Police | 6 | 0 | N | Belt bomb | 13 | During search at Scorpion checkpoint | Pape/NCTC |
| 2-Jul-05 | Tanzim | Hillah | Iraq | Govt/Police | 0 | 26 | N | Belt bomb | 13 | Follow-on bombing to first | MIPT/SLPD |
| 3-Jul-05 | Unknown | Ramadi | Iraq | Military | 0 | 2 | Y | Car bomb | 13 | US military patrol/Al Jumhuri area | AS |
| 4-Jul-05 | Unknown | Bande Sarde | Afghanistan | Civilian | 1 | 1 | N | Bike bomb | 12 | Target Turkish engineer's car | MIPT/XNA |
| 4-Jul-05 | Tanzim | Falluja | Iraq | Military | 2 | 2 | N | Car bomb | 13 | Iraqi Army convoy/Shahada area | Pape/AP |
| 5-Jul-05 | Unknown | Ayodhya | India | Religious site | 0 | 0 | N | Car bomb | 9 | Bomb used to crash shrine fence | AP/TG |
| 5-Jul-05 | Unknown | Hit | Iraq | Military | 0 | 5 | Y | Car bomb | 13 | US military base | STR |
| 5-Jul-05 | Unknown | Kirkuk | Iraq | Military | 1 | 3 | N | Car bomb | 13 | Iraqi Army checkpoint | NYT |
| 6-Jul-05 | Unknown | Jbeila | Iraq | Market^ | 6 | 15 | N | Car bomb | 13 | Coordinated attack | NCTC |
| 6-Jul-05 | Unknown | Jbeila | Iraq | Market^ | 6 | 15 | N | Car bomb | 13 | 2nd bomb targeted first responders | NCTC |
| 7-Jul-05 | Abu Hafs | London | England | Train | 6 | 120 | N | Bag bomb | 7 | Edgware Road station | NCTC/MIPT |
| 7-Jul-05 | Abu Hafs | London | England | Train | 7 | 100 | N | Bag bomb | 7 | Liverpool Street/Aldgate Circle | NCTC/MIPT |
| 7-Jul-05 | Abu Hafs | London | England | Train | 26 | 200 | N | Bag bomb | 7 | Picadilly line | NCTC/MIPT |

| | | | | | | | | | | | |
|---|---|---|---|---|---|---|---|---|---|---|---|
| 7-Jul-05 | Abu Hafs | London | England | Bus | 13 | 46 | N | Bag bomb | 7 | No. 30 double-decker bus | NCTC/MIPT |
| 8-Jul-05 | Unknown | Baghdad | Iraq | Govt/Police | 0 | 0 | N | Car bomb | 13 | Western security convoy/foiled by fire | NCTC |
| 9-Jul-05 | Tanzim | Hit | Iraq | Military | 0 | 1 | Y | Car bomb | 13 | US military patrol | SITE |
| 10-Jul-05 | Tanzim | Baghdad | Iraq | Military | 24 | 47 | N | Belt bomb | 13 | Army recruiting center/Al-Muthanna | Pape/RFE |
| 10-Jul-05 | Tanzim | Falluja | Iraq | Military | 3 | 2 | Y | Car bomb | 13 | US military convoy | TI/BT |
| 10-Jul-05 | Tanzim | Iraq/Syria border | Iraq | Govt/Police | 3 | 0 | N | Car bomb | 13 | Border officials | MIPT/TI |
| 10-Jul-05 | Tanzim | Iraq/Syria border | Iraq | Govt/Police | 4 | 0 | N | Car bomb | 13 | Border officials | MIPT/TI |
| 10-Jul-05 | Unknown | Kirkuk | Iraq | Govt/Police** | 4 | 15 | N | Car bomb | 13 | Municipal building/target mayor | RFE/MIPT |
| 10-Jul-05 | Tanzim | Mosul | Iraq | Govt/Police** | 5 | 3 | N | Car bomb | 13 | Mosul police chief Saleh Mishaal | Pape/RFE |
| 10-Jul-05 | Unknown | Ramadi | Iraq | Military | 0 | 0 | Y | Car bomb | 13 | US military base | TI/BT |
| 11-Jul-05 | Unknown | Baghdad | Iraq | Military | 3 | 1 | N | Truck bomb | 13 | Iraq Army checkpoint | TDN |
| 12-Jul-05 | PIJ | Netanya | Israel | Mall | 5 | 40 | N | Belt bomb | 4 | Hasharon Mall | CSS/NCTC |
| 12-Jul-05 | PIJ | Settlement | West Bank | Civilian | 0 | 0 | N | Car bomb | 4 | Early detonation/bomber arrested | MIPT/CT |
| 12-Jul-05 | Unknown | Diyala | Iraq | Religious site | 1 | 16 | N | Belt bomb | 13 | Jawawla Mosque/early detonation | Pape/NCTC |
| 12-Jul-05 | Tanzim | Mosul | Iraq | Military | 0 | 3 | Y | Car bomb | 13 | US military patrol | AS/SITE |
| 13-Jul-05 | Unknown | Baghdad | Iraq | Civilian | 42 | 50 | Y | Car bomb | 13 | US troops giving out candy/al-Khalij | Pape/NCTC |
| 14-Jul-05 | Tanzim | Baghdad | Iraq | Govt/Police | 1 | 9 | N | Car bomb | 13 | 3 bombers/Green Zone checkpoint | NCTC/RFE |
| 14-Jul-05 | Tanzim | Baghdad | Iraq | Govt/Police | 1 | 0 | N | Belt bomb | 13 | 3 bombers/Green Zone checkpoint | RFE/MIPT |
| 14-Jul-05 | Tanzim | Baghdad | Iraq | Govt/Police | 0 | 0 | N | Belt bomb | 13 | 3 bombers/1 shot and arrested | RFE/MIPT |
| 14-Jul-05 | Unknown | Baghdad | Iraq | Govt/Police** | 0 | 0 | N | Belt bomb | 13 | Interior Minister/bomber arrested | MIPT/AIW |
| 15-Jul-05 | Tanzim | Baghdad | Iraq | Govt/Police | 4 | 9 | N | Car bomb | 13 | Near President Talabani's house | NCTC/MIPT |
| 15-Jul-05 | Tanzim | Baghdad | Iraq | Religious site | 0 | 5 | N | Belt bomb | 13 | Shiite mosque in Jabila | NCTC/MIPT |
| 15-Jul-05 | Tanzim | Baghdad | Iraq | Military | 2 | 14 | N | Car bomb | 13 | Defense Ministry/North Baghdad | NCTC/MIPT |
| 15-Jul-05 | Tanzim | Baghdad | Iraq | Govt/Police | 8 | 43 | N | Car bomb | 13 | Iraqi police commando patrol | NCTC/MIPT |
| 15-Jul-05 | Tanzim | Baghdad | Iraq | Govt/Police | 10 | 24 | N | Car bomb | 13 | Police patrol/Sadiya district | NCTC/MIPT |
| 15-Jul-05 | Tanzim | Baghdad | Iraq | Military | 0 | 9 | Y | Car bomb | 13 | US military patrol | NCTC/NYT |
| 15-Jul-05 | Tanzim | Baghdad | Iraq | Military | 0 | 3 | N | Car bomb | 13 | US military checkpoint | NCTC/SUNT |
| 15-Jul-05 | Tanzim | Baghdad | Iraq | Military | 2 | 6 | N | Car bomb | 13 | Iraq Army patrol/Andalus Square | NPII/GU |
| 15-Jul-05 | Tanzim | Baghdad | Iraq | Military | 7 | 8 | N | Car bomb | 13 | Iraq Army base/Shaab district | NPII/GU |
| 15-Jul-05 | Tanzim | Baghdad | Iraq | Govt/Police | 2 | 4 | N | Car bomb | 13 | Iraqi police checkpoint | SUNT/TR |
| 15-Jul-05 | Unknown | Baghdad | Iraq | Military | 1 | 2 | Y | Car bomb | 13 | US military convoy/Rustmiyah area | GU/AP |
| 15-Jul-05 | Tanzim | Baghdad | Iraq | Military | 1 | 1 | Y | Car bomb | 13 | US military patrol | TR/TI |
| 15-Jul-05 | Unknown | Kirkuk | Iraq | Unknown | 1 | 0 | N | Car bomb | 13 | Premature detonation/2 bombers in car | NCTC/MIPT |
| 16-Jul-05 | Unknown | Baghdad | Iraq | Govt/Police | 2 | 0 | N | Car bomb | 13 | Police checkpoint | NCTC/IPCS |
| 16-Jul-05 | Unknown | Baghdad | Iraq | Civilian | 0 | 0 | N | Car bomb | 13 | Arrested before detonation at funeral | MIPT/NYT |
| 16-Jul-05 | Unknown | Baghdad | Iraq | Govt/Police | 4 | 20 | N | Car bomb | 13 | Police patrol/Dora area | NCTC/RFE |
| 16-Jul-05 | Unknown | Baghdad | Iraq | Military | 0 | 1 | Y | Car bomb | 13 | US military convoy | AS/HC |
| 16-Jul-05 | Unknown | Hillah | Iraq | Govt/Police | 9 | 20 | N | Car bomb | 13 | Army/Police checkpoint/Iskandariyah | NCTC/MIPT |
| 16-Jul-05 | Tanzim | Mosul | Iraq | Govt/Police | 7 | 20 | N | Belt bomb | 13 | Hammam al-Alil Police station | Pape/RFE |
| 16-Jul-05 | Tanzim | Musayyib | Iraq | Religious site | 98 | 200 | N | Truck bomb | 13 | Ignited fuel tanker near mosque | Pape/NCTC |
| 17-Jul-05 | Tanzim | Baghdad | Iraq | Govt/Police | 6 | 13 | N | Car bomb | 13 | Police patrol/Hai al-Bayaa area | NCTC/RFE |
| 17-Jul-05 | Tanzim | Baghdad | Iraq | Bus | 7 | 8 | Y | Car bomb | 13 | Bus station | NCTC/RFE |
| 17-Jul-05 | Tanzim | Baghdad | Iraq | Govt/Police | 3 | 8 | N | Car bomb | 13 | Police patrol/dead bodies as lure | NCTC/RFE |

| Date | Group | City | Country | Target | Killed | Wounded | ? | Weapon | # | Notes | Source |
|---|---|---|---|---|---|---|---|---|---|---|---|
| 17-Jul-05 | Tanzim | Baghdad | Iraq | Govt/Police | 6 | 7 | N | Car bomb | 13 | Electoral commission/east Baghdad | Pape/NCTC |
| 17-Jul-05 | Unknown | Mahmudiyah | Iraq | Military | 5 | 9 | Y | Car bomb | 13 | Missed US convoy/hit civilian bus | Pape/NCTC |
| 18-Jul-05 | Tanzim | Rawah | Iraq | Military | 1 | 0 | Y | Car bomb | 13 | US military patrol | SDU/SPI |
| 18-Jul-05 | Tanzim | Rawah | Iraq | Military | 0 | 0 | Y | Car bomb | 13 | US military patrol | AP/SITE |
| 19-Jul-05 | Unknown | Heart | Afghanistan | Govt/Police** | 0 | 0 | N | Belt bomb | 12 | Enjil District Governor Kwaja Esa | NCTC/RFE |
| 19-Jul-05 | Unknown | Rawah | Iraq | Military | 0 | 0 | Y | Car bomb | 13 | US military patrol (near Stryker) | AFT |
| 20-Jul-05 | Hizbul M | Srinagar | Kashmir/India | Military | 3 | 17 | N | Car bomb | 9 | Rammed Indian Army car | NCTC/SATP |
| 20-Jul-05 | Tanzim | Baghdad | Iraq | Govt/Police | 9 | 21 | N | Belt bomb | 13 | Army recruiting center/Al-Muthanna | Pape/NCTC |
| 21-Jul-05 | Unknown | London | England | Bus | 0 | 0 | N | Bag bomb | 7 | 4 bombers/Failed to detonate | AP/CNN |
| 21-Jul-05 | Unknown | London | England | Train | 0 | 0 | N | Bag bomb | 7 | 4 bombers/Failed to detonate | AP/CNN |
| 21-Jul-05 | Unknown | London | England | Train | 0 | 0 | N | Bag bomb | 7 | 4 bombers/Failed to detonate | AP/CNN |
| 21-Jul-05 | Unknown | London | England | Train | 0 | 0 | N | Bag bomb | 7 | 4 bombers/Failed to detonate | AP/CNN |
| 21-Jul-05 | Tanzim | Baghdad | Iraq | Govt/Police | 2 | 10 | N | Car bomb | 13 | Interior Ministry checkpoint/Bueitha | NCTC/MIPT |
| 21-Jul-05 | Unknown | Mahmudiyah | Iraq | Military | 5 | 16 | N | Car bomb | 13 | Iraqi Army post | NCTC/NPII |
| 23-Jul-05 | Unknown | Tel Aviv | Israel | Unknown | 0 | 0 | N | Belt bomb | 4 | Arrested en route/5kg belt bomb? | RFE/AP |
| 23-Jul-05 | Al-Tawhid | Sharm ash Shaykh | Egypt | Restaurant^ | 27 | 42 | N | Car bomb | 5 | Old Market coffee shop | HC/TM |
| 23-Jul-05 | Al-Tawhid | Sharm ash Shaykh | Egypt | Hotel^ | 27 | 42 | N | Car bomb | 5 | Ghaala Gardens Hotel | IHT/HC |
| 24-Jul-05 | Unknown | Baghdad | Iraq | Govt/Police | 38 | 30 | N | Truck bomb | 13 | al-Rashad police station | Pape/NCTC |
| 25-Jul-05 | Tanzim | Baghdad | Iraq | Hotel | 11 | 18 | N | Bus bomb | 13 | Sadeer Hotel used by Westerners | Pape/IPCS |
| 25-Jul-05 | Unknown | Baghdad | Iraq | Govt/Police | 3 | 9 | N | Car bomb | 13 | Police commando CP/Green Zone | IPCS/NCTC |
| 27-Jul-05 | Unknown | Baghdad | Iraq | Govt/Police | 0 | 4 | N | Car bomb | 13 | Iraqi police/al-Suaiyb area | NCTC/XNA |
| 27-Jul-05 | Tanzim | Baghdad | Iraq | Military | 5 | 8 | N | Car bomb | 13 | Iraqi Army patrol | NCTC/NPII |
| 27-Jul-05 | Tanzim | Baghdad | Iraq | Govt/Police | 1 | 4 | N | Car bomb | 13 | Police commando checkpoint | NCTC/MIPT |
| 27-Jul-05 | Unknown | Baghdad | Iraq | Govt/Police | 4 | 10 | N | Belt bomb | 13 | Police checkpoint/Numaa hospital | IPCS/NCTC |
| 28-Jul-05 | Chechen sep | Grozny | Russia | Unknown | 0 | 0 | N | Belt bomb | 6 | Detonated when police approach | NCTC/MIPT |
| 28-Jul-05 | Unknown | Baghdad | Iraq | Military | 1 | 1 | N | Car bomb | 13 | Iraq Army convoy/Al-Tarmiyah area | NPII |
| 29-Jul-05 | Unknown | Baghdad | Iraq | Govt/Police | 6 | 20 | N | Car bomb | 13 | Police patrol/Al-Sarafiyah district | Pape/NPII |
| 29-Jul-05 | Unknown | Balad | Iraq | Military | 2 | 2 | N | Bike bomb | 13 | Bus with Iraq Army trainees | NPII |
| 29-Jul-05 | Unknown | Mosul | Iraq | Military | 1 | 11 | Y | Car bomb | 13 | US military convoy | DTL/TOO |
| 29-Jul-05 | Tanzim | Rabia | Iraq | Military | 51 | 93 | N | Belt bomb | 13 | Army recruiting center | Pape/IPCS |
| 31-Jul-05 | Unknown | Baghdad | Iraq | Govt/Police | 3 | 29 | N | Car bomb | 13 | Iraq police convoy | NCTC/CNN |
| 31-Jul-05 | Unknown | Iskandariyah | Iraq | Govt/Police | 0 | 0 | N | Car bomb | 13 | Iraqi police patrol | NCTC |
| 1-Aug-05 | Tanzim | Hit | Iraq | Military | 2 | 6 | Y | Belt bomb | 13 | RCT-2 combat operations | CC/Pape |
| 1-Aug-05 | Tanzim | Syrian border | Iraq | Military | 0 | 6 | Y | Car bomb | 13 | U.S. soldiers and embedded journalist | NPII/NBC |
| 2-Aug-05 | Tanzim | Baghdad | Iraq | Military | 3 | 23 | Y | Car bomb | 13 | Near US military convoy/Al-Tayaran | IPCS/RFE |
| 2-Aug-05 | Unknown | Baquba | Iraq | Govt/Police | 1 | 8 | N | Car bomb | 13 | Iraqi police patrol | NCTC/IPCS |
| 2-Aug-05 | Unknown | Mosul | Iraq | Govt/Police | 6 | 8 | N | Car bomb | 13 | Iraqi police vehicle at checkpoint | NCTC/IPCS |
| 3-Aug-05 | Unknown | Baquba | Iraq | Govt/Police | 3 | 6 | N | Car bomb | 13 | Police checkpoint | IPCS/KTI |
| 3-Aug-05 | Unknown | Mosul | Iraq | Civilian | 6 | 0 | N | Car bomb | 13 | Humanitarian food convoy | NCTC |
| 4-Aug-05 | Unknown | Balad | Iraq | Military | 1 | 5 | N | Tractor | 13 | Iraqi Army | IPCS/MAS |
| 4-Aug-05 | Unknown | Baquba | Iraq | Military | 4 | 6 | N | Car bomb | 13 | Iraqi Army checkpoint | NCTC/IPCS |
| 5-Aug-05 | Unknown | Baghdad | Iraq | Military | 1 | 1 | N | Car bomb | 13 | Iraq Army/Southern Baghdad | NPII/AP |

| Date | Group | Location | Country | Target | Killed | Wounded | S | Type | Code | Notes | Source |
|---|---|---|---|---|---|---|---|---|---|---|---|
| 5-Aug-05 | Unknown | Rawah | Iraq | Military | 0 | 0 | Y | Car bomb | 13 | US military patrol | XNA |
| 6-Aug-05 | Unknown | Pakistan border | Afghanistan | Military | 0 | 0 | Y | Belt bomb | 12 | Arrested/foiled attack on US base | RFE/CNN |
| 6-Aug-05 | Unknown | Ameriyah | Iraq | Military | 1 | 2 | Y | Car bomb | 13 | US military patrol/RCT-8 | WN/AS |
| 6-Aug-05 | Unknown | Baghdad | Iraq | Military | 0 | 3 | Y | Car bomb | 13 | US military convoy/East Baghdad | NPII/XNA |
| 6-Aug-05 | Unknown | Hillah | Iraq | Govt/Police | 2 | 2 | N | Car bomb | 13 | Police checkpoint | NCTC/MI |
| 7-Aug-05 | Unknown | Baghdad | Iraq | Military | 1 | 3 | N | Car bomb | 13 | Iraqi Army checkpoint | IPCS/AP |
| 7-Aug-05 | Tanzim | Sinjar | Iraq | Military | 0 | 2 | Y | Car bomb | 13 | US military patrol | SITE |
| 7-Aug-05 | Unknown | Tikrit | Iraq | Military | 5 | 15 | N | Truck bomb | 13 | Iraqi Army HQ | NCTC/IPC |
| 8-Aug-05 | None | Fuzhou | China | Bus | 0 | 23 | N | Bag bomb | x | Man with lung cancer | XNA/CBN |
| 9-Aug-05 | Unknown | Baghdad | Iraq | Military | 6 | 93 | Y | Car bomb | 13 | US mil convoy/Taiyaran Square | NCTC/IPC |
| 10-Aug-05 | Unknown | Baghdad | Iraq | Govt/Police | 5 | 16 | N | Car bomb | 13 | Iraqi Army/police patrol/Gazaliyah area | Pape/IPC |
| 11-Aug-05 | Unknown | Baghdad | Iraq | Military | 0 | 0 | Y | Car bomb | 13 | US military patrol | IPCS |
| 12-Aug-05 | Unknown | Baghdad | Iraq | Govt/Police | 0 | 14 | N | Car bomb | 13 | Iraqi police convoy/Ad Dawrah area | NCTC |
| 12-Aug-05 | Unknown | Mosul | Iraq | Govt/Police | 0 | 0 | N | Belt bomb | 13 | Police killed 3 bombers | MIPT/AP |
| 13-Aug-05 | Unknown | Baghdad | Iraq | Military | 1 | 7 | Y | Car bomb | 13 | US military vehicle | NCTC/IPC |
| 14-Aug-05 | Unknown | Baghdad | Iraq | Market | 1 | 4 | N | Belt bomb | 13 | Detonated/shot by police/al-Mahwil | NCTC/RF |
| 15-Aug-05 | Unknown | Baghdad | Iraq | Restaurant | 0 | 15 | N | Motorcycle | 13 | Iraqi police/Abu Ahmed's restaurant | NCTC/IPC |
| 17-Aug-05 | Tanzim | Baghdad | Iraq | Govt/Police^ | 15 | 19 | N | Car bomb | 13 | 1st attack - police patrol | NCTC/EIV |
| 17-Aug-05 | Tanzim | Baghdad | Iraq | Bus^ | 15 | 19 | N | Car bomb | 13 | 2nd attack - al-Nahda bus depot | NCTC/IPC |
| 17-Aug-05 | Tanzim | Baghdad | Iraq | Govt/Police^ | 15 | 19 | N | Car bomb | 13 | 3rd attack - first responders | NCTC/XN |
| 17-Aug-05 | Unknown | Baghdad | Iraq | Hospital^ | 15 | 19 | N | Car bomb | 13 | 4th attack -al-Kindi hospital | NCTC/AI |
| 17-Aug-05 | Unknown | Baghdad | Iraq | Hospital^ | 15 | 19 | N | Car bomb | 13 | 5th attack -al-Kindi hospital | NCTC/EIV |
| 21-Aug-05 | Unknown | Baghdad | Iraq | Govt/Police | 0 | 0 | N | Car bomb | 13 | 0839/Police convoy | NCTC |
| 22-Aug-05 | Unknown | Spin Boldak | Afghanistan | Unknown | 0 | 0 | | Car bomb | 12 | Detonated while police pursued | NCTC/RF |
| 22-Aug-05 | Unknown | Baghdad | Iraq | Govt/Police | 8 | 4 | N | Car bomb | 13 | Police checkpoint | NCTC/MI |
| 23-Aug-05 | Tanzim | Baquba | Iraq | Govt/Police | 6 | 20 | Y | Belt bomb | 13 | US/Iraqi Joint Coordination Post | CC/IPCS |
| 23-Aug-05 | Unknown | Karmah | Iraq | Military | 0 | 4 | Y | Car bomb | 13 | US military patrol | NYT |
| 23-Aug-05 | Unknown | Ramadi | Iraq | Military^ | 0 | 11 | Y | Truck bomb | 13 | US military post/also small arms fire | SDU/REL |
| 24-Aug-05 | Unknown | Baghdad | Iraq | Govt/Police^ | 7 | 28 | N | Car bomb | 13 | Police checkpoint/armed attack | IPCS/MIP |
| 24-Aug-05 | Unknown | Baghdad | Iraq | Govt/Police^ | 7 | 28 | N | Car bomb | 13 | Police checkpoint/armed attack | IPCS/MIP |
| 24-Aug-05 | Unknown | Baghdad | Iraq | Govt/Police** | 6 | 6 | N | Car bomb | 13 | Defense Minister's convoy | MIPT/GN |
| 26-Aug-05 | Unknown | Falluja | Iraq | Military | 0 | 1 | Y | Car bomb | 13 | US military patrol | AJ/AFP |
| 28-Aug-05 | Hamas | Beer Sheba | West Bank | Bus | 0 | 50 | N | Bag bomb | 4 | Partially foiled by security | NCTC/MI |
| 28-Aug-05 | Unknown | Mosul | Iraq | Military | 2 | 5 | Y | Car bomb | 13 | US military patrol/Al Dubbat area | NCTC/AS |
| 30-Aug-05 | Unknown | Samarra | Iraq | Govt/Police | 2 | 5 | N | Car bomb | 13 | Police patrol/Al Tharthar checkpoint | NCTC/MI |
| 3-Sep-05 | Unknown | Baghdad | Iraq | Govt/Police | 1 | 2 | N | Car bomb | 13 | 1100/1 police car destroyed | NCTC |
| 4-Sep-05 | Unknown | Baghdad | Iraq | Govt/Police | 1 | 2 | N | Car bomb | 13 | Police checkpoint/Iskandariyah | NCTC/MI |
| 5-Sep-05 | Tanzim | Hit | Iraq | Military | 11 | 16 | N | Car bomb | 13 | MNF-I base | IPCS/NC |
| 6-Sep-05 | Unknown | Haqlaniyah | Iraq | Military | 0 | 3 | Y | Car bomb | 13 | US military patrol | NPII/IPCS |
| 6-Sep-05 | Unknown | Talafar | Iraq | Military | 4 | 10 | N | Belt bomb | 13 | Iraqi Army | NCTC/IPC |
| 7-Sep-05 | Unknown | Girishk | Afghanistan | Military | 0 | 4 | N | Car bomb | 12 | Failed attack on US military patrol | NCTC/CD |
| 7-Sep-05 | Unknown | al Khalis | Iraq | Military | 5 | 5 | N | Car bomb | 13 | 0710/Iraqi Army checkpoint | NCTC/KT |
| 7-Sep-05 | Unknown | Baghdad | Iraq | Civilian | 2 | 3 | N | Car bomb | 13 | Probable premature detonation | NCTC/XN |

| Date | Group | City | Country | Target | Killed | Wounded | S | Weapon | Region | Notes | Source |
|---|---|---|---|---|---|---|---|---|---|---|---|
| 7-Sep-05 | Unknown | Basra | Iraq | Restaurant | 16 | 21 | N | Car bomb | 13 | Hayaniyah area restaurant | Pape/NCTC |
| 8-Sep-05 | Unknown | Baghdad | Iraq | Govt/Police | 0 | 5 | Y | Car bomb | 13 | US security guard convoy | NCTC/MIPT |
| 9-Sep-05 | Unknown | Mahaweel | Iraq | Govt/Police^ | 5 | 2 | N | Car bomb | 13 | 1804/2 bombs/police patrol | MIPT/NCTC |
| 9-Sep-05 | Unknown | Mahaweel | Iraq | Govt/Police^ | 6 | 2 | N | Car bomb | 13 | 1804/2 bombs/police patrol | MIPT/NCTC |
| 9-Sep-05 | Unknown | Musayyib | Iraq | Govt/Police | 8 | 4 | N | Car bomb | 13 | Iraqi police/Coalition military | NCTC/XNA |
| 11-Sep-05 | Tanzim | al-Karama | Iraq | Military | 0 | 1 | Y | Car bomb | 13 | US military patrol | SITE |
| 11-Sep-05 | Tanzim | Baghdad | Iraq | Military | 0 | 0 | Y | Car bomb | 13 | US military patrol | SITE |
| 11-Sep-05 | Unknown | Baghdad | Iraq | Military | 0 | 6 | Y | Car bomb | 13 | US military convoy/Ghazaliyah area | XNA |
| 12-Sep-05 | Tanzim | Abu Ghraib | Iraq | Military | 0 | 1 | Y | Car bomb | 13 | US military patrol | SITE |
| 12-Sep-05 | Tanzim | Abu Ghraib | Iraq | Military | 0 | 0 | Y | Car bomb | 13 | US military patrol/bomb failed | SITE |
| 14-Sep-05 | Unknown | Samzai | Pakistan | Civilian | 0 | 2 | N | Belt bomb | 10 | Sunni madrasa/premature detonation | NCTC/AFP |
| 14-Sep-05 | Tanzim | Baghdad | Iraq | Civilian | 114 | 227 | N | Car bomb | 13 | Shiite day laborers/Uruba Square | IPCS/NCTC |
| 14-Sep-05 | Tanzim | Baghdad | Iraq | Civilian | 4 | 23 | N | Car bomb | 13 | Shiite cleric's office | NCTC/RFE |
| 14-Sep-05 | Tanzim | Baghdad | Iraq | Civilian | 10 | 14 | N | Car bomb | 13 | Gas station/Huriya district | NCTC/RFE |
| 14-Sep-05 | Tanzim | Baghdad | Iraq | Govt/Police | 3 | 3 | N | Car bomb | 13 | Police patrol/Adil district | NCTC/RFE |
| 14-Sep-05 | Tanzim | Baghdad | Iraq | Military | 2 | 6 | Y | Car bomb | 13 | US mil convoy/Al-Salihiyah | RFE/NPII |
| 14-Sep-05 | Tanzim | Baghdad | Iraq | Market | 4 | 23 | N | Car bomb | 13 | Shiite market/northwest Baghdad | NCTC/RFE |
| 14-Sep-05 | Tanzim | Baghdad | Iraq | Govt/Police | 7 | 4 | N | Car bomb | 13 | Police patrol/Al-Waziriyah | NCTC/RFE |
| 14-Sep-05 | Tanzim | Baghdad | Iraq | Govt/Police | 6 | 1 | N | Car bomb | 13 | Police patrol/Al-Ameriyah | NCTC/RFE |
| 14-Sep-05 | Tanzim | Baghdad | Iraq | Military | 2 | 7 | Y | Car bomb | 13 | Central Baghdad/near US patrol | RFE/NPII |
| 14-Sep-05 | Tanzim | Baghdad | Iraq | Govt/Police | 0 | 14 | N | Car bomb | 13 | Iraqi police/Al-Allawi | NCTC/RFE |
| 14-Sep-05 | Tanzim | Baghdad | Iraq | Military | 0 | 0 | Y | Car bomb | 13 | Bomb malfunctioned/US tank target | NCTC/MIPT |
| 15-Sep-05 | Tanzim | Baghdad | Iraq | Govt/Police^ | 4 | 6 | N | Car bomb | 13 | Police patrol | IPCS/NCTC |
| 15-Sep-05 | Tanzim | Baghdad | Iraq | Govt/Police^ | 5 | 6 | N | Car bomb | 13 | Police patrol/Dora area | IPCS/NCTC |
| 15-Sep-05 | Tanzim | Baghdad | Iraq | Govt/Police | 21 | 21 | N | Car bomb | 13 | Police commando convoy | IPCS/NCTC |
| 16-Sep-05 | Unknown | Haswa | Iraq | Govt/Police | 3 | 6 | N | Car bomb | 13 | Police patrol | NCTC/MIPT |
| 16-Sep-05 | Unknown | Tuz Khormato | Iraq | Religious site | 11 | 24 | N | Car bomb | 13 | Al-Rasul Al-Aadham Mosque | Pape/IPCS |
| 16-Sep-05 | Unknown | Tuz Khormato | Iraq | Religious site | 0 | 0 | N | Belt bomb | 13 | Arrested before detonation | MIPT/AA |
| 17-Sep-05 | Unknown | Abu Ghraib | Iraq | Military | 0 | 0 | Y | Car bomb | 13 | US military patrol near Abu Ghraib | XNA/SM |
| 17-Sep-05 | Unknown | Baquba | Iraq | Military | 0 | 17 | N | Car bomb | 13 | Iraqi Army | NCTC/SM |
| 17-Sep-05 | Unknown | Falluja | Iraq | Military | 0 | 3 | Y | Car bomb | 13 | US/Iraqi patrol | XNA/AAIW |
| 18-Sep-05 | Unknown | Khost | Afghanistan | Govt/Police | 0 | 0 | N | Belt bomb | 12 | 2 bombers lived/polling station | MIPT/PAN |
| 18-Sep-05 | Unknown | Taji | Iraq | Military | 1 | 6 | N | Car bomb | 13 | US/Iraqi Army patrol | CBS |
| 19-Sep-05 | Unknown | Latifiyah | Iraq | Govt/Police | 7 | 2 | N | Belt bomb | 13 | Police checkpoint | IPCS/NCTC |
| 19-Sep-05 | Unknown | Mahmudiyah | Iraq | Govt/Police | 0 | 10 | N | Belt bomb | 13 | Police checkpoint | IPCS/MIPT |
| 19-Sep-05 | Tanzim | Mosul | Iraq | Military | 4 | 0 | Y | Car bomb | 13 | US State Department convoy/Al Zera | Pape/BH |
| 20-Sep-05 | Unknown | Baghdad | Iraq | Govt/Police | 5 | 8 | N | Car bomb | 13 | 1950/Iraqi police checkpoint | NCTC |
| 23-Sep-05 | Unknown | Baghdad | Iraq | Bus | 7 | 20 | N | Car bomb | 13 | Tayaran Square bus station | IPCS/NCTC |
| 23-Sep-05 | Unknown | Musayyib | Iraq | Govt/Police | 4 | 5 | N | Car bomb | 13 | Iraqi police checkpoint | IPCS/NCTC |
| 23-Sep-05 | Unknown | Sinjar | Iraq | Govt/Police | 2 | 2 | N | Car bomb | 13 | Iraqi police checkpoint | NCTC/BBC |
| 24-Sep-05 | Unknown | Baghdad | Iraq | Military | 3 | 5 | N | Car bomb | 13 | Iraq Army convoy/by al-Fendan café | XNA/BBC |
| 24-Sep-05 | Unknown | Latifiyah | Iraq | Military | 1 | 3 | N | Car bomb | 13 | Iraq Army checkpoint | SM/AJ |
| 25-Sep-05 | Tanzim | Baghdad | Iraq | Govt/Police | 12 | 12 | N | Car bomb | 13 | Police commando convoy/al-Ghadier | Pape/IPCS |
| 25-Sep-05 | Unknown | Hillah | Iraq | Market | 4 | 49 | N | Bike bomb | 13 | Crowd at vegetable market | IPCS/NCTC |

| | | | | | | | | | | | |
|---|---|---|---|---|---|---|---|---|---|---|---|
| 25-Sep-05 | Unknown | Musayyib | Iraq | Civilian | 5 | 19 | N | Motorcycle | 13 | Near Shiite shrine | RFE/MIPT |
| 26-Sep-05 | Unknown | Baghdad | Iraq | Govt/Police | 9 | 36 | N | Car bomb | 13 | Oil ministry or Police Academy | IPCS/NCTC |
| 27-Sep-05 | Unknown | Baghdad | Iraq | Govt/Police | 0 | 0 | Y | Car bomb | 13 | Arrested before detonation/Green Zone | IPCS/MIPT |
| 27-Sep-05 | Tanzim | Baquba | Iraq | Govt/Police | 9 | 26 | N | Belt bomb | 13 | Police recruits for QRPF | Pape/IPCS |
| 28-Sep-05 | Taliban | Pol-e Charki | Afghanistan | Military | 9 | 40 | N | Motorcycle | 12 | Bus of military recruits | RFE/XNA |
| 28-Sep-05 | Unknown | Baquba | Iraq | Govt/Police | 1 | 14 | N | Car bomb | 13 | Police mobile checkpoint | CC/MIPT |
| 28-Sep-05 | Tanzim | Talafar | Iraq | Military | 8 | 53 | N | Belt bomb | 13 | First known Iraq female/Army recruits | Pape/IPCS |
| 29-Sep-05 | Tanzim | Balad | Iraq | Mall^ | 33 | 50 | N | Car bomb | 13 | Coordinated attack | Pape/IPCS |
| 29-Sep-05 | Tanzim | Balad | Iraq | Bank^ | 33 | 50 | N | Car bomb | 13 | Coordinated attack | Pape/IPCS |
| 29-Sep-05 | Tanzim | Balad | Iraq | Market^ | 33 | 50 | N | Car bomb | 13 | Coordinated attack | Pape/IPCS |
| 30-Sep-05 | Unknown | Baghdad | Iraq | Market | 0 | 0 | N | Belt bomb | 13 | Female arrested at checkpoint | MIPT/AP |
| 30-Sep-05 | Unknown | Mahaweel/Hillah | Iraq | Military | 3 | 10 | N | Car bomb | 13 | Coalition base checkpoint | NCTC/TG |
| 1-Oct-05 | JI | Bali | Indonesia | Restaurant^ | 8 | 43 | N | Belt bomb | 7 | 3 bombers/Menega seafood café | NCTC/MIPT |
| 1-Oct-05 | JI | Bali | Indonesia | Restaurant^ | 9 | 43 | N | Belt bomb | 7 | 3 bombers/Nyoman café | NCTC/MIPT |
| 1-Oct-05 | JI | Bali | Indonesia | Restaurant^ | 9 | 43 | N | Belt bomb | 7 | 3 bombers/Raja restaurant | NCTC/MIPT |
| 1-Oct-05 | Unknown | al-Qaim | Iraq | Military | 0 | 0 | Y | Car bomb | 13 | US military patrol | REUT/SDU |
| 1-Oct-05 | Unknown | Oklahoma | United States | Civilian | 0 | 0 | Y | Belt bomb | x | Early detonation/outside football game | EIW/AP |
| 3-Oct-05 | Unknown | Mosul | Iraq | Military | 1 | 6 | Y | Car bomb | 13 | US military patrol | AS |
| 4-Oct-05 | Unknown | Baghdad | Iraq | Govt/Police | 2 | 7 | N | Car bomb | 13 | Green Zone checkpoint | IPCS/NCTC |
| 4-Oct-05 | Unknown | Baghdad | Iraq | Govt/Police | 0 | 3 | N | Car bomb | 13 | Iraq Intelligence Agency | NCTC/MIPT |
| 4-Oct-05 | MSC | Ramadi | Iraq | Military | 0 | 0 | Y | Car bomb | 13 | US military patrol | SITE |
| 5-Oct-05 | Unknown | Kandahar | Afghanistan | Military | 1 | 1 | N | Car bomb | 12 | ISAF convoy (Canadian) | NCTC/RFE |
| 5-Oct-05 | Unknown | Haditha | Iraq | Military | 0 | 1 | Y | Car bomb | 13 | US military patrol | JU |
| 5-Oct-05 | Unknown | Hillah | Iraq | Religious site | 35 | 95 | N | Car bomb | 13 | Shiite mosque | Pape/NCTC |
| 5-Oct-05 | Unknown | Rawah | Iraq | Military | 0 | 3 | Y | Car bomb | 13 | US military checkpoint | AP |
| 6-Oct-05 | Unknown | Baghdad | Iraq | Govt/Police | 10 | 11 | N | Belt bomb | 13 | Bus near police patrol/Oil Ministry | NCTC/RFE |
| 6-Oct-05 | Tanzim | Baghdad | Iraq | Civilian | 3 | 8 | Y | Car bomb | 13 | Western (US) convoy/Nidhal St. | Pape/IPCS |
| 6-Oct-05 | Unknown | Samarra | Iraq | Military | 1 | 0 | Y | Car bomb | 13 | US military patrol | CC |
| 7-Oct-05 | Tanzim | Talafar | Iraq | Govt/Police | 0 | 6 | N | Car bomb | 13 | Iraqi police checkpoint | UPI/SITE |
| 8-Oct-05 | Unknown | Baghdad | Iraq | Govt/Police | 6 | 16 | N | Car bomb | 13 | Police patrol at traffic accident site | IPCS/NCTC |
| 9-Oct-05 | Taliban | Kandahar | Afghanistan | Govt/Police | 0 | 4 | N | Car bomb | 12 | UK Customs officials | NCTC/RFE |
| 9-Oct-05 | Unknown | Basra | Iraq | Civilian | 2 | 3 | N | Car bomb | 13 | Badr Brigade apartments | IPCS/AP |
| 9-Oct-05 | Unknown | Haditha | Iraq | Military | 0 | 2 | Y | Car bomb | 13 | US military checkpoint | CC |
| 9-Oct-05 | Unknown | Dushambe | Tajikistan | Airport | 0 | 0 | N | Belt bomb | x | Female lived/arrested | AP/ITAR |
| 10-Oct-05 | Taliban | Kandahar | Afghanistan | Govt/Police* | 4 | 8 | N | Belt bomb | 12 | Militia leader Shah Agah | NCTC/RFE |
| 10-Oct-05 | Unknown | Kandahar | Afghanistan | Unknown | 0 | 0 | N | Belt bomb | 12 | Detonated after police challenge | NCTC/RFE |
| 10-Oct-05 | Unknown | Baghdad | Iraq | Govt/Police | 1 | 3 | N | Car bomb | 13 | Green Zone checkpoint | CC/IPCS |
| 10-Oct-05 | Tanzim | Baghdad | Iraq | Govt/Police | 6 | 0 | N | Car bomb | 13 | Police checkpoint | Pape/NCTC |
| 10-Oct-05 | Unknown | Baghdad | Iraq | Govt/Police | 0 | 4 | N | Car bomb | 13 | Iraqi police station/Hay al-Amil | NCTC/MIPT |
| 10-Oct-05 | Unknown | Baghdad | Iraq | Govt/Police | 3 | 0 | N | Car bomb | 13 | Police patrol/Al Tu'ma Street | NCTC/MIPT |
| 10-Oct-05 | Unknown | Baquba | Iraq | Military | 0 | 8 | N | Car bomb | 13 | Iraqi Army checkpoint | IHT |
| 10-Oct-05 | MSC | Khalidiya | Iraq | Military | 3 | 14 | N | Car bomb | 13 | Iraqi Army patrol | SDU/SITE |
| 11-Oct-05 | Unknown | Baghdad | Iraq | Military** | 0 | 6 | N | Car bomb | 13 | Iraqi State Min for provinces | IPCS/NCTC |
| 11-Oct-05 | Unknown | Baghdad | Iraq | Market | 8 | 4 | N | Car bomb | 13 | Police patrol/Ameriyah area | IPCS/EIW |

| Date | Group | City | Country | Target | Killed | Wounded | Suicide | Weapon | Code | Notes | Source |
|---|---|---|---|---|---|---|---|---|---|---|---|
| 11-Oct-05 | Tanzim | Mosul | Iraq | Military | 1 | 4 | Y | Car bomb | 13 | First female car bomber/US mil convoy | AP/AIW |
| 11-Oct-05 | Tanzim | Mosul | Iraq | Military | 0 | 0 | Y | Car bomb | 13 | US military patrol | AP/SITE |
| 11-Oct-05 | Tanzim | Talafar | Iraq | Market | 29 | 45 | N | Car bomb | 13 | Vegetable market | IPCS/NCTC |
| 12-Oct-05 | Unknown | Baghdad | Iraq | Govt/Police | 1 | 6 | N | Car bomb | 13 | Iraq Army checkpoint/Bakriyah area | AP |
| 12-Oct-05 | Unknown | Baghdad | Iraq | Govt/Police** | 0 | 10 | N | Car bomb | 13 | Province Affairs Min. Saad al-Hardan | XNA/AA |
| 12-Oct-05 | Unknown | Baghdad | Iraq | Military | 0 | 4 | Y | Car bomb | 13 | US military convoy/Gazaliyah area | XNA/DR |
| 12-Oct-05 | Unknown | Baquba | Iraq | Military | 0 | 8 | N | Car bomb | 13 | Iraq Army patrol | AP/DR |
| 12-Oct-05 | Tanzim | Talafar | Iraq | Govt/Police | 29 | 35 | N | Belt bomb | 13 | Army recruiting center | Pape/IPCS |
| 13-Oct-05 | JeM | Awantipora | Kashmir/India | Bank | 0 | 0 | N | Belt bomb | 9 | Early detonation/first woman | IPCS/XNA |
| 13-Oct-05 | Unknown | Kirkuk | Iraq | Govt/Police | 5 | 5 | N | Car bomb | 13 | Police patrol/al-Wasiti area | NCTC/MIPT |
| 13-Oct-05 | Unknown | Kirkuk | Iraq | Govt/Police | 2 | 2 | N | Car bomb | 13 | Police patrol | NCTC/MIPT |
| 17-Oct-05 | Unknown | Samarra | Iraq | Civilian | 2 | 1 | N | Car bomb | 13 | Funeral procession/Sheikh Mumtaz | NCTC/MIPT |
| 19-Oct-05 | Unknown | Karabilah | Iraq | Military | 1 | 5 | Y | Car bomb | 13 | US military operations RCT-2 | CC/AP |
| 20-Oct-05 | Tanzim | Baquba | Iraq | Govt/Police | 7 | 13 | N | Car bomb | 13 | Governor's compound | MIPT/AP |
| 20-Oct-05 | Tanzim | Khalis | Iraq | Govt/Police | 1 | 8 | N | Car bomb | 13 | Police checkpoint | NCTC/MIPT |
| 23-Oct-05 | Tanzim | Baghdad | Iraq | Govt/Police | 3 | 13 | N | Car bomb | 13 | Police patrol/Tahrir Square | NCTC/MIPT |
| 23-Oct-05 | Unknown | Kirkuk | Iraq | Military | 1 | 13 | Y | Car bomb | 13 | US military convoy | Pape/NCTC |
| 24-Oct-05 | Tanzim | Baghdad | Iraq | Hotel^ | 6 | 13 | N | Car bomb | 13 | Coordinated attack/Palestine hotel | Pape/NCTC |
| 24-Oct-05 | Tanzim | Baghdad | Iraq | Hotel^ | 7 | 13 | N | Car bomb | 13 | Coordinated attack/Sheraton hotel | Pape/NCTC |
| 24-Oct-05 | Tanzim | Baghdad | Iraq | Hotel^ | 7 | 14 | N | Truck bomb | 13 | Coordinated attack/al-Sadir hotel | Pape/NCTC |
| 24-Oct-05 | Unknown | Baghdad | Iraq | Govt/Police | 2 | 5 | N | Car bomb | 13 | Police patrol/Shaab area | NCTC/MIPT |
| 24-Oct-05 | Unknown | Musayyib | Iraq | Govt/Police | 0 | 2 | N | Car bomb | 13 | Iraqi police | NCTC |
| 25-Oct-05 | Unknown | Baquba | Iraq | Bus | 4 | 4 | N | Belt bomb | 13 | Near Kan'an intersection | NCTC/MIPT |
| 25-Oct-05 | Unknown | Kirkuk | Iraq | Military | 3 | 2 | N | Car bomb | 13 | Iraqi Army patrol | IHT |
| 25-Oct-05 | Tanzim | Sulaimaniyah | Iraq | Govt/Police | 9 | 4 | N | Car bomb | 13 | Peshmerga Affairs building | NCTC/MIPT |
| 25-Oct-05 | Tanzim | Sulaimaniyah | Iraq | Govt/Police** | 0 | 3 | N | Car bomb | 13 | 2 bombs/PUK official Bakhtiyar | NCTC/MIPT |
| 25-Oct-05 | Tanzim | Sulaimaniyah | Iraq | Govt/Police** | 1 | 3 | N | Car bomb | 13 | 2 bombs/PUK official Bakhtiyar | NCTC/MIPT |
| 26-Oct-05 | PIJ | Hadera | Israel | Market | 6 | 30 | N | Belt bomb | 4 | Near food stand | CSS/NCTC |
| 26-Oct-05 | Unknown | Baghdad | Iraq | Military | 1 | 3 | Y | Car bomb | 13 | US military patrol/Karada area | BBC |
| 29-Oct-05 | Unknown | Howaider | Iraq | Market | 29 | 42 | N | Truck bomb | 13 | Shiite area/Fake date sale | Pape/IPCS |
| 29-Oct-05 | Tanzim | Mosul | Iraq | Military | 0 | 9 | N | Car bomb | 13 | Iraqi Army convoy | SITE |
| 30-Oct-05 | Unknown | Khasavyurt | Russia | Unknown | 0 | 0 | N | Belt bomb | 6 | Arrested by police after car stop | ITAR |
| 30-Oct-05 | Unknown | Sinjar | Iraq | Govt/Police | 1 | 7 | N | Car bomb | 13 | Police checkpoint near Syrian border | MIPT/AP |
| 31-Oct-05 | Unknown | Baghdad | Iraq | Govt/Police | 0 | 4 | N | Car bomb | 13 | Early detonation/target police patrol | NCTC/MIPT |
| 31-Oct-05 | Unknown | Falluja | Iraq | Military | 0 | 1 | Y | Car bomb | 13 | US military patrol | DTL |
| 1-Nov-05 | JeM | Srinagar | Kashmir/India | Govt/Police** | 9 | 18 | N | Car bomb | 9 | Chief Minister Mufti Sayeed | IPCS/NCTC |
| 1-Nov-05 | Unknown | Kirkuk | Iraq | Govt/Police** | 0 | 4 | N | Belt bomb | 13 | Kirkuk police chief | IPCS/NCTC |
| 2-Nov-05 | Unknown | Musayyib | Iraq | Market | 21 | 61 | N | Car bomb | 13 | Market/restaurant/mosque area | Pape/AP |
| 5-Nov-05 | Unknown | Husaybah | Iraq | Military | 0 | 0 | Y | Car bomb | 13 | US military patrol | ABC |
| 7-Nov-05 | Taliban | Lashkar Gar | Afghanistan | Govt/Police* | 0 | 1 | N | Car bomb | 12 | Helmand governor, bomber lived | MIPT/CDI |
| 7-Nov-05 | Tanzim | Baghdad | Iraq | Military | 4 | 1 | Y | Car bomb | 13 | US military checkpoint | CC/AIW |
| 7-Nov-05 | Unknown | Baghdad | Iraq | Govt/Police | 8 | 10 | N | Car bomb | 13 | Iraqi police patrol/Dora area | NCTC/XNA |
| 7-Nov-05 | Unknown | Kirkuk | Iraq | Military | 2 | 7 | N | Car bomb | 13 | Iraq Army unit guarding oil pipeline | AP/NYT |

| Date | Group | City | Country | Target | Killed | Wounded | US? | Type | Code | Notes | Source |
|---|---|---|---|---|---|---|---|---|---|---|---|
| 7-Nov-05 | Tanzim | Mosul | Iraq | Military | 0 | 6 | Y | Car bomb | 13 | US military patrol | CNN/SDU |
| 9-Nov-05 | Tanzim | Amman | Jordan | Hotel | 0 | 0 | N | Belt bomb | 7 | Coordinated attack/bomb failed | NCTC/MI |
| 9-Nov-05 | Tanzim | Amman | Jordan | Hotel^ | 21 | 33 | N | Belt bomb | 7 | Coordinated attack/Radisson | NCTC/MI |
| 9-Nov-05 | Tanzim | Amman | Jordan | Hotel^ | 21 | 33 | N | Belt bomb | 7 | Coordinated attack/Grand Hyatt | NCTC/MI |
| 9-Nov-05 | Tanzim | Amman | Jordan | Hotel^ | 21 | 33 | N | Belt bomb | 7 | Coordinated attack/Days Inn | NCTC/MI |
| 9-Nov-05 | Unknown | Baghdad | Iraq | Military | 0 | 1 | Y | Car bomb | 13 | US convoy/Belgian female bomber | IPCS/CSN |
| 9-Nov-05 | Unknown | Baghdad | Iraq | Govt/Police^ | 5 | 0 | N | Car bomb | 13 | 2 bombs/Al Shaab police station | USA/SDU |
| 9-Nov-05 | Unknown | Baghdad | Iraq | Religious site^ | 6 | 1 | N | Car bomb | 13 | 2 bombs/Al Sharoofi mosque | USA/SDU |
| 9-Nov-05 | Unknown | Baquba | Iraq | Govt/Police | 7 | 9 | N | Car bomb | 13 | Police patrol | NCTC/MI |
| 10-Nov-05 | Tanzim | Baghdad | Iraq | Restaurant | 34 | 25 | N | Bag bomb | 13 | Qadduri Police-related restaurant | Pape/NC |
| 10-Nov-05 | Unknown | Tikrit | Iraq | Govt/Police | 6 | 13 | N | Car bomb | 13 | Army recruiting center | MIPT/CT |
| 11-Nov-05 | Unknown | Baghdad | Iraq | Military | 1 | 11 | Y | Car bomb | 13 | US military patrol | AP/AAL |
| 14-Nov-05 | Taliban | Kabul | Afghanistan | Military | 2 | 7 | N | Car bomb | 12 | Target German troops | NCTC/RF |
| 14-Nov-05 | Taliban | Kabul | Afghanistan | Military | 2 | 4 | N | Car bomb | 12 | 2nd bomber at election office | NCTC/RF |
| 14-Nov-05 | Jamatul | Jhalakathi | Bangladesh | Govt/Police | 2 | 0 | N | Belt bomb | 15 | Two judges Ahmed/Pandey | DSB/UNB |
| 15-Nov-05 | Chechen sep | St. Petersburg | Russia | Govt/Police | 1 | 0 | N | Belt bomb | 6 | 1500/police barracks | NCTC |
| 15-Nov-05 | Unknown | Al Karma | Iraq | Military | 1 | 3 | Y | Car bomb | 13 | US Marine patrol near Falluja/RCT-8 | CC/XNA |
| 15-Nov-05 | Unknown | Mahmudiyah | Iraq | Military | 4 | 7 | N | Car bomb | 13 | Iraq Army checkpoint | NCTC/XN |
| 16-Nov-05 | Unknown | Kandahar | Afghanistan | Military | 1 | 3 | Y | Car bomb | 12 | US convoy/Afghan civilian KIA | XNA/AIW |
| 18-Nov-05 | Tanzim | Baghdad | Iraq | Hotel^ | 3 | 21 | N | Car bomb | 13 | 2 bombs/near Interior Min/al-Hamra | CC/NCTC |
| 18-Nov-05 | Tanzim | Baghdad | Iraq | Hotel^ | 3 | 22 | N | Truck bomb | 13 | 2 bombs/near Interior Min/water truck | CC/NCTC |
| 18-Nov-05 | Unknown | Kan'an/Baquba | Iraq | Military | 4 | 9 | Y | Car bomb | 13 | Missed US/Iraqi patrol/hit civilians | NCTC/XN |
| 18-Nov-05 | Unknown | Khanaqin | Iraq | Religious site^ | 44 | 75 | N | Belt bomb | 13 | 2 bombs/Sheik Murad Shia mosque | Pape/NC |
| 18-Nov-05 | Unknown | Khanaqin | Iraq | Religious site^ | 44 | 75 | N | Belt bomb | 13 | 2 bombs/Khanaqin Grand mosque | Pape/NC |
| 18-Nov-05 | Unknown | Khanaqin | Iraq | Religious site | 0 | 0 | N | Belt bomb | 13 | Arrested before detonation | MIPT/AP |
| 19-Nov-05 | Unknown | Abu Saida/Baquba | Iraq | Civilian | 50 | 75 | N | Car bomb | 13 | Tribal chief funeral tent | Pape/NC |
| 19-Nov-05 | Unknown | Baghdad | Iraq | Govt/Police | 0 | 10 | N | Car bomb | 13 | Police convoy | NCTC/MI |
| 21-Nov-05 | Unknown | Baquba | Iraq | Military | 2 | 3 | Y | Car bomb | 13 | US military convoy | AP/BBC |
| 22-Nov-05 | Unknown | Kirkuk | Iraq | Govt/Police | 21 | 24 | N | Car bomb | 13 | Target first responders | Pape/IPC |
| 24-Nov-05 | Partisans | Hillah | Iraq | Market | 13 | 23 | N | Car bomb | 13 | Crowd at market/near soda stand | IPCS/NC |
| 24-Nov-05 | Unknown | Mahmudiyah | Iraq | Hospital | 33 | 39 | Y | Car bomb | 13 | US troops at Iraqi hospital | CC/IPCS |
| 25-Nov-05 | Unknown | Talash Chowk | Afghanistan | Unknown | 0 | 1 | N | Belt bomb | 12 | Premature detonation | NCTC/MI |
| 26-Nov-05 | Unknown | Samarra | Iraq | Civilian | 5 | 16 | N | Car bomb | 13 | Gas station | Pape/NC |
| 28-Nov-05 | Tanzim | Baquba | Iraq | Military | 0 | 4 | Y | Car bomb | 13 | US military patrol | CNN/DWS |
| 29-Nov-05 | Tanzim | Moshahada | Iraq | Military | 1 | 4 | N | Car bomb | 13 | Iraqi Army convoy | SITE |
| 29-Nov-05 | Unknown | Rawah | Iraq | Military | 0 | 0 | Y | Car bomb | 13 | US military patrol | AIW |
| 29-Nov-05 | Jamatul | Chittagong | Bangladesh | Govt/Police | 2 | 17 | N | Belt bomb | 15 | Coordinated attack/bomber lived | NCTC/MI |
| 29-Nov-05 | Jamatul | Gazipur | Bangladesh | Govt/Police | 6 | 50 | N | Belt bomb | 15 | Coordinated attack | NCTC/MI |
| 1-Dec-05 | Jamatul | Gazipur | Bangladesh | Govt/Police | 1 | 29 | N | Belt bomb | 15 | Bomber survived/Near Govt office | MIPT/JTI |
| 2-Dec-05 | Tanzim | Samarra | Iraq | Govt/Police | 0 | 2 | N | Belt bomb | 13 | Iraqi police checkpoint | DWS/KM |
| 4-Dec-05 | Unknown | Kandahar | Afghanistan | Military | 1 | 3 | Y | Belt bomb | 12 | US convoy/Bomber hit by motorcycle | NCTC/RF |
| 5-Dec-05 | PIJ | Netanya | Israel | Mall | 5 | 40 | N | Bag bomb | 4 | Partially foiled by security | CSS/NCT |
| 6-Dec-05 | Tanzim | Baghdad | Iraq | Govt/Police^ | 19 | 36 | N | Belt bomb | 13 | 2 females/Baghdad Police Academy | Pape/IPC |

| Date | Group | City | Country | Target | Killed | Wounded | ? | Weapon | # | Notes | Source |
|---|---|---|---|---|---|---|---|---|---|---|---|
| 6-Dec-05 | Tanzim | Baghdad | Iraq | Govt/Police^ | 20 | 37 | N | Belt bomb | 13 | 2 females/Baghdad Police Academy | Pape/IPCS |
| 6-Dec-05 | Unknown | Baghdad | Iraq | Restaurant | 2 | 20 | N | Belt bomb | 13 | Police-related café | IPCS/NCTC |
| 7-Dec-05 | Jamatul | Netrakona | Bangladesh | Govt/Police | 6 | 46 | N | Bike bomb | 15 | Communist Party Office (Udichi) | NCTC/MIPT |
| 8-Dec-05 | Unknown | Baghdad | Iraq | Bus | 31 | 44 | N | Belt bomb | 13 | Bus to Nasiriya/Al Nahdha garage | Pape/NCTC |
| 8-Dec-05 | Unknown | Mosul | Iraq | Military | 0 | 8 | Y | Car bomb | 13 | US military patrol | NH |
| 8-Dec-05 | Unknown | Salman Pak | Iraq | Govt/Police | 0 | 4 | N | Car bomb | 13 | Police patrol near Salman Pak | NCTC/MIPT |
| 9-Dec-05 | Unknown | Baghdad | Iraq | Military | 1 | 12 | Y | Car bomb | 13 | US military CP/Abu Ghraib area | CC/XNA |
| 10-Dec-05 | Unknown | Baghdad | Iraq | Military | 2 | 8 | Y | Car bomb | 13 | US military patrol | XNA |
| 11-Dec-05 | Unknown | Kandahar | Afghanistan | Military | 1 | 3 | Y | Belt bomb | 12 | US mil convoy/3 civilian wounded | RFE/XNA |
| 11-Dec-05 | Unknown | Ramadi | Iraq | Military | 1 | 2 | Y | Car bomb | 13 | US military patrol | CC/XNA |
| 12-Dec-05 | Unknown | Baghdad | Iraq | Military | 0 | 5 | N | Car bomb | 13 | Iraqi Army patrol | AIW |
| 12-Dec-05 | Tanzim | Falluja | Iraq | Military | 0 | 1 | Y | Car bomb | 13 | US military patrol/east Falluja | XNA/AIW |
| 14-Dec-05 | Unknown | Mazar-e-Sharif | Afghanistan | Religious site | 0 | 0 | N | Belt bomb | 12 | Hazrat Ali shrine/Blue Mosque | NCTC/RFE |
| 14-Dec-05 | Unknown | Baghdad | Iraq | Military | 3 | 5 | N | Car bomb | 13 | UK checkpoint | Pape |
| 15-Dec-05 | Unknown | Baghdad | Iraq | Civilian | 0 | 0 | N | Car bomb | 13 | Bomber killed by police | MIPT/REUT |
| 16-Dec-05 | Taliban | Kabul | Afghanistan | Military | 0 | 2 | N | Car bomb | 12 | Premature detonation/Norwegian ISAF | NCTC/AP |
| 18-Dec-05 | Unknown | al Ameriyah | Iraq | Unknown | 0 | 0 | N | Belt bomb | 13 | Premature detonation | NCTC/SDU |
| 18-Dec-05 | Unknown | Baghdad | Iraq | Govt/Police | 1 | 5 | N | Car bomb | 13 | Police checkpoint at Interior Ministry | NCTC/MIPT |
| 19-Dec-05 | Unknown | Baghdad | Iraq | Govt/Police** | 2 | 11 | N | Car bomb | 13 | District police chief for al-Dora | NCTC/MIPT |
| 20-Dec-05 | Taliban | Herat | Afghanistan | Military | 0 | 3 | N | Belt bomb | 12 | ISAF convoy | RFE/XNA |
| 21-Dec-05 | Tanzim | Haswa | Iraq | Military | 5 | 13 | N | Car bomb | 13 | Iraqi Army checkpoint at base | SDU/SITE |
| 22-Dec-05 | Mujahideen A | Falluja | Iraq | Military | 0 | 0 | Y | Car bomb | 13 | US military patrol | SITE |
| 22-Dec-05 | Unknown | Falluja | Iraq | Govt/Police | 0 | 7 | N | Car bomb | 13 | Iraqi police checkpoint | SABC |
| 23-Dec-05 | Unknown | Balad Ruz | Iraq | Religious site | 9 | 3 | N | Belt bomb | 13 | Mosque, partly foiled by security | NCTC/MIPT |
| 26-Dec-05 | Unknown | Baghdad | Iraq | Govt/Police | 1 | 2 | N | Car bomb | 13 | Karadah district | CC/AIW |
| 26-Dec-05 | Unknown | Baghdad | Iraq | Govt/Police | 0 | 6 | N | Car bomb | 13 | Central Baghdad | CC/AIW |
| 26-Dec-05 | Unknown | Baghdad | Iraq | Civilians | 2 | 4 | N | Motorcycle | 13 | Shiite funeral procession | NBC/AIW |
| 26-Dec-05 | Unknown | Falluja | Iraq | Military | 0 | 2 | Y | Belt bomb | 13 | Checkpoint at US/Iraqi CMOC | AIW |
| 26-Dec-05 | Unknown | Falluja | Iraq | Govt/Police | 2 | 0 | N | Belt bomb | 13 | Police recruits/grenades first then belt | NCTC/MIPT |
| 27-Dec-05 | Unknown | Baquba | Iraq | Unknown | 0 | 0 | N | Belt bomb | 13 | Arrested before detonation | MIPT/CNN |
| 29-Dec-05 | PIJ | Tulkarm | West Bank | Military | 3 | 8 | N | Belt bomb | 4 | Checkpoint/Premature detonation | CSS/NCTC |
| 29-Dec-05 | Chechen sep | Makhachkala | Russia | Religious site | 0 | 1 | N | Belt bomb | 6 | Early detonation/target funeral | NCTC/RFE |
| 29-Dec-05 | Unknown | Spin Boldak | Afghanistan | Unknown | 0 | 0 | N | Belt bomb | 12 | 2 killed while donning explosives | MIPT/XNA |
| 29-Dec-05 | Sunna | Baghdad | Iraq | Govt/Police | 5 | 6 | N | Belt bomb | 13 | Police checkpoint Interior Ministry | NCTC/RFE |
| 30-Dec-05 | Unknown | Baghdad | Iraq | Govt/Police | 3 | 2 | N | Car bomb | 13 | Police patrol/Al Kifah Street | MIPT/AP |
| 1-Jan-06 | Unknown | al-Qaim | Iraq | Military | 0 | 2 | Y | Car bomb | 13 | US military convoy | XNA/IPCS |
| 1-Jan-06 | Unknown | Baghdad | Iraq | Market | 0 | 2 | N | Car bomb | 13 | Commercial area near copy shop | MIPT/CNN |
| 1-Jan-06 | Unknown | Kirkuk | Iraq | Military | 1 | 6 | Y | Car bomb | 13 | US/Iraqi patrol | XNA/UPI |
| 1-Jan-06 | Unknown | Kirkuk | Iraq | Unknown | 0 | 0 | N | Car bomb | 13 | Premature detonation | UPI/DTI |
| 2-Jan-06 | Unknown | Kandahar | Afghanistan | Military | 0 | 2 | Y | Car bomb | 12 | US military convoy | RFE/XNA |
| 2-Jan-06 | Tanzim | Baquba | Iraq | Govt/Police | 6 | 13 | N | Car bomb | 13 | Police recruit bus | CC/IPCS |
| 2-Jan-06 | Unknown | Kirkuk | Iraq | Military | 1 | 0 | N | Car bomb | 13 | Army base/troops fired on bomber | IPCS/DWS |
| 3-Jan-06 | Unknown | Karbala | Iraq | Civilian | 0 | 0 | N | Car bomb | 13 | Arrested before detonation | MIPT/AP |

| Date | Group | City | Country | Target | Killed | Wounded | US? | Type | Code | Notes | Source |
|---|---|---|---|---|---|---|---|---|---|---|---|
| 4-Jan-06 | Unknown | Baghdad | Iraq | Govt/Police | 0 | 6 | N | Car bomb | 13 | Iraqi police patrol | XNA/AP |
| 4-Jan-06 | Unknown | Muqdadiyah | Iraq | Civilian | 35 | 42 | N | Belt bomb | 13 | Funeral, also mortars | IPCS/RFE |
| 5-Jan-06 | Taliban | Tarin Khot | Afghanistan | Govt/Police | 9 | 50 | N | Car bomb | 12 | Uruzgon Governor offce/cattle market | RFE/MIPT |
| 5-Jan-06 | Unknown | Baghdad | Iraq | Military^ | 1 | 3 | N | Car bomb | 13 | 2 bombs/police patrol near mosque | MIPT/XNA |
| 5-Jan-06 | Unknown | Baghdad | Iraq | Military^ | 1 | 3 | N | Car bomb | 13 | 2 bombs/police patrol near mosque | MIPT/XNA |
| 5-Jan-06 | Tanzim | Karbala | Iraq | Civilian | 62 | 120 | N | Belt bomb | 13 | Near Imam Hussein shrine | IPCS/RFE |
| 5-Jan-06 | Unknown | Ramadi | Iraq | Govt/Police | 55 | 60 | N | Belt bomb | 13 | Police recruits | IPCS/RFE |
| 6-Jan-06 | Unknown | Baghdad | Iraq | Govt/Police | 1 | 4 | N | Car bomb | 13 | Iraq police patrol/Zeafraniya area | XNA/AS |
| 6-Jan-06 | Unknown | Mosul | Iraq | Govt/Police | 0 | 10 | N | Car bomb | 13 | Iraqi police patrol | MIPT/NCTC |
| 7-Jan-06 | LTTE | Trincomalee | Sri Lanka | Naval vessel | 13 | 2 | N | Boat bomb | 3 | Navy gunboat | SATP/TG |
| 7-Jan-06 | Unknown | Baghdad | Iraq | Govt/Police | 0 | 13 | N | Car bomb | 13 | Police commando patrol | MIPT/AP |
| 7-Jan-06 | None | Gansu | China | Govt/Police | 4 | 22 | N | Belt bomb | x | Farmer in courtroom arguing | TOL/AP |
| 8-Jan-06 | Unknown | Baghdad | Iraq | Govt/Police | 1 | 5 | N | Car bomb | 13 | National security advisor convoy | MIPT/XNA |
| 8-Jan-06 | Unknown | Baghdad | Iraq | Govt/Police | 1 | 7 | N | Belt bomb | 13 | Police commando CP/Al-Jadida area | MIPT/NCTC |
| 9-Jan-06 | Tanzim | Baghdad | Iraq | Govt/Police^ | 13 | 12 | N | Belt bomb | 13 | Police Day celebration | IPCS/MIPT |
| 9-Jan-06 | Tanzim | Baghdad | Iraq | Govt/Police^ | 14 | 13 | N | Belt bomb | 13 | Police Day celebration | IPCS/MIPT |
| 12-Jan-06 | Unknown | Jenin | West Bank | Military | 0 | 0 | N | Belt bomb | 4 | Detonated when IDF approached | AP/JP |
| 13-Jan-06 | Unknown | Baquba | Iraq | Govt/Police | 2 | 5 | N | Car bomb | 13 | Iraqi police patrol | KM/AFP |
| 13-Jan-06 | Tanzim | Falluja | Iraq | Military | 0 | 10 | Y | Car bomb | 13 | US military patrol | AS/NCTC |
| 14-Jan-06 | Unknown | Helmand | Afghanistan | Military | 0 | 1 | Y | Car bomb | 12 | US/Afghan military patrol | RFE/AP |
| 15-Jan-06 | Taliban | Kandahar | Afghanistan | Military | 3 | 13 | N | Car bomb | 12 | Canadian military convoy/diplomat | RFE/XNA |
| 16-Jan-06 | Taliban | Kandahar | Afghanistan | Military | 7 | 14 | N | Belt bomb | 12 | Afghan Army patrol vehicle | RFE/CDI |
| 16-Jan-06 | Unknown | Spin Boldak | Afghanistan | Civilian | 21 | 27 | N | Motorcycle | 12 | Wrestling match | RFE/MIPT |
| 16-Jan-06 | Unknown | Muqdadiyah | Iraq | Military | 10 | 13 | N | Car bomb | 13 | Iraqi police checkpoint | AIW |
| 18-Jan-06 | Unknown | Baghdad | Iraq | Govt/Police | 2 | 5 | N | Car bomb | 13 | Police patrol near Shiite politician | NCTC |
| 19-Jan-06 | PIJ | Tel Aviv | Israel | Market | 0 | 22 | N | Bag bomb | 4 | Sandwich stand/Central Bus Station | AP/REUT |
| 19-Jan-06 | Unknown | Baghdad | Iraq | Restaurant | 15 | 21 | N | Belt bomb | 13 | Coffee shop on Saadoun Street | IPCS/MIPT |
| 19-Jan-06 | Unknown | Shahyat | Iraq | Military | 0 | 0 | Y | Car bomb | 13 | US military convoy | AS |
| 20-Jan-06 | Unknown | Haqlaniyah | Iraq | Military | 2 | 0 | Y | Car bomb | 13 | US Marines/ 2 MARDIV | CC/XNA |
| 21-Jan-06 | Unknown | Baghdad | Iraq | Civilian | 0 | 4 | N | Car bomb | 13 | Possible premature detonation/market | SFC/AP |
| 21-Jan-06 | Unknown | Baquba | Iraq | Govt/Police | 2 | 8 | N | Car bomb | 13 | Iraqi police checkpoint | KM/CNN |
| 23-Jan-06 | Unknown | Baghdad | Iraq | Govt/Police | 0 | 0 | Y | Car bomb | 13 | US/Iraqi patrol/al-Swaiyb area | XNA/AIW |
| 23-Jan-06 | MSC | Baghdad | Iraq | Govt/Police | 3 | 7 | N | Car bomb | 13 | Green Zone checkpoint/Iran Embassy | MIPT/XNA |
| 24-Jan-06 | Unknown | Mosul | Iraq | Military | 0 | 0 | Y | Car bomb | 13 | US military patrol | SDU/IHT |
| 28-Jan-06 | Unknown | Tikrit | Iraq | Govt/Police | 4 | 6 | N | Car bomb | 13 | Iraqi police checkpoint | AIW/KTI |
| 30-Jan-06 | Unknown | Kandahar | Afghanistan | Military | 0 | 0 | Y | Bus bomb | 12 | US base/arrested on tip/55kg bomb | RFE/CSM |
| 30-Jan-06 | MSC | Nasiriya | Iraq | Govt/Police | 2 | 30 | N | Car bomb | 13 | Police commando training center | MIPT/JTIC |
| 1-Feb-06 | Unknown | Khost | Afghanistan | Military | 3 | 8 | N | Car bomb | 12 | Army checkpoint/2 bombers in car | RFE/CDI |
| 1-Feb-06 | Unknown | Baghdad | Iraq | Civilian | 3 | 61 | N | Car bomb | 13 | Waiting workers near mosque | IPCS/TES |
| 2-Feb-06 | Unknown | Baghdad | Iraq | Civilian^ | 8 | 45 | N | Car bomb | 13 | 2 bombs/Gas station/Al Amin | NCTC/MIP |
| 2-Feb-06 | Unknown | Baghdad | Iraq | Market^ | 8 | 45 | N | Car bomb | 13 | 2 bombs/market/Al Amin | NCTC/MIP |
| 5-Feb-06 | MSC | Mosul | Iraq | Military | 0 | 2 | Y | Car bomb | 13 | US military patrol | SITE |
| 6-Feb-06 | Unknown | Mazar-e-Sharif | Afghanistan | Govt/Police** | 0 | 0 | N | Belt bomb | 12 | Bomber arrested, Governor target | RFE/MIPT |

| Date | Group | Location | Country | Target | Killed | Wounded | ? | Type | # | Notes | Source |
|---|---|---|---|---|---|---|---|---|---|---|---|
| 6-Feb-06 | Unknown | Kosovska M | Serbia | Restaurant | 0 | 0 | N | Belt bomb | x | Sienna café | NCTC/SSB |
| 7-Feb-06 | Taliban | Kandahar | Afghanistan | Govt/Police | 13 | 13 | N | Belt bomb | 12 | Tried to enter police station | RFE/MIPT |
| 7-Feb-06 | Unknown | Baghdad | Iraq | Military | 0 | 0 | Y | Car bomb | 13 | US military convoy (1-66 AR) | CC/JTIC |
| 8-Feb-06 | Unknown | New Ubaydi | Iraq | Govt/Police | 5 | 3 | N | Car bomb | 13 | Vehicle checkpoint | CC/XNA |
| 9-Feb-06 | Unknown | Hangu | Pakistan | Religious site | 22 | 50 | N | Belt bomb | 10 | Shiite Muharram procession | MIPT/SATP |
| 11-Feb-06 | LTTE | Mannar | Sri Lanka | Naval vessel | 0 | 1 | N | Boat bomb | 3 | Detonated after interception | SATP/NYT |
| 12-Feb-06 | Unknown | Baghdad | Iraq | Govt/Police | 0 | 8 | N | Belt bomb | 13 | Iraqi police commando patrol | MIPT/XNA |
| 12-Feb-06 | Unknown | Baghdad | Iraq | Govt/Police | 3 | 4 | N | Belt bomb | 13 | Police checkpoint | MIPT/CTC |
| 13-Feb-06 | Unknown | Baghdad | Iraq | Bank | 9 | 40 | N | Belt bomb | 13 | Line outside Istethemar bank | MIPT/BBC |
| 14-Feb-06 | Unknown | Al-Qaim | Iraq | Military | 2 | 1 | Y | Car bomb | 13 | 2 x US military | CC/AIW |
| 16-Feb-06 | Unknown | Baghdad | Iraq | Govt/Police | 0 | 3 | N | Car bomb | 13 | Iraqi police patrol | SDU |
| 19-Feb-06 | Unknown | Baghdad | Iraq | Govt/Police | 2 | 6 | N | Car bomb | 13 | Green Zone checkpoint | RTE/KNA |
| 19-Feb-06 | Unknown | Baghdad | Iraq | Military | 0 | 4 | N | Belt bomb | 13 | Iraqi Army checkpoint/Al-Jumhuriyah | MIPT/NCTC |
| 20-Feb-06 | Unknown | Nagarhar | Afghanistan | Unknown | 0 | 0 | N | Belt bomb | 12 | Premature detonation | MIPT/NYT |
| 20-Feb-06 | Unknown | Baghdad | Iraq | Bus | 11 | 15 | N | Belt bomb | 13 | Mostly Shiite riders/Kadimiyah area | MIPT/XNA |
| 20-Feb-06 | MSC | Mosul | Iraq | Restaurant | 4 | 21 | N | Belt bomb | 13 | Abu Ali Police-related restaurant | MIPT/XNA |
| 21-Feb-06 | Unknown | Baghdad | Iraq | Military | 1 | 13 | Y | Car bomb | 13 | US military base | NCTC |
| 23-Feb-06 | Unknown | Shaw Wali Kot | Afghanistan | Military | 0 | 0 | Y | Car bomb | 12 | US mil convoy/failed to detonate | CDI/FOX |
| 23-Feb-06 | MSC | Baquba | Iraq | Govt/Police | 10 | 15 | N | Car bomb | 13 | Police checkpoint at market | SITE |
| 24-Feb-06 | al-Qaeda | Abqaiq | Saudi Arabia | Oil Refinery^ | 0 | 4 | N | Car bomb | 7 | 2 car bombs/Oil refinery | RFE/MIPT |
| 24-Feb-06 | al-Qaeda | Abqaiq | Saudi Arabia | Oil Refinery^ | 2 | 4 | N | Car bomb | 7 | 2 car bombs/Oil refinery | RFE/MIPT |
| 25-Feb-06 | Unknown | Karbala | Iraq | Market | 5 | 52 | N | Car bomb | 13 | Busy shopping street | RTE/AFP |
| 28-Feb-06 | Unknown | Baghdad | Iraq | Civilian | 22 | 51 | N | Car bomb | 13 | Line as gas station/Shiite area | RFE/MIPT |
| 28-Feb-06 | Unknown | Baghdad | Iraq | Religious site | 5 | 16 | N | Car bomb | 13 | Shiite Timimi mosque/Karada area | MIPT/NCTC |
| 1-Mar-06 | Unknown | Baghdad | Iraq | Civilian | 23 | 58 | N | Car bomb | 13 | East Baghdad/near cinema | CNN |
| 1-Mar-06 | Unknown | Ramadi | Iraq | Govt/Police | 1 | 6 | N | Car bomb | 13 | 2 bombs/Iraq police checkpoint | SPPP |
| 2-Mar-06 | Unknown | Karachi | Pakistan | Govt/Police* | 3 | 50 | Y | Car bomb | 7 | U.S. Diplomat David Fyfe | RFE/MIPT |
| 2-Mar-06 | Unknown | Baghdad | Iraq | Market | 4 | 10 | N | Car bomb | 13 | Shiites in Sadr City market | NCTC/CC |
| 3-Mar-06 | Taliban | Daman | Afghanistan | Military | 0 | 5 | N | Car bomb | 12 | Canadian patrol vehicle | XNA/NP |
| 4-Mar-06 | Unknown | Sakran | Iraq | Military | 0 | 1 | N | Car bomb | 13 | Iraqi Army checkpoint | AS |
| 6-Mar-06 | Unknown | Baghdad | Iraq | Govt/Police | 1 | 5 | N | Car bomb | 13 | Police patrol/Dora area | MIPT/XNA |
| 6-Mar-06 | Unknown | Baghdad | Iraq | Govt/Police | 2 | 3 | N | Car bomb | 13 | Police patrol/al-Mustansiriyah | MIPT/CNN |
| 7-Mar-06 | Unknown | Baquba | Iraq | Govt/Police | 0 | 1 | N | Car bomb | 13 | Iraq police patrol/Tahrir area | CNN |
| 8-Mar-06 | Unknown | Baghdad | Iraq | Military | 0 | 5 | Y | Car bomb | 13 | US military patrol | DWS |
| 9-Mar-06 | Unknown | Van | Turkey | Govt/Police | 3 | 16 | N | Belt bomb | 8 | Police car near sports center | UPI/BBC |
| 9-Mar-06 | None | Amur | Russia | Bank | 0 | 4 | N | Belt bomb | x | Bankrupt businessman | MOS/ITAR |
| 10-Mar-06 | MSC | Falluja | Iraq | Military | 1 | 0 | Y | Car bomb | 13 | US Marines guarding building | SFC/CNN |
| 10-Mar-06 | Unknown | Falluja | Iraq | Military | 10 | 11 | Y | Car bomb | 13 | US/Iraqi checkpoint | AP/MIPT |
| 10-Mar-06 | Unknown | Mishahda | Iraq | Military | 0 | 2 | Y | Car bomb | 13 | US military patrol | FOR |
| 10-Mar-06 | Unknown | Samarra | Iraq | Govt/Police | 0 | 6 | N | Car bomb | 13 | Iraqi police | CNN |
| 12-Mar-06 | Unknown | Kabul | Afghanistan | Govt/Police** | 2 | 3 | N | Car bomb | 12 | Afghan Parliament head Mojadidi | JTIC/XNA |
| 12-Mar-06 | Unknown | Baghdad | Iraq | Market^ | 8 | 25 | N | Car bomb | 13 | 2 bombers/Sadr City | MIPT/CNN |
| 12-Mar-06 | Unknown | Baghdad | Iraq | Market^ | 9 | 25 | N | Car bomb | 13 | 2 bombers/Sadr City | MIPT/CNN |
| 13-Mar-06 | Unknown | Baghdad | Iraq | Civilian | 1 | 4 | N | Car bomb | 13 | UK security company convoy (AEGIS) | MIPT/XNA |

| Date | Group | City | Country | Target | Killed | Wounded | F | Type | Region | Notes | Source |
|---|---|---|---|---|---|---|---|---|---|---|---|
| 14-Mar-06 | Unknown | Baghdad | Iraq | School | 0 | 0 | N | Belt bomb | 13 | Stopped by security guard | MIPT/AS |
| 14-Mar-06 | MSC | Talafar | Iraq | Civilian | 1 | 4 | N | Car bomb | 13 | UK security company convoy (AEGIS) | NCTC/SIT |
| 15-Mar-06 | Unknown | Baquba | Iraq | Govt/Police | 2 | 6 | N | Bike bomb | 13 | Police patrol, early detonation/Al Amin | IPCS/MIP |
| 17-Mar-06 | Unknown | Baghdad | Iraq | Bus | 1 | 4 | N | Belt bomb | 13 | Bus driver killed | MIPT/AS |
| 18-Mar-06 | MSC | Talafar | Iraq | Military | 0 | 0 | Y | Car bomb | 13 | Near U.S. base | CBS/BNS |
| 19-Mar-06 | Taliban | Spin Boldak | Afghanistan | Military | 0 | 0 | N | Car bomb | 12 | French ISAF vehicle/failed to detonate | AIP/CDI |
| 20-Mar-06 | MSC | Baquba | Iraq | Govt/Police | 1 | 2 | N | Car bomb | 13 | Iraqi police checkpoint near hospital | MIPT/NCT |
| 22-Mar-06 | MSC | Falluja | Iraq | Military | 0 | 7 | Y | Car bomb | 13 | US military patrol | SITE |
| 22-Mar-06 | MSC | Mosul | Iraq | Military | 1 | 0 | Y | Car bomb | 13 | US military patrol | SITE |
| 23-Mar-06 | MSC | Baghdad | Iraq | Govt/Police | 24 | 32 | N | Car bomb | 13 | Baghdad Police Major Crime Unit | MIPT/XNA |
| 23-Mar-06 | Unknown | Hit | Iraq | Govt/Police | 6 | 6 | N | Car bomb | 13 | Iraqi police CP/Ayn al-Asad base | MIPT/NCT |
| 24-Mar-06 | Unknown | Falluja | Iraq | Unknown | 0 | 0 | N | Car bomb | 13 | Probable premature detonation | DWS/AS |
| 25-Mar-06 | LTTE | Puttalam | Sri Lanka | Naval vessel | 8 | 11 | N | Boat bomb | 3 | 6 bombers in boat | SATP/SPR |
| 27-Mar-06 | Unknown | Kandahar | Afghanistan | Unknown | 0 | 0 | N | Belt bomb | 12 | 2 detonated/police approached | RFE/MIPT |
| 27-Mar-06 | MSC | Talafar | Iraq | Govt/Police | 40 | 30 | N | Belt bomb | 13 | Army recruiting/Tamarat base | IPCS/MIP |
| 28-Mar-06 | MSC | Iskandariyah | Iraq | Govt/Police | 0 | 12 | N | Car bomb | 13 | Police station | MIPT/AP |
| 30-Mar-06 | Fatah | Kedumim | West Bank | Civilian | 4 | 0 | N | Suitcase | 4 | Entrance of Israeli settlement | JA/MIPT |
| 30-Mar-06 | Taliban | Kandahar | Afghanistan | Military | 2 | 8 | N | Car bomb | 12 | Early detonation/Canadian convoy | AP/XNA |
| 30-Mar-06 | Unknown | Baghdad | Iraq | Govt/Police | 6 | 1 | N | Car bomb | 13 | Police commandos | MIPT/XNA |
| 30-Mar-06 | Unknown | Baghdad | Iraq | Govt/Police | 1 | 7 | N | Car bomb | 13 | Police commando convoy/Yarmuk | MIPT/NCT |
| 31-Mar-06 | Taliban | Zormat | Afghanistan | Govt/Police | 0 | 1 | N | Belt bomb | 12 | Detonated after arrest | MIPT/JTIC |
| 1-Apr-06 | Unknown | Maiwand | Afghanistan | Military | 0 | 1 | Y | Car bomb | 12 | ISAF/Afghan convoy on Herat Road | AIW/AP |
| 3-Apr-06 | Taliban | Arghandab | Afghanistan | Govt/Police** | 0 | 0 | N | Belt bomb | 12 | Shot before detonation/district chief | RFE/MIPT |
| 3-Apr-06 | Unknown | Baghdad | Iraq | Religious site | 10 | 38 | N | Truck bomb | 13 | Al-Shoofri Shiite mosque | AP/LAT |
| 5-Apr-06 | Unknown | Falluja | Iraq | Military | 5 | 6 | N | Car bomb | 13 | US military patrol | AS/NCTC |
| 7-Apr-06 | Unknown | Lashkar Gar | Afghanistan | Military | 0 | 3 | Y | Car bomb | 12 | US military leaving base | XNA/AP |
| 7-Apr-06 | Unknown | Tej | Afghanistan | Military | 0 | 6 | N | Car bomb | 12 | Afghan military patrol | PAN/WS |
| 7-Apr-06 | Unknown | Baghdad | Iraq | Religious site^ | 30 | 55 | N | Belt bomb | 13 | 3 bombers/Baratha Shiite mosque | IPCS/MIP |
| 7-Apr-06 | Unknown | Baghdad | Iraq | Religious site^ | 30 | 55 | N | Belt bomb | 13 | 3 bombers/Baratha Shiite mosque | IPCS/MIP |
| 7-Apr-06 | Unknown | Baghdad | Iraq | Religious site^ | 30 | 55 | N | Belt bomb | 13 | 3 bombers/Baratha Shiite mosque | IPCS/MIP |
| 7-Apr-06 | None | Guangyuan | China | Govt/Police | 0 | 1 | N | Belt bomb | x | Miner unhappy with judge's ruling | UPI/SCM |
| 7-Apr-06 | Unknown | Ordu | Turkey | Religious site | 0 | 6 | N | Belt bomb | x | Girl's Koran school/early detonation | MIPT/JTIC |
| 8-Apr-06 | Taliban | Herat | Afghanistan | Military | 3 | 7 | N | Car bomb | 12 | Italian peacekeeper base | BBC/AP |
| 9-Apr-06 | Unknown | Angora Ada | Afghanistan | Military | 1 | 5 | N | Car bomb | 12 | Afghan Army checkpoint | PAN/AIP |
| 11-Apr-06 | Unknown | Karachi | Pakistan | Religious site | 56 | 200 | N | Bag bomb | 10 | Religious Ceremony/Nishtar Park | MIPT/SAT |
| 11-Apr-06 | Unknown | Rawah | Iraq | Military | 1 | 2 | Y | Belt bomb | 13 | US military patrol near market | CNN/DOD |
| 12-Apr-06 | Unknown | Howaider | Iraq | Religious site | 30 | 70 | N | Car bomb | 13 | Shiite mosque/police opened fire | MIPT/NC |
| 12-Apr-06 | Unknown | Talafar | Iraq | Market | 3 | 7 | N | Car bomb | 13 | Vegetable market | MIPT/AP |
| 14-Apr-06 | Unknown | Helmand | Afghanistan | Military | 0 | 3 | N | Belt bomb | 12 | 2 UK military wounded at base | AP/Reuter |
| 14-Apr-06 | Unknown | Mosul | Iraq | Govt/Police | 0 | 9 | N | Car bomb | 13 | Iraqi police station | XNA/AA |
| 14-Apr-06 | Unknown | Shaibah | Iraq | Military | 2 | 5 | N | Car bomb | 13 | UK military convoy | DM/TM |
| 15-Apr-06 | Unknown | Mosul | Iraq | Govt/Police | 2 | 5 | N | Car bomb | 13 | Partially foiled by police fire | RFE/MIP |
| 16-Apr-06 | Unknown | Mahmudiyah | Iraq | Market | 13 | 19 | N | Car bomb | 13 | Mahmudiyah market | TI |

| Date | Group | Location | Country | Target | Killed | Wounded | ? | Type | Code | Notes | Source |
|---|---|---|---|---|---|---|---|---|---|---|---|
| 17-Apr-06 | PIJ/Fatah | Tel Aviv | Israel | Restaurant | 12 | 49 | N | Belt bomb | 4 | Near Central Bus Station | JA/MIPT |
| 17-Apr-06 | Unknown | Ramadi | Iraq | Military^ | 0 | 1 | Y | Car bomb | 13 | 2 car bombs led assault on Govt bldg | MIPT/CNN |
| 17-Apr-06 | Unknown | Ramadi | Iraq | Military^ | 0 | 2 | Y | Car bomb | 13 | 2 car bombs led assault on Govt bldg | MIPT/CNN |
| 17-Apr-06 | Unknown | Rawah | Iraq | Military | 1 | 1 | N | Car bomb | 13 | Iraqi Army checkpoint | FOX/JP |
| 19-Apr-06 | Unknown | Baghdad | Iraq | Military | 2 | 8 | Y | Car bomb | 13 | US military/near airport | Pape |
| 20-Apr-06 | Unknown | Zarai | Afghanistan | Govt/Police | 0 | 3 | N | Car bomb | 12 | Afghan police convoy | MIPT/PAN |
| 20-Apr-06 | Unknown | Basra | Iraq | Military | 2 | 5 | N | Car bomb | 13 | US military convoy | NCTC/DWS |
| 21-Apr-06 | Unknown | Talafar | Iraq | Govt/Police | 5 | 11 | N | Car bomb | 13 | Police patrol | MIPT/AP |
| 22-Apr-06 | Unknown | Pulwama | Kashmir/India | Military | 0 | 0 | N | Car bomb | 13 | Early detonation/Indian mil convoy | NCTC/SATP |
| 24-Apr-06 | Unknown | Baghdad | Iraq | School^ | 4 | 11 | N | Car bomb | 13 | Al Mustansarya University | XNA/DWS |
| 24-Apr-06 | Unknown | Baghdad | Iraq | Govt/Police | 2 | 25 | N | Car bomb | 13 | Police patrol/near Ministry of Health | MIPT/REUT |
| 25-Apr-06 | LTTE | Columbo | Sri Lanka | Military** | 8 | 27 | N | Belt bomb | 3 | Army commander LTG Fonseka | SATP/SPUR |
| 26-Apr-06 | Unknown | Al-Shaykh Zuwayd | Egypt | Govt/Police** | 0 | 0 | N | Motorcycle | 5 | Town police chief | MIPT/XNA |
| 26-Apr-06 | Unknown | Rafah crossing | Egypt | Military | 0 | 0 | N | Belt bomb | 5 | Multinational troops (Norwegian) | CNN/XNA |
| 26-Apr-06 | Unknown | Baghdad | Iraq | Unknown | 0 | 0 | N | Belt bomb | 13 | 2 bombers killed by police | NCTC |
| 28-Apr-06 | Unknown | Rawah | Iraq | Military | 0 | 0 | N | Belt bomb | 13 | Iraqi Army checkpoint at Rawa bridge | ALB |
| 29-Apr-06 | Unknown | Al Qaim | Iraq | Military | 3 | 4 | N | Car bomb | 13 | Iraqi Army base | NCTC |
| 1-May-06 | Unknown | Helmand | Afghanistan | Military | 0 | 0 | N | Belt bomb | 12 | Afghan Army patrol | RFE/XNA |
| 1-May-06 | Unknown | Kandahar | Afghanistan | Military | 2 | 2 | N | Car bomb | 12 | ISAF convoy | RFE/XNA |
| 1-May-06 | Unknown | Khost | Afghanistan | Unknown | 1 | 0 | N | Car bomb | 12 | Early detonation/target ceremony | RFE/MIPT |
| 1-May-06 | Unknown | Baghdad | Iraq | Military | 0 | 2 | Y | Car bomb | 13 | Near US convoy/early detonation | SDU |
| 2-May-06 | Taliban | Kabul | Afghanistan | Military | 1 | 0 | N | Belt bomb | 12 | NATO convoy (Canadian) | RFE/AP |
| 2-May-06 | Unknown | Baghdad | Iraq | Military | 0 | 0 | Y | Belt bomb | 13 | Guard detonated during U.S. raid | CNN |
| 2-May-06 | Unknown | Ramadi | Iraq | Govt/Police** | 10 | 6 | N | Car bomb | 13 | Anbar governor Mamoun Rashid | MIPT/CNN |
| 3-May-06 | Unknown | Falluja | Iraq | Govt/Police | 17 | 30 | N | Belt bomb | 13 | Sunni police recruits | IPCS/RFE |
| 3-May-06 | Unknown | Mosul | Iraq | Military^ | 1 | 5 | Y | Car bomb | 13 | 2 car bombs on US/Iraqi Army patrol | CNN/AS |
| 3-May-06 | Unknown | Mosul | Iraq | Military^ | 2 | 5 | Y | Car bomb | 13 | 2 car bombs on US/Iraqi Army patrol | CNN/AS |
| 4-May-06 | Unknown | Baghdad | Iraq | Govt/Police | 9 | 52 | N | Belt bomb | 13 | Civil Court building | MIPT/SUN |
| 6-May-06 | Unknown | Tikrit | Iraq | Military | 3 | 1 | N | Belt bomb | 13 | Iraqi Army base | CNN/AP |
| 7-May-06 | Unknown | Baghdad | Iraq | Govt/Police | 9 | 15 | N | Car bomb | 13 | Iraqi Army patrol/Azamiyah area | IPCS/XNA |
| 7-May-06 | Unknown | Baghdad | Iraq | Govt/Police | 1 | 5 | N | Car bomb | 13 | Near al-Sabah newspaper office | IPCS/MIPT |
| 7-May-06 | Unknown | Karbala | Iraq | Govt/Police | 20 | 52 | N | Car bomb | 13 | Province government building | IPCS/MIPT |
| 9-May-06 | Unknown | Talafar | Iraq | Market | 23 | 134 | N | Truck bomb | 13 | Drew Shia crowd with fake flour sale | IPCS/MIPT |
| 11-May-06 | LTTE | Point Pedru | Sri Lanka | Naval vessel | 17 | 0 | N | Boat bomb | 3 | Escort (P418) for troop ship | SPUR/BL |
| 14-May-06 | Unknown | Baghdad | Iraq | Airport^ | 6 | 3 | N | Car bomb | 13 | BIAP Coordinated attack/ 2 bombers | IPCS/MIPT |
| 14-May-06 | Unknown | Baghdad | Iraq | Airport^ | 6 | 3 | N | Car bomb | 13 | BIAP Coordinated attack/ 2 bombers | IPCS/MIPT |
| 14-May-06 | Unknown | Mosul | Iraq | Military | 2 | 9 | Y | Car bomb | 13 | 1330/US military patrol | NCTC |
| 16-May-06 | Unknown | Baghdad | Iraq | Market | 21 | 33 | N | Car bomb | 13 | Al Shaeb market | ABC/UPI |
| 17-May-06 | Chechen sep | Ingushetia | Russia | Govt/Police* | 7 | 6 | N | Car bomb | 6 | Interior Ministry official Kostoyev | MOS/XNA |
| 17-May-06 | Taliban | Kandahar | Afghanistan | Govt/Police | 0 | 2 | N | Car bomb | 12 | UN demining convoy near airport | MIPT/XNA |
| 17-May-06 | Unknown | Ramadi | Iraq | Military | 0 | 0 | Y | Car bomb | 13 | US military at Government Center | URU |
| 17-May-06 | MSC | Ramadi | Iraq | Military | 0 | 3 | N | Car bomb | 13 | Iraqi Army base | SITE |
| 18-May-06 | Unknown | Ghazni | Afghanistan | Military | 1 | 5 | Y | Car bomb | 12 | Afghan Army/PRT base | XNA/TG |

| Date | Group | City | Country | Target | Killed | Wounded | ? | Weapon | Region | Notes | Source |
|---|---|---|---|---|---|---|---|---|---|---|---|
| 18-May-06 | Taliban | Herat | Afghanistan | Govt/Police | 2 | 5 | Y | Car bomb | 12 | American advisor to Afghan police | MIPT/CNN |
| 19-May-06 | MSC | Falluja | Iraq | Military | 0 | 0 | Y | Car bomb | 13 | US military post | SITE |
| 20-May-06 | Unknown | Al-Qaim | Iraq | Govt/Police | 5 | 10 | N | Belt bomb | 13 | Police station near Syrian border | IPCS/MIPT |
| 20-May-06 | Unknown | Falluja | Iraq | Military | 0 | 2 | N | Car bomb | 13 | Iraq Army post near bridge | URU |
| 20-May-06 | MSC | Mosul | Iraq | Military | 3 | 6 | Y | Car bomb | 13 | US military convoy/Sukor area | AP/SITE |
| 21-May-06 | LeT | Srinagar | Kashmir/India | Civilian | 5 | 22 | N | Grenades | 9 | Youth Congress political rally in park | UPI/TOI |
| 21-May-06 | Unknown | Kabul | Afghanistan | Unknown | 2 | 6 | N | Car comb | 12 | Probable premature detonation | MIPT/CNN |
| 21-May-06 | MSC | Baghdad | Iraq | Restaurant | 12 | 17 | N | Belt bomb | 13 | Safwan Police-related restaurant | IPCS/MIPT |
| 22-May-06 | Unknown | Baghdad | Iraq | Civilian^ | 2 | 5 | N | Car bomb | 13 | 2 bombs/near market | XNA |
| 22-May-06 | Unknown | Baghdad | Iraq | Civilian^ | 3 | 5 | N | Car bomb | 13 | 2 bombs/near market | XNA |
| 22-May-06 | Unknown | Husaybah | Iraq | Govt/Police | 0 | 4 | N | Car bomb | 13 | Iraq Border Police station | SAS |
| 23-May-06 | Hizbul M | Hyderpora | Kashmir/India | Govt/Police | 0 | 25 | N | Car bomb | 9 | Police patrol/PM scheduled to visit | MIPT/SATP |
| 29-May-06 | Unknown | Jerusalem | Israel | Unknown | 0 | 0 | N | Belt bomb | 4 | Arrested before detonation/7 kg bomb | MIPT/XNA |
| 29-May-06 | Unknown | Baghdad | Iraq | Govt/Police | 2 | 5 | N | Car bomb | 13 | Police patrol/Masbah district | MIPT/XNA |
| 29-May-06 | Unknown | Baghdad | Iraq | Military | 4 | 7 | Y | Car bomb | 13 | US mil convoy with journalists | IPCS/AT |
| 30-May-06 | Unknown | Hillah | Iraq | Military | 12 | 30 | N | Car bomb | 13 | Iraq Army checkpoint near car shop | XNA/AAIW |
| 30-May-06 | Unknown | Husaybah | Iraq | Unknown | 0 | 0 | N | Belt bomb | 13 | Premature detonation | SAS |
| 30-May-06 | Unknown | Mosul | Iraq | Govt/Police | 0 | 0 | N | Car bomb | 13 | Early detonation/police opened fire | IPCS/TN |
| 1-Jun-06 | Unknown | Farah | Afghanistan | Unknown | 0 | 0 | N | Car bomb | 12 | Detonated after police chase | RFE/MIPT |
| 1-Jun-06 | Unknown | Baquba | Iraq | Govt/Police | 4 | 5 | N | Car bomb | 13 | Iraqi government convoy | IPCS/DWS |
| 1-Jun-06 | Unknown | Kirkuk | Iraq | Govt/Police | 1 | 11 | Y | Car bomb | 13 | US Dip convoy at Northern Oil | IPCS/DWS |
| 2-Jun-06 | Unknown | Bakakhel | Pakistan | Military | 5 | 7 | N | Car bomb | 10 | Pakistani Army convoy in NWFP | SATP/PPI |
| 2-Jun-06 | Taliban | Gul Qalacha | Afghanistan | Military | 3 | 0 | N | Car bomb | 12 | Missed ISAF convoy (Canadian) | CDI/PAN |
| 3-Jun-06 | Unknown | Basra | Iraq | Market | 27 | 62 | N | Car bomb | 13 | Crowded market in evening | IPCS/MIPT |
| 3-Jun-06 | None | Jixian | China | Civilian | 8 | 5 | N | Belt bomb | x | Ex-wife's wedding | AP/TOI |
| 4-Jun-06 | Taliban | Kandahar | Afghanistan | Govt/Police** | 3 | 12 | N | Car bomb | 12 | Kandahar governor Asadullah Khalid | RFE/MIPT |
| 5-Jun-06 | Unknown | Mosul | Iraq | Military | 0 | 1 | Y | Car bomb | 13 | US military patrol | URU |
| 6-Jun-06 | Unknown | Band-e Sarda | Afghanistan | Unknown | 0 | 0 | N | Belt bomb | 12 | Premature detonation/Turkish workers | MIPT/XNA |
| 6-Jun-06 | Unknown | Ghazni | Afghanistan | Unknown | 0 | 7 | N | Motorcycle | 12 | Detonated while being prepared | MIPT/NBC |
| 6-Jun-06 | Taliban | Khost | Afghanistan | Military | 0 | 3 | Y | Car bomb | 12 | US military convoy | RFE/CNN |
| 6-Jun-06 | Unknown | Baghdad | Iraq | Civilian | 4 | 16 | N | Car bomb | 13 | Funeral procession | SDU/AJ |
| 11-Jun-06 | Unknown | Baghdad | Iraq | Military | 0 | 24 | N | Car bomb | 13 | Iraqi police checkpoint | WP |
| 11-Jun-06 | Unknown | Baquba | Iraq | Military | 4 | 8 | N | Car bomb | 13 | Iraqi Army checkpoint | IPCS/XNA |
| 11-Jun-06 | Unknown | Mosul | Iraq | Military | 1 | 6 | N | Car bomb | 13 | Iraqi Army patrol | WP |
| 12-Jun-06 | Unknown | Talafar | Iraq | Civilian | 3 | 40 | N | Car bomb | 13 | Gas station | MIPT/AP |
| 13-Jun-06 | MSC | Kirkuk | Iraq | Govt/Police** | 4 | 6 | N | Car bomb | 13 | Police commander MG Torhan Yussef | IPCS/MIPT |
| 13-Jun-06 | MSC | Kirkuk | Iraq | Govt/Police** | 1 | 7 | N | Car bomb | 13 | Hurriyah police chief Taher Salaeh | IPCS/MIPT |
| 13-Jun-06 | MSC | Kirkuk | Iraq | Govt/Police | 0 | 4 | N | Car bomb | 13 | PUK HQ/3rd car | MIPT/NCTC |
| 13-Jun-06 | MSC | Kirkuk | Iraq | Govt/Police | 3 | 0 | N | Car bomb | 13 | PUK HQ/partly foiled by security | MIPT/NCTC |
| 13-Jun-06 | MSC | Kirkuk | Iraq | Govt/Police | 0 | 0 | N | Car bomb | 13 | PUK HQ/2nd car/shot by police | MIPT/NCTC |
| 14-Jun-06 | Unknown | Kirkuk | Iraq | Govt/Police | 0 | 0 | N | Car bomb | 13 | Police checkpoint/shot by police | MIPT/REUT |
| 16-Jun-06 | Tanzim | Baghdad | Iraq | Religious site | 12 | 28 | N | Belt bomb | 13 | Shiite Buratha mosque | IPCS/MIPT |
| 17-Jun-06 | Unknown | Pushte Rud | Afghanistan | Military | 1 | 5 | N | Motorcycle | 12 | Afghan Army convoy | FOX/TA |

| Date | Group | City | Country | Target | Killed | Wounded | S | Weapon | Region | Notes | Source |
|---|---|---|---|---|---|---|---|---|---|---|---|
| 17-Jun-06 | Unknown | Baghdad | Iraq | Govt/Police | 5 | 10 | N | Car bomb | 13 | Iraqi police patrol | DTL/IPCS |
| 17-Jun-06 | Unknown | Baghdad | Iraq | Civilian | 10 | 15 | N | Car bomb | 13 | Iraqi civilians | DTL/IPCS |
| 17-Jun-06 | Unknown | Baghdad | Iraq | Govt/Police | 4 | 5 | N | Car bomb | 13 | Iraqi Police HQ | DTL/IPCS |
| 17-Jun-06 | Unknown | Baghdad | Iraq | Govt/Police | 3 | 11 | N | Car bomb | 13 | Iraqi Police checkpoint/Karradah | AS/NCTC |
| 17-Jun-06 | MSC | Mahmudiyah | Iraq | Govt/Police | 3 | 15 | N | Car bomb | 13 | Police checkpoint/towed car | MIPT/AP |
| 18-Jun-06 | MSC | Mosul | Iraq | Military | 1 | 19 | Y | Car bomb | 13 | US military patrol | NCTC/SITE |
| 19-Jun-06 | Unknown | Baghdad | Iraq | Military | 4 | 10 | N | Car bomb | 13 | Iraqi Army patrol | IPCS/DTL |
| 20-Jun-06 | Unknown | Basra | Iraq | Civilian | 2 | 3 | N | Belt bomb | 13 | Home for elderly women | AP/Reuters |
| 21-Jun-06 | Unknown | Kandahar | Afghanistan | Military | 1 | 9 | N | Car bomb | 12 | ISAF convoy (Canada)/early detonation | XNA/CDI |
| 23-Jun-06 | Unknown | Basra | Iraq | Civilian | 9 | 18 | N | Car bomb | 13 | Gas line/Bashar Street | XNA/NCTC |
| 24-Jun-06 | Unknown | Baghdad | Iraq | Military | 0 | 4 | Y | Car bomb | 13 | US military convoy at Iraqi checkpoint | XNA/NCTC |
| 24-Jun-06 | Unknown | Balad | Iraq | Military | 3 | 11 | N | Bus bomb | 13 | Iraqi Army checkpoint | XNA/NCTC |
| 24-Jun-06 | Unknown | Ramadi | Iraq | Military | 1 | 1 | N | Car bomb | 13 | Iraqi Army checkpoint | XNA |
| 25-Jun-06 | Unknown | Baghdad | Iraq | Govt/Police | 1 | 3 | N | Car bomb | 13 | Iraqi police commando CP/Zayouna | XNA |
| 25-Jun-06 | Unknown | Baghdad | Iraq | Govt/Police | 1 | 9 | N | Car bomb | 13 | Iraqi police checkpoint/Zayoona area | MIPT/NCTC |
| 26-Jun-06 | LTTE | Columbo | Sri Lanka | Military* | 4 | 8 | N | Belt bomb | 3 | Sri Lanka Army COS Kulatunga | SATP/NYT |
| 26-Jun-06 | Chechen sep | Shali | Russia | Bus | 0 | 0 | N | Grenades | 6 | Foiled by passengers/arrested | MIPT/INT |
| 26-Jun-06 | Unknown | Miramshah | Pakistan | Military | 7 | 20 | N | Car bomb | 10 | Pakistan military checkpoint in FATA | RFE/SATP |
| 26-Jun-06 | Taliban | Kabul | Afghanistan | Military | 0 | 2 | Y | Car bomb | 12 | Premature detonation/US mil convoy | AP/CDI |
| 26-Jun-06 | Unknown | Baghdad | Iraq | Govt/Police | 4 | 11 | N | Belt bomb | 13 | Police commando CP/Saidiyah area | MIPT/NCTC |
| 26-Jun-06 | Unknown | Baquba | Iraq | Market | 17 | 20 | N | Motorcycle | 13 | Khairnabat shoppers | DWS/REUT |
| 27-Jun-06 | Unknown | Konduz | Afghanistan | Military | 4 | 5 | N | Car bomb | 12 | ISAF convoy (German) | RFE/AP |
| 27-Jun-06 | Unknown | Kirkuk | Iraq | Civilian | 2 | 21 | N | Car bomb | 13 | Gas station for government workers | NYT/MIPT |
| 28-Jun-06 | Unknown | Qalat | Afghanistan | Military | 1 | 1 | N | Car bomb | 12 | ISAF convoy on Ring Road | XNA/AIP |
| 28-Jun-06 | Unknown | Anah | Iraq | Military | 2 | 10 | Y | Car bomb | 13 | US/Iraqi patrol | INDY |
| 28-Jun-06 | Unknown | Baquba | Iraq | Civilian | 3 | 12 | N | Car bomb | 13 | Day laborers near Sunni mosque | MIPT/NCTC |
| 29-Jun-06 | Unknown | Kirkuk | Iraq | Civilian | 6 | 31 | N | Car bomb | 13 | Funeral for Shiite soldier | MIPT/XNA |
| 30-Jun-06 | Unknown | Ramadi | Iraq | Military | 0 | 4 | Y | Car bomb | 13 | US/Iraqi Army patrol | DWS |
| 1-Jul-06 | Unknown | Baghdad | Iraq | Market | 62 | 120 | N | Car bomb | 13 | Market in Shiite slum | IPCS/NYT |
| 1-Jul-06 | Unknown | Mosul | Iraq | Govt/Police | 2 | 6 | N | Car bomb | 13 | Police patrol | MIPT/REUT |
| 2-Jul-06 | Unknown | Baghdad | Iraq | Military | 0 | 0 | N | Car bomb | 13 | Iraqi security checkpoint/Ghazaliyah | XNA/NCTC |
| 2-Jul-06 | Unknown | Baghdad | Iraq | Govt/Police | 5 | 3 | N | Car bomb | 13 | Iraqi police checkpoint | XNA |
| 2-Jul-06 | Unknown | Tamim | Iraq | Govt/Police | 1 | 2 | N | Car bomb | 13 | Iraqi police patrol | NCTC |
| 3-Jul-06 | Unknown | Kandahar | Afghanistan | Govt/Police | 1 | 6 | N | Belt bomb | 12 | Police post at governor's house | WP/MIPT |
| 3-Jul-06 | Unknown | Baghdad | Iraq | Military | 3 | 5 | N | Car bomb | 13 | Iraq Army checkpoint/Kendi hospital | XNA/NCTC |
| 3-Jul-06 | Unknown | Baghdad | Iraq | Govt/Police | 0 | 5 | N | Car bomb | 13 | Army/Police patrol | MIPT/AP |
| 3-Jul-06 | Unknown | Mosul | Iraq | Govt/Police | 8 | 23 | N | Car bomb | 13 | Iraqi police station | IPCS/NYT |
| 5-Jul-06 | PIJ | Barkan | West Bank | Unknown | 0 | 0 | N | Belt bomb | 4 | Arrested before detonation | MIPT/VOI |
| 5-Jul-06 | Unknown | Mosul | Iraq | Govt/Police | 1 | 4 | N | Car bomb | 13 | Police checkpoint | IPCS/MIPT |
| 6-Jul-06 | Unknown | Ana | Iraq | Military | 0 | 2 | Y | Car bomb | 13 | US/Iraqi checkpoint | AP/AIW |
| 6-Jul-06 | Unknown | Kufa | Iraq | Religious site | 13 | 38 | N | Car bomb | 13 | Maytham al-Tammar shrine | IPCS/WP |
| 9-Jul-06 | Unknown | Ramadi | Iraq | Military | 0 | 4 | Y | Car bomb | 13 | US military patrol | JP |
| 10-Jul-06 | Chechen sep | Nazran | Russia | Unknown | 0 | 0 | N | Belt bomb | 6 | Arrested before detonation | MIPT |

| Date | Group | City | Country | Target | Killed | Wounded | ? | Type | ? | Notes | Source |
|---|---|---|---|---|---|---|---|---|---|---|---|
| 10-Jul-06 | Unknown | Baghdad | Iraq | Civilian | 8 | 41 | N | Belt bomb | 13 | Bomb was second explosion/Sadr City | MIPT/XNA |
| 10-Jul-06 | Unknown | Kirkuk | Iraq | Govt/Police | 4 | 12 | N | Truck bomb | 13 | PUK offices | IPCS/MIP |
| 11-Jul-06 | IAI | Baghdad | Iraq | Govt/Police^ | 6 | 5 | N | Car bomb | 13 | Coordinated attack/Green Zone ECP | MIPT/XNA |
| 11-Jul-06 | MSC | Baghdad | Iraq | Govt/Police^ | 5 | 4 | N | Belt bomb | 13 | Coordinated attack/Green Zone ECP | NYT/IPCS |
| 11-Jul-06 | MSC | Baghdad | Iraq | Govt/Police^ | 5 | 4 | N | Belt bomb | 13 | Coordinated attack/Green Zone ECP | NYT/IPCS |
| 11-Jul-06 | Unknown | Baghdad | Iraq | Govt/Police | 4 | 12 | N | Car bomb | 13 | Iraqi police base | NYT/AP |
| 11-Jul-06 | MSC | Mosul | Iraq | Military | 2 | 4 | Y | Car bomb | 13 | US/Iraqi military patrol | NYT/SITE |
| 12-Jul-06 | Taliban | Yaqubi | Afghanistan | Military | 1 | 6 | N | Car bomb | 12 | ISAF convoy | RFE/MIPT |
| 12-Jul-06 | Unknown | Baghdad | Iraq | Military | 1 | 1 | N | Car bomb | 13 | Iraqi Army checkpoint | AS |
| 12-Jul-06 | Unknown | Baghdad | Iraq | Restaurant | 7 | 30 | N | Belt bomb | 13 | Falih Abu-Al-Amra restaurant | RFE/MIPT |
| 13-Jul-06 | MSC | Abi Saida | Iraq | Govt/Police | 6 | 3 | N | Bike bomb | 13 | Village Council building | MIPT/XNA |
| 13-Jul-06 | Unknown | Karabilah | Iraq | Military | 0 | 0 | Y | Car bomb | 13 | US military checkpoint | WP |
| 13-Jul-06 | Unknown | Mosul | Iraq | Govt/Police | 5 | 5 | N | Car bomb | 13 | Police patrol | MIPT/AP |
| 14-Jul-06 | Unknown | Abbas | Pakistan | Govt/Police* | 2 | 3 | N | Belt bomb | 10 | Shiite leader Allama Hassan Turabi | IPCS/NYT |
| 14-Jul-06 | Taliban | Khost | Afghanistan | Govt/Police | 0 | 1 | N | Belt bomb | 12 | Bomber approached police vehicle | RFE/MIPT |
| 14-Jul-06 | Unknown | Mosul | Iraq | Govt/Police | 4 | 4 | N | Car bomb | 13 | Police patrol | MIPT/REU |
| 15-Jul-06 | MSC | Baghdad | Iraq | Govt/Police | 0 | 6 | N | Car bomb | 13 | Police patrol | MIPT/AP |
| 15-Jul-06 | Unknown | Baghdad | Iraq | Govt/Police | 2 | 4 | N | Car bomb | 13 | Police commando CP/Ghadier bridge | MIPT/XNA |
| 15-Jul-06 | Unknown | Ramadi | Iraq | Military | 1 | 2 | Y | Car bomb | 13 | US/Iraqi checkpoint | SFC/URU |
| 16-Jul-06 | Taliban | Gardez | Afghanistan | Govt/Police | 4 | 23 | N | Belt bomb | 12 | Gardez government building | XNA/JTIC |
| 16-Jul-06 | Unknown | Paktia | Afghanistan | Military | 2 | 1 | N | Belt bomb | 12 | Afghan Army convoy | RFE/AFP |
| 16-Jul-06 | MSC | Mosul | Iraq | Military | 3 | 10 | Y | Belt bomb | 13 | US/Iraqi patrol | IPCS/NYT |
| 16-Jul-06 | MSC | Tuz Khormato | Iraq | Restaurant | 25 | 22 | N | Belt bomb | 13 | Targeted Shiites near mosque | BBC/IPCS |
| 17-Jul-06 | Unknown | Lashkar Gar | Afghanistan | Govt/Police | 2 | 9 | N | Belt bomb | 12 | Provincial center/building collapsed | AP/UPI |
| 17-Jul-06 | Unknown | Ubaydi | Iraq | Military | 2 | 2 | N | Belt bomb | 13 | Iraqi Army post at hospital | URU |
| 18-Jul-06 | MSC | Kufa | Iraq | Civilian | 58 | 105 | N | Truck bomb | 13 | Targeted Shiite laborers | AP/MIPT |
| 18-Jul-06 | MSC | Mosul | Iraq | Military | 4 | 3 | N | Car bomb | 13 | Iraqi Army | AP/NCTC |
| 19-Jul-06 | Unknown | Al-Qaim | Iraq | Military | 0 | 4 | Y | Belt bomb | 13 | US checkpoint | REUT/IPC |
| 19-Jul-06 | Unknown | Baghdad | Iraq | Govt/Police | 3 | 3 | N | Car bomb | 13 | Iraqi police patrol | REUT/SF |
| 19-Jul-06 | Unknown | Kirkuk | Iraq | Govt/Police | 3 | 5 | N | Car bomb | 13 | Iraqi police patrol | NCTC |
| 21-Jul-06 | Unknown | Falluja | Iraq | Govt/Police | 6 | 13 | N | Car bomb | 13 | Police post | REUT/IPC |
| 21-Jul-06 | Unknown | Samarra | Iraq | Govt/Police** | 0 | 3 | N | Belt bomb | 13 | Council head As'ad Ali Yasin | MIPT/AS |
| 22-Jul-06 | Taliban | Kandahar | Afghanistan | Military | 3 | 15 | N | Car bomb | 12 | ISAF convoy (Canadian) | LAT/NYT |
| 22-Jul-06 | Taliban | Kandahar | Afghanistan | Civilian | 6 | 20 | N | Belt bomb | 12 | Targeted crowd from 1st bomb | LAT/NYT |
| 22-Jul-06 | MSC | Mosul | Iraq | Military | 0 | 1 | N | Car bomb | 13 | Iraqi Army base | DWS/SIT |
| 23-Jul-06 | Unknown | Gholam Khan | Afghanistan | Unknown | 1 | 3 | N | Belt bomb | 12 | Premature detonation in taxi | MIPT/PAI |
| 23-Jul-06 | Unknown | Baghdad | Iraq | Govt/Police | 33 | 72 | N | Bus bomb | 13 | Police station at al-Jamilah market | WSJ/MIP |
| 23-Jul-06 | Unknown | Kirkuk | Iraq | Govt/Police | 17 | 100 | N | Car bomb | 13 | Kirkuk courthouse | UPI/XNA |
| 24-Jul-06 | Unknown | Daman | Afghanistan | Military | 0 | 2 | N | Car bomb | 12 | NATO convoy | AP/AIP |
| 24-Jul-06 | Unknown | Farah | Afghanistan | Unknown | 3 | 0 | N | Motorcycle | 12 | 3 bombers killed/detonated at base | MIPT/CD |
| 24-Jul-06 | Unknown | Mosul | Iraq | Govt/Police | 5 | 4 | N | Car bomb | 13 | Police patrol | REUT/NY |
| 24-Jul-06 | MSC | Samarra | Iraq | Govt/Police | 2 | 17 | N | Car bomb | 13 | Police patrol | REUT/IPC |
| 25-Jul-06 | Unknown | Kabul | Afghanistan | Civilian | 1 | 3 | N | Belt bomb | 12 | Afghan girl killed | CC/BLM |
| 25-Jul-06 | MSC | Baghdad | Iraq | Govt/Police | 3 | 0 | N | Car bomb | 13 | Iraqi Army/Police checkpoint | AP/NCTC |

| Date | Group | Location | Country | Target | Killed | Wounded | S | Type | Code | Notes | Source |
|---|---|---|---|---|---|---|---|---|---|---|---|
| 25-Jul-06 | MSC | Mosul | Iraq | Military | 0 | 11 | N | Car bomb | 13 | US military patrol | REUT/IPCS |
| 25-Jul-06 | None | Heilongjiang | China | Restaurant | 3 | 0+ | N | Belt bomb | x | Man with marital problems | TM |
| 26-Jul-06 | MSC | al-Baghdadi | Iraq | Military | 0 | 0 | Y | Car bomb | 13 | US/Iraqi Army checkpoint | SITE |
| 29-Jul-06 | Unknown | al Anbar | Iraq | Military | 4 | 4 | Y | Truck bomb | 13 | US Marines building search | LAT/MNFI |
| 29-Jul-06 | Unknown | Al-Qaim | Iraq | Govt/Police | 0 | 2 | N | Bike bomb | 13 | Iraqi police checkpoint | NCTC |
| 29-Jul-06 | Unknown | Falluja | Iraq | Military | 0 | 3 | Y | Car bomb | 13 | US military patrol | ALB |
| 29-Jul-06 | Unknown | Falluja | Iraq | Military | 0 | 0 | Y | Car bomb | 13 | US military at site of 1st bomb | ALB |
| 29-Jul-06 | Unknown | Rawah | Iraq | Military | 4 | 4 | Y | Car bomb | 13 | US military patrol | FB/MIPT |
| 30-Jul-06 | MSC | Mosul | Iraq | Govt/Police | 1 | 3 | N | Car bomb | 13 | Police patrol | KNA/IPCS |
| 31-Jul-06 | MSC | Mosul | Iraq | Military | 4 | 6 | N | Car bomb | 13 | Iraqi Army checkpoint | WP/AS |
| 1-Aug-06 | MSC | Baghdad | Iraq | Military | 0 | 0 | Y | Car bomb | 13 | US military patrol | SITE |
| 1-Aug-06 | MSC | Baghdad | Iraq | Military | 0 | 7 | Y | Car bomb | 13 | Joint Iraqi/U.S. military patrol | XNA/SITE |
| 1-Aug-06 | MSC | Baghdad | Iraq | Govt/Police | 10 | 22 | N | Car bomb | 13 | Security forces at bank/Urizdi | NYT/IPCS |
| 1-Aug-06 | MSC | Mosul | Iraq | Military | 3 | 3 | N | Car bomb | 13 | Iraqi Army patrol base | TNL/YN |
| 3-Aug-06 | Taliban | Panjwayi | Afghanistan | Market | 21 | 15 | N | Car bomb | 12 | NATO convoy nearby | NYT/WP |
| 3-Aug-06 | MSC | Hadrah | Iraq | Govt/Police | 9 | 15 | N | Car bomb | 13 | Police soccer game | CNN/AP |
| 4-Aug-06 | Taliban | Maiwand | Afghanistan | Military | 0 | 0 | N | Car bomb | 12 | NATO convoy (Canadian) | CDI/TES |
| 4-Aug-06 | Unknown | Mosul | Iraq | Govt/Police | 7 | 11 | N | Car bomb | 13 | Iraqi police station | EIW/AP |
| 6-Aug-06 | Unknown | Daman | Afghanistan | Military | 0 | 1 | N | Car bomb | 12 | NATO convoy | XNA/AP |
| 6-Aug-06 | MSC | al-Ameriyah | Iraq | Military | 1 | 5 | Y | Car bomb | 13 | Iraq Army base | CC/Pape |
| 6-Aug-06 | MSC | Falluja | Iraq | Military | 0 | 11 | Y | Car bomb | 13 | US military patrol | AP/ABC |
| 6-Aug-06 | Unknown | Tikrit | Iraq | Civilian | 14 | 18 | N | Belt bomb | 13 | Funeral | IPCS/MNFI |
| 6-Aug-06 | Unknown | Hub | Pakistan | Unknown | 0 | 0 | N | Bike bomb | x | Premature detonation | IPCS/MIPT |
| 6-Aug-06 | Unknown | Hub | Pakistan | Unknown | 0 | 0 | N | Belt bomb | x | Premature detonation | AP/PPI |
| 7-Aug-06 | Unknown | Samarra | Iraq | Govt/Police | 10 | 18 | N | Truck bomb | 13 | Police commando station/Muatsim | IPCS/MIPT |
| 9-Aug-06 | Unknown | Habaniyah | Iraq | Govt/Police | 3 | 7 | N | Car bomb | 13 | Police station | MIPT/REUT |
| 10-Aug-06 | Tanzim | Najaf | Iraq | Religious site | 34 | 122 | N | Belt bomb | 13 | Police checkpoint at Imam Ali Shrine | IPCS/LAT |
| 11-Aug-06 | Taliban | Kandahar | Afghanistan | Military | 1 | 0 | N | Car bomb | 12 | NATO convoy (Canadian) | NYT/TM |
| 13-Aug-06 | Unknown | Baghdad | Iraq | Unknown | 0 | 15 | N | Car bomb | 13 | Probable premature detonation | NCTC |
| 13-Aug-06 | Unknown^ | Baghdad | Iraq | Market^ | 15 | 37 | N | Motorcycle | 13 | Coordinated with mortars/gunfire | NYT/IPCS |
| 13-Aug-06 | MSC | Talafar | Iraq | Govt/Police | 0 | 9 | N | Car bomb | 13 | Police checkpoint | REUT/IPCS |
| 14-Aug-06 | LTTE | Columbo | Sri Lanka | Govt/Police** | 7 | 17 | N | Belt bomb | 3 | Pakistan High Commissioner | SATP/DWS |
| 14-Aug-06 | Unknown | Barmal | Afghanistan | Market | 0 | 16 | N | Car bomb | 12 | Bazaar/6 soldiers wounded | RFE/XNA |
| 14-Aug-06 | Unknown | Kabul | Afghanistan | Military | 1 | 6 | N | Car bomb | 12 | 4 NATO wounded/north Kabul | RFE/XNA |
| 14-Aug-06 | Unknown | Logar | Afghanistan | Govt/Police | 0 | 0 | N | Bike bomb | 12 | Bomber wounded then arrested | AP/SDU |
| 15-Aug-06 | MSC | Mosul | Iraq | Govt/Police | 9 | 36 | N | Truck bomb | 13 | PUK headquarters | REUT/IPCS |
| 16-Aug-06 | MSC | Muqdadiyah | Iraq | Military | 6 | 20 | Y | Belt bomb | 13 | Joint Iraqi/U.S. military patrol/female | PS/SITE |
| 17-Aug-06 | Taliban | Kandahar | Afghanistan | Military | 0 | 1 | Y | Car bomb | 12 | NATO convoy (US) | WP/RFE |
| 17-Aug-06 | Unknown | Tarin Khot | Afghanistan | Military | 1 | 6 | N | Belt bomb | 12 | NATO patrol | RFE/XNA |
| 17-Aug-06 | Unknown | Baghdad | Iraq | Govt/Police | 0 | 5 | N | Car bomb | 13 | Iraqi police patrol | NCTC |
| 17-Aug-06 | Unknown | Mosul | Iraq | Govt/Police | 0 | 9 | N | Belt bomb | 13 | Iraqi Army/police patrol | REUT/IPCS |
| 17-Aug-06 | MSC | Sinjar | Iraq | Govt/Police | 5 | 4 | N | Car bomb | 13 | Kurd peshmerga checkpoint | NCTC |
| 18-Aug-06 | Unknown | Baghdad | Iraq | Religious site | 1 | 5 | N | Car bomb | 13 | Shiite worshipers | CNN/NYT |
| 19-Aug-06 | Unknown | Balad | Iraq | Military | 3 | 3 | N | Motorcycle | 13 | Iraqi Army checkpoint | IPCS |

| Date | Group | City | Country | Target | Killed | Wounded | ? | Type | # | Notes | Source |
|---|---|---|---|---|---|---|---|---|---|---|---|
| 21-Aug-06 | Unknown | Ramadi | Iraq | Govt/Police | 4 | 29 | Y | Car bomb | 13 | Joint Iraqi police/U.S. base | URU |
| 22-Aug-06 | Taliban | Kandahar | Afghanistan | Military | 1 | 5 | N | Car bomb | 12 | NATO convoy (Canadian) | XNA/CNN |
| 23-Aug-06 | Unknown | Baghdad | Iraq | Govt/Police | 2 | 9 | N | Car bomb | 13 | Iraqi police checkpoint/Mashtal area | SDU/TPC |
| 23-Aug-06 | Unknown | Mosul | Iraq | Govt/Police | 1 | 10 | N | Belt bomb | 13 | Police HQ | MNFI/MIPT |
| 24-Aug-06 | Unknown | Baghdad | Iraq | Govt/Police | 2 | 9 | N | Car bomb | 13 | Al-Rashad Police station | MIPT/AP |
| 27-Aug-06 | MSC | Baghdad | Iraq | Civilian | 2 | 20 | N | Car bomb | 13 | Al-Sabah Newspaper office | NYT/MIPT |
| 27-Aug-06 | Unknown | Kirkuk | Iraq | Govt/Police^ | 3 | 11 | N | Car bomb | 13 | 2 car bombs/Police commander Tayib | MIPT/EIW |
| 27-Aug-06 | Unknown | Kirkuk | Iraq | Govt/Police^ | 4 | 11 | N | Car bomb | 13 | 2 car bombs/Peyrut Talabani | AP/NYT |
| 27-Aug-06 | Unknown | Kirkuk | Iraq | Govt/Police | 2 | 16 | N | Car bomb | 13 | PUK building | AP/NYT |
| 28-Aug-06 | Taliban | Lashkar Gar | Afghanistan | Market* | 21 | 43 | N | Belt bomb | 12 | Former police chief Nan Khan Noorzai | NYT/MIPT |
| 28-Aug-06 | MSC | Baghdad | Iraq | Govt/Police | 15 | 63 | N | Car bomb | 13 | Interior Ministry checkpoint | WP/MIPT |
| 28-Aug-06 | Unknown | Baghdad | Iraq | Bus | 8 | 18 | N | Belt bomb | 13 | Near Palestine hotel | AP/IPCS |
| 29-Aug-06 | Taliban | Kandahar | Afghanistan | Military | 2 | 1 | N | Car bomb | 12 | NATO/Afghan convoy/airport road | RFE/XNA |
| 31-Aug-06 | Taliban | Qalat | Afghanistan | Govt/Police** | 1 | 4 | N | Belt bomb | 12 | Deputy Interior Minister Abdul Khaled | MIPT/CDI |
| 31-Aug-06 | Unknown | Baghdad | Iraq | Civilian | 2 | 13 | N | Belt bomb | 13 | Gas station/police patrol nearby | MIPT/AP |
| 1-Sep-06 | LTTE | Kankesanthurai | Sri Lanka | Naval vessel | 0 | 2 | N | Boat bomb | 3 | 5 suicide boats damage 2 boats | SATP/DWS |
| 2-Sep-06 | Unknown | Spin Khowar | Afghanistan | Military | 0 | 2 | Y | Car bomb | 12 | NATO (US)/Afghan convoy | PAN/AIP |
| 2-Sep-06 | Unknown | Baghdad | Iraq | Govt/Police | 4 | 13 | N | Truck bomb | 13 | Tunis police station | XNA |
| 3-Sep-06 | Unknown | Mosul | Iraq | Govt/Police | 0 | 3 | N | Car bomb | 13 | Iraqi police patrol | NCTC |
| 3-Sep-06 | MSC | Mosul | Iraq | Govt/Police | 2 | 5 | N | Car bomb | 13 | Police patrol/Al-Karamah area | MIPT/AS |
| 4-Sep-06 | Unknown | Kabul | Afghanistan | Military | 5 | 9 | N | Car bomb | 12 | NATO convoy (UK)/2 bombers in car | TI/NYT |
| 4-Sep-06 | MSC | Mosul | Iraq | Military** | 0 | 0 | Y | Car bomb | 13 | US/Iraqi convoy with US general officer | SITE |
| 6-Sep-06 | Taliban | Khost | Afghanistan | Govt/Police** | 2 | 2 | N | Car bomb | 12 | Ya'Qubi district head | RFE/MIPT |
| 6-Sep-06 | Unknown | Baghdad | Iraq | Govt/Police | 6 | 29 | N | Car bomb | 13 | Iraqi police checkpoint | CNN/AP |
| 6-Sep-06 | Unknown | Sinjar | Iraq | Govt/Police | 6 | 6 | N | Car bomb | 13 | Border police patrol | CNN/KHA |
| 7-Sep-06 | Unknown | Baghdad | Iraq | Govt/Police | 12 | 39 | N | Car bomb | 13 | Police refueling center | XNA/MIPT |
| 7-Sep-06 | Unknown | Baghdad | Iraq | Govt/Police | 3 | 15 | N | Car bomb | 13 | Police patrol near Taiyran Square | XNA/MIPT |
| 8-Sep-06 | Taliban | Kabul | Afghanistan | Military | 17 | 29 | Y | Car bomb | 12 | US convoy near US Embassy | NYT/BP |
| 8-Sep-06 | Unknown | Kandahar | Afghanistan | Military | 0 | 0 | N | Car bomb | 12 | 10 min after NATO convoy passed | XNA/CDI |
| 9-Sep-06 | MSC | Baghdad | Iraq | Govt/Police | 1 | 13 | N | Car bomb | 13 | Police patrol near Nidaa mosque | XNA/CNN |
| 9-Sep-06 | Unknown | Baghdad | Iraq | Military | 0 | 4 | Y | Car bomb | 13 | US military patrol | XNA |
| 10-Sep-06 | Taliban | Gardez | Afghanistan | Govt/Police* | 4 | 6 | N | Belt bomb | 12 | Paktia governor Hakim Taniwal | NYT/CT |
| 10-Sep-06 | Tanzim | Baghdad | Iraq | Govt/Police | 2 | 14 | N | Car bomb | 13 | Police patrol at bombing site | CNN/MIPT |
| 11-Sep-06 | Unknown | Barmal | Afghanistan | Govt/Police | 0 | 0 | N | Belt bomb | 12 | Detonated after stop at District HQ | EIW/PAN |
| 11-Sep-06 | Unknown | Hisarak | Afghanistan | Civilian | 7 | 30 | N | Belt bomb | 12 | Governor Hakim Taniwal's funeral | CT/IHT |
| 11-Sep-06 | Unknown | Baghdad | Iraq | Govt/Police | 16 | 7 | N | Belt bomb | 13 | Army recruits on bus | NYT/XNA |
| 12-Sep-06 | Unknown | Damascus | Syria | Embassy | 0 | 0 | Y | Car bomb | 7 | Failed to detonate/US Embassy | DT/CNN |
| 12-Sep-06 | Unknown | Baghdad | Iraq | Military | 3 | 14 | Y | Car bomb | 13 | US military patrol | AJ |
| 13-Sep-06 | Unknown | Kandahar | Afghanistan | Religious site | 1 | 0 | N | Belt bomb | 12 | Sydan mosque destroyed | XNA/FOX |
| 13-Sep-06 | MSC | Mosul | Iraq | Military | 1 | 21 | Y | Car bomb | 13 | US military patrol | SITE |
| 14-Sep-06 | Unknown | Baghdad | Iraq | Military | 3 | 30 | Y | Truck bomb | 13 | US military base at electric plant | CC/MC |
| 14-Sep-06 | MSC | Baghdad | Iraq | Military | 0 | 3 | Y | Car bomb | 13 | US military patrol/by al-Rashid market | XNA/SITE |
| 14-Sep-06 | MSC | Talafar | Iraq | Govt/Police | 1 | 2 | N | Belt bomb | 13 | Police checkpoint | MIPT/REU |

| Date | Group | City | Country | Target | Killed | Wounded | ? | Weapon | Code | Notes | Source |
|---|---|---|---|---|---|---|---|---|---|---|---|
| 15-Sep-06 | al-Qaeda | Hadramout | Yemen | Oil Refinery | 1 | 0 | N | Car bomb | 7 | Security foiled/oil export terminal | WPA/NYT |
| 15-Sep-06 | al-Qaeda | Marib | Yemen | Oil Refinery | 0 | 0 | N | Car bomb | 7 | Security foiled/oil, gas production | WPA/NYT |
| 15-Sep-06 | MSC | Mosul | Iraq | Military | 0 | 10 | Y | Car bomb | 13 | US military patrol | REUT/NCTC |
| 16-Sep-06 | Unknown | Khost | Afghanistan | Govt/Police | 0 | 0 | N | Belt bomb | 12 | Early detonation at police checkpoint | CDI/ABC |
| 16-Sep-06 | Unknown | Baghdad | Iraq | Govt/Police | 1 | 22 | Y | Car bomb | 13 | US/Iraqi patrol at police station/Dora | XNA/MIPT |
| 16-Sep-06 | Unknown | Ramadi | Iraq | Govt/Police | 3 | 0 | N | Motorcycle | 13 | Police at hospital | MIPT/AP |
| 17-Sep-06 | Unknown | Kabul | Afghanistan | Military | 1 | 4 | Y | Belt bomb | 12 | US mil convoy/17-year-old bomber | SL/XNA |
| 17-Sep-06 | Unknown | Kandahar | Afghanistan | Military | 1 | 11 | N | Car bomb | 12 | NATO convoy (Canadian) | SL/XNA |
| 17-Sep-06 | Tanzim | Falluja | Iraq | Military^ | 1 | 2 | Y | Car bomb | 13 | US military base | WP |
| 17-Sep-06 | Tanzim | Falluja | Iraq | Military^ | 2 | 3 | Y | Car bomb | 13 | US military base | WP |
| 17-Sep-06 | Unknown | Kirkuk | Iraq | Govt/Police | 18 | 58 | N | Truck bomb | 13 | PUK/KDP HQ/city court | TNL/WP |
| 17-Sep-06 | Unknown | Kirkuk | Iraq | Military | 3 | 8 | Y | Car bomb | 13 | US/Iraqi Army patrol | TNL/WP |
| 17-Sep-06 | Unknown | Kirkuk | Iraq | Govt/Police | 11 | 50 | N | Car bomb | 13 | Police investigation HQ | XNA/WP |
| 17-Sep-06 | Unknown | Kirkuk | Iraq | Civilian | 3 | 10 | N | Car bomb | 13 | Children's organization | XNA/CNN |
| 17-Sep-06 | Unknown | Kirkuk | Iraq | Civilian | 2 | 5 | N | Car bomb | 13 | House of pro-Saddam tribal leader | WP |
| 17-Sep-06 | Unknown | Kirkuk | Iraq | Govt/Police^ | 0 | 6 | N | Car bomb | 13 | Police patrol southern Kirkuk | WP |
| 17-Sep-06 | Unknown | Kirkuk | Iraq | Govt/Police^ | 1 | 6 | N | Car bomb | 13 | Police patrol central Kirkuk | WP |
| 18-Sep-06 | Unknown | Herat | Afghanistan | Religious site | 11 | 18 | N | Bike bomb | 12 | Herat Great Mosque | ADR/IHT |
| 18-Sep-06 | Unknown | Kabul | Afghanistan | Govt/Police | 8 | 8 | N | Car bomb | 12 | Detonated as police approached | ADR/IHT |
| 18-Sep-06 | Taliban | Pashmul | Afghanistan | Military | 4 | 38 | N | Bike bomb | 12 | Canadian troops giving out candy | ADR/IHT |
| 18-Sep-06 | Unknown | Ramadi | Iraq | Govt/Police | 2 | 26 | N | Car bomb | 13 | Iraqi police station/recruiting center | NYT/WP |
| 18-Sep-06 | Unknown | Ramadi | Iraq | Govt/Police | 0 | 0 | N | Car bomb | 13 | Follow-up attack | NYT/MIPT |
| 18-Sep-06 | Unknown | Talafar | Iraq | Civilian | 20 | 17 | N | Belt bomb | 13 | Propane gas line | NYT/WP |
| 18-Sep-06 | Unknown | Baidoa | Somalia | Govt/Police** | 5 | 24 | N | Car bomb | 16 | President Yusaf/6 bombers killed | TG/NYT |
| 19-Sep-06 | MSC | Mosul | Iraq | Military | 1 | 2 | Y | Car bomb | 13 | US military vehicle/89th MP BDE | CC/FTU |
| 19-Sep-06 | Unknown | Mosul | Iraq | Military | 0 | 3 | Y | Car bomb | 13 | US military patrol | SDU/WP |
| 19-Sep-06 | Unknown | Sharqat | Iraq | Civilian | 21 | 50 | N | Belt bomb | 13 | Civilian crowd after roadside bomb | NCTC |
| 20-Sep-06 | Taliban | Nesh | Afghanistan | Govt/Police | 0 | 8 | N | Motorcycle | 12 | Niashb government building | XNA/PAN |
| 20-Sep-06 | Unknown | Baghdad | Iraq | Govt/Police | 3 | 14 | N | Car bomb | 13 | Police patrol/north Baghdad | XNA/AP |
| 20-Sep-06 | MSC | Baghdad | Iraq | Govt/Police | 7 | 11 | N | Truck bomb | 13 | Dora police station/near oil refinery | TNL/TES |
| 20-Sep-06 | Unknown | Mosul | Iraq | Govt/Police | 9 | 18 | N | Car bomb | 13 | Target responders from earlier blast | TNL/EIW |
| 20-Sep-06 | Unknown | Samarra | Iraq | Civilian | 8 | 28 | N | Car bomb | 13 | Sunni leader Khalid al-Fulalli's house | XNA/LAT |
| 21-Sep-06 | Unknown | Ramadi | Iraq | Military | 13 | 9 | N | Car bomb | 13 | Iraqi police headquarters | BLM |
| 21-Sep-06 | Unknown | Talafar | Iraq | Govt/Police | 0 | 0 | N | Belt bomb | 13 | Detonated as police fired | CC |
| 23-Sep-06 | Prophet C | Baghdad | Iraq | Civilian | 37 | 31 | N | Cart bomb | 13 | al-Dakhil Kerosene line/female bomber | WP/XNA |
| 24-Sep-06 | Unknown | Ramadi | Iraq | Military | 0 | 1 | Y | Car bomb | 13 | US military patrol | GU |
| 24-Sep-06 | Unknown | Talafar | Iraq | Military | 2 | 2 | N | Belt bomb | 13 | Iraqi Army checkpoint | CNN/XNA |
| 25-Sep-06 | Unknown | Khost | Afghanistan | Civilian | 0 | 1 | N | Car bomb | 12 | Security workers/early detonation | XNA/AFX |
| 25-Sep-06 | Unknown | Paktika | Afghanistan | Military | 0 | 0 | N | Car bomb | 12 | NATO convoy (US) | AFX/EIW |
| 25-Sep-06 | Unknown | Babil | Iraq | Govt/Police | 3 | 12 | N | Car bomb | 13 | Jurf As Sakhr police station | CNN/MIPT |
| 25-Sep-06 | Unknown | Ramadi | Iraq | Govt/Police | 7 | 7 | N | Car bomb | 13 | Police checkpoint | AP/MIPT |
| 26-Sep-06 | Unknown | Kabul | Afghanistan | Military | 0 | 0 | N | Car bomb | 12 | Target responders/fired at by troops | XNA/AP |
| 26-Sep-06 | Taliban | Lashkar Gar | Afghanistan | Govt/Police | 18 | 17 | N | Belt bomb | 12 | Provincial governor's compound | TH/HC |

| Date | Group | City | Country | Target | Killed | Wounded | Suicide | Weapon | Region | Notes | Source |
|---|---|---|---|---|---|---|---|---|---|---|---|
| 26-Sep-06 | Unknown | Baghdad | Iraq | Govt/Police | 4 | 18 | N | Motorcycle | 13 | Communist Party HQ/Andalus Square | XNA/AS |
| 27-Sep-06 | Unknown | Kandahar | Afghanistan | Military | 0 | 1 | N | Car bomb | 12 | NATO convoy/Dorahi area | TH/XNA |
| 27-Sep-06 | Unknown | Baghdad | Iraq | Unknown | 5 | 8 | N | Car bomb | 13 | South Baghdad | CNN/JTIC |
| 28-Sep-06 | Unknown | Baghdad | Iraq | Military | 0 | 2 | N | Car bomb | 13 | Iraqi Army checkpoint | DWS |
| 28-Sep-06 | Unknown | Baghdad | Iraq | Military | 2 | 25 | N | Car bomb | 13 | Iraq Army checkpoint/Shaab area | XNA/AP |
| 28-Sep-06 | Unknown | Kirkuk | Iraq | Govt/Police | 1 | 8 | N | Car bomb | 13 | Police checkpoint at US base | MIPT/AS |
| 28-Sep-06 | Unknown | Ramadi | Iraq | Military | 0 | 2 | Y | Car bomb | 13 | US military patrol | CNN |
| 29-Sep-06 | MSC | Falluja | Iraq | Military | 0 | 3 | Y | Car bomb | 13 | US military convoy | SITE |
| 30-Sep-06 | Taliban | Kabul | Afghanistan | Govt/Police | 12 | 42 | N | Belt bomb | 12 | Interior Ministry gate | AP/NYT |
| 30-Sep-06 | Unknown | Talafar | Iraq | Market | 2 | 30 | N | Car bomb | 13 | Busy market | WP/MIPT |
| 1-Oct-06 | MSC | Falluja | Iraq | Military | 4 | 2 | Y | Car bomb | 13 | US/Iraqi checkpoint at base | NDC/SITE |
| 2-Oct-06 | Taliban | Kabul | Afghanistan | Military | 0 | 6 | N | Belt bomb | 12 | NATO convoy | XNA/GRF |
| 2-Oct-06 | Unknown | Kabul | Afghanistan | Military | 0 | 0 | N | Motorcycle | 12 | Overpowered before detonation | PAN |
| 3-Oct-06 | Taliban | Kandahar | Afghanistan | Military | 0 | 4 | N | Bike bomb | 12 | NATO convoy (Canadian) | XNA/RFE |
| 3-Oct-06 | Unknown | Baghdad | Iraq | Market | 3 | 19 | N | Belt bomb | 13 | Sadiyah fish market | WP/AS |
| 4-Oct-06 | MSC | Mosul | Iraq | Govt/Police | 4 | 15 | N | Car bomb | 13 | Bus of Iraq Army recruits | SITE |
| 4-Oct-06 | Unknown | Ramadi | Iraq | Military | 19 | 10 | N | Truck bomb | 13 | Iraqi Army base/guards fired | REUT/CN |
| 4-Oct-06 | MSC | Talafar | Iraq | Military | 0 | 14 | N | Car bomb | 13 | Iraqi Army base | SITE |
| 5-Oct-06 | Unknown | Bala Buluk | Afghanistan | Govt/Police** | 0 | 0 | N | Car bomb | 12 | Regional police chief | AP/PAN |
| 5-Oct-06 | Unknown | Baghdad | Iraq | Govt/Police | 1 | 7 | N | Car bomb | 13 | Early detonation under police fire | CNN |
| 5-Oct-06 | MSC | Haditha | Iraq | Military | 0 | 2 | Y | Car bomb | 13 | US military patrol | SITE |
| 6-Oct-06 | Unknown | Khost | Afghanistan | Govt/Police | 1 | 3 | N | Belt bomb | 12 | Detonate in taxi after police stop | BP/CNN |
| 6-Oct-06 | Unknown | Khost | Afghanistan | Govt/Police | 0 | 16 | N | Belt bomb | 12 | Police station | BP/NYT |
| 6-Oct-06 | Unknown | Baghdad | Iraq | Govt/Police | 2 | 10 | N | Car bomb | 13 | Iraqi police checkpoint | CG |
| 7-Oct-06 | Unknown | Khost | Afghanistan | Military | 0 | 0 | Y | Car bomb | 12 | US military patrol | CNN/CDI |
| 7-Oct-06 | Unknown | Talafar | Iraq | Govt/Police | 13 | 13 | N | Truck bomb | 13 | Iraqi Army CP/Hai al-Salamm area | AP/WP |
| 8-Oct-06 | Unknown | Maqdadiya | Iraq | Hospital | 1 | 13 | N | Belt bomb | 13 | Outside hospital | CNN |
| 9-Oct-06 | Unknown | Talafar | Iraq | Govt/Police | 2 | 12 | N | Car bomb | 13 | Army/police checkpoint | AP/XNA |
| 9-Oct-06 | Unknown | Tribil | Iraq | Govt/Police | 0 | 13 | N | Car bomb | 13 | Iraqi police patrol base/Syrian border | AJ/MIPT |
| 10-Oct-06 | Unknown | Baghdad | Iraq | Govt/Police | 2 | 7 | N | Car bomb | 13 | Police checkpoint/Seleikh area | CNN |
| 12-Oct-06 | Unknown | Khost | Afghanistan | Military | 1 | 15 | N | Belt bomb | 12 | Afghan Army convoy | XNA/IHT |
| 12-Oct-06 | Unknown | Tani | Afghanistan | Military | 0 | 3 | Y | Car bomb | 12 | US military patrol | XNA/GRF |
| 12-Oct-06 | Unknown | Kirkuk | Iraq | Govt/Police | 0 | 0 | N | Car bomb | 13 | Bomber killed by police | IHT |
| 13-Oct-06 | Taliban | Kandahar | Afghanistan | Military | 8 | 8 | Y | Car bomb | 12 | NATO convoy/mostly U.S. troops | NYT/WP |
| 13-Oct-06 | Unknown | al-Qaim | Iraq | Govt/Police | 2 | 5 | N | Belt bomb | 13 | Iraqi police post | MNFI/XN |
| 15-Oct-06 | Unknown | Kirkuk | Iraq | Market | 3 | 8 | N | Car bomb | 13 | Market in south of city | AP/MIPT |
| 15-Oct-06 | Unknown | Kirkuk | Iraq | School | 2 | 25 | N | Belt bomb | 13 | Kurd al-Mallamin girls' school | REUT/WP |
| 15-Oct-06 | Unknown | Kirkuk | Iraq | Govt/Police | 5 | 10 | N | Truck bomb | 13 | FPS HQ/refrigerated truck bomb | WP/MIPT |
| 15-Oct-06 | Unknown | Talafar | Iraq | Govt/Police | 1 | 5 | N | Belt bomb | 13 | Police checkpoint at market | WP |
| 16-Oct-06 | LTTE | Habanara | Sri Lanka | Military | 115 | 160 | N | Truck bomb | 3 | Navy convoy/sailors on leave | PTI/LAT |
| 16-Oct-06 | Taliban | Kabul | Afghanistan | Airport | 0 | 3 | N | Car bomb | 12 | Police cornered bomber | AP/NYT |
| 16-Oct-06 | Taliban | Kandahar | Afghanistan | Military | 4 | 5 | N | Car bomb | 12 | NATO convoy | NYT/DP |
| 16-Oct-06 | Unknown | al-Qaim | Iraq | Military | | | Y | | 13 | US military convoy | AA |
| 16-Oct-06 | Unknown | Baghdad | Iraq | Civilian | 19 | 27 | N | Car bomb | 13 | Shiite funeral tent | MIPT/AP |

| Date | Group | City | Country | Target | Killed | Wounded | ? | Weapon | # | Notes | Source |
|---|---|---|---|---|---|---|---|---|---|---|---|
| 1-Dec-06 | LTTE | Colombo | Sri Lanka | Military** | 2 | 15 | N | Car bomb | 3 | Defense Min Gothabaya Rajapaksa | CNN/WP |
| 1-Dec-06 | Unknown | Peshawar | Pakistan | Military | 0 | 0 | N | Motorcycle | 10 | Military HQ parking lot | WP/PTI |
| 1-Dec-06 | Unknown | Kirkuk | Iraq | Military | 2 | 4 | Y | Car bomb | 13 | US military convoy/Al-Tis'in area | CNN/WP |
| 3-Dec-06 | Unknown | Kandahar | Afghanistan | Military | 3 | 9 | N | Car bomb | 12 | NATO military convoy (UK) | CNN/WP |
| 3-Dec-06 | Unknown | Kirkuk | Iraq | Military | 3 | 1 | Y | Belt bomb | 13 | US military convoy | LAT/NYT |
| 3-Dec-06 | Unknown | Mosul | Iraq | Govt/Police | 2 | 4 | N | Car bomb | 13 | Iraqi police station | NYT/XNA |
| 4-Dec-06 | Unknown | Speen Tangi | Pakistan | Govt/Police | 1 | 0 | N | Belt bomb | 12 | Uzbek/detonated after police stop | XNA/DT |
| 4-Dec-06 | Unknown | Mosul | Iraq | Military | 0 | 5 | Y | Car bomb | 13 | US military convoy/Al-Mithaq area | AP/XNA |
| 5-Dec-06 | Taliban | Kandahar | Afghanistan | Civilian | 11 | 3 | Y | Belt bomb | 12 | In front of USPI Security Company | CNN/LAT |
| 5-Dec-06 | Unknown | Baghdad | Iraq | Govt/Police | 6 | 13 | N | Car bomb | 13 | Iraqi police station/NE Baghdad | CNN |
| 5-Dec-06 | Unknown | Baghdad | Iraq | Civilian | 0 | 0 | N | Car bomb | 13 | Target victims from earlier bomb on bus | WP/LAT |
| 6-Dec-06 | Unknown | Kandahar | Afghanistan | Military | 2 | 8 | N | Car bomb | 12 | NATO military convoy (UK) | NYT/UPI |
| 6-Dec-06 | Unknown | Baghdad | Iraq | Market | 15 | 25 | N | Car bomb | 13 | Sadr City marketplace/used taxi | WP/REUT |
| 6-Dec-06 | Unknown | Baghdad | Iraq | Govt/Police | 4 | 7 | N | Car bomb | 13 | Iraqi police station/Al Thadeeb area | XNA/AS |
| 7-Dec-06 | Unknown | Kandahar | Afghanistan | Military | 2 | 11 | N | Car bomb | 12 | NATO convoy | WP/AP |
| 7-Dec-06 | Unknown | Mosul | Iraq | Military | | | Y | Truck bomb | 13 | US military patrol/Muthanna area | XNA |
| 8-Dec-06 | Unknown | Talafar | Iraq | Military | 3 | 15 | N | Car bomb | 13 | Iraqi Army checkpoint/Muthnan area | WP/CNN |
| 9-Dec-06 | Unknown | Karbala | Iraq | Market | 7 | 44 | N | Car bomb | 13 | Shiite market near Al-Abbas shrine | WP/REUT |
| 11-Dec-06 | Unknown | Baghdad | Iraq | Govt/Police | 1 | 7 | N | Car bomb | 13 | Iraqi police outpost/Tadhwaniya | WP/CNN |
| 12-Dec-06 | Taliban | Helmand | Afghanistan | Govt/Police** | 8 | 8 | N | Belt bomb | 12 | Helmand Governor Daud's compound | WP/AP |
| 12-Dec-06 | Unknown | Baghdad | Iraq | Civilian | 71 | 220 | N | Car bomb | 13 | Day laborers/Tayaran Square | BG/CNN |
| 12-Dec-06 | Unknown | Kirkuk | Iraq | Military | 4 | 14 | N | Car bomb | 13 | Iraqi Army base | XNA/KST |
| 13-Dec-06 | Unknown | Riyadh | Iraq | Military^ | 3 | 7 | N | Truck bomb | 13 | 2 bombs/Iraqi Army base | CNN/NYT |
| 13-Dec-06 | Unknown | Riyadh | Iraq | Military^ | 4 | 8 | N | Truck bomb | 13 | 2 bombs/Iraqi Army base | CNN/NYT |
| 14-Dec-06 | Taliban | Qalat | Afghanistan | Govt/Police | 4 | 24 | N | Belt bomb | 12 | Police car near market | CNN/NYT |
| 14-Dec-06 | MSC | Baghdad | Iraq | Military | 2 | 9 | N | Car bomb | 13 | Iraq Army checkpoint | KCS/AP |
| 15-Dec-06 | Unknown | Paktia | Afghanistan | Military | 2 | 2 | N | Car bomb | 12 | NATO/Afghan military convoy | NYT/WP |
| 15-Dec-06 | Unknown | Paktika | Afghanistan | Military | 0 | 3 | N | Belt bomb | 12 | Man in burqa/Afghan military patrol | NYT/WP |
| 15-Dec-06 | Unknown | Ramadi | Iraq | Military | 2 | | Y | Car bomb | 13 | US military checkpoint | PI/AP |
| 15-Dec-06 | Unknown | Ramadi | Iraq | Military | 2 | | Y | Car bomb | 13 | US military checkpoint | PI/AP |
| 17-Dec-06 | Taliban | Khost | Afghanistan | Military | 1 | 2 | Y | Car bomb | 12 | US military convoy | KCS/AP |
| 18-Dec-06 | Taliban | Kandahar | Afghanistan | Military | 0 | 2 | Y | Car bomb | 12 | US military convoy | WP/AP |
| 19-Dec-06 | Unknown | Mosul | Iraq | Military | 0 | 2 | Y | Car bomb | 13 | US military convoy | WP/AP |
| 20-Dec-06 | Unknown | Baghdad | Iraq | Govt/Police | 1 | 4 | N | Car bomb | 13 | Passport office near Kasra market | WP/LAT |
| 20-Dec-06 | Unknown | Baghdad | Iraq | Govt/Police | 11 | 30 | N | Car bomb | 13 | Iraq police commando CP/Jadriyah | CNN/WP |
| 21-Dec-06 | Unknown | Baghdad | Iraq | Military | 2 | 7 | N | Belt bomb | 13 | Iraq Army checkpoint/Adhamiyah | WP |
| 21-Dec-06 | Tanzim | Baghdad | Iraq | Military | 15 | 15 | N | Belt bomb | 13 | Iraq Army recruit center | CNN/LAT |
| 22-Dec-06 | Unknown | Kandahar | Afghanistan | Govt/Police** | 2 | 7 | N | Belt bomb | 12 | Parliament Member Zadran's home | KCS/WP |
| 24-Dec-06 | Unknown | Muqdadiyah | Iraq | Govt/Police | 7 | 30 | N | Belt bomb | 13 | Iraqi Police station | KCS/AP |
| 24-Dec-06 | Unknown | Ramadi | Iraq | Govt/Police | 2 | 5 | N | Belt bomb | 13 | Police CP at Al Anbar University | CNN/WP |
| 25-Dec-06 | Unknown | Baghdad | Iraq | Bus | 2 | 20 | N | Belt bomb | 13 | Bus in Northeast Baghdad | CNN/NYT |
| 27-Dec-06 | Unknown | Mosul | Iraq | Govt/Police | 2 | 19 | N | Car bomb | 13 | KDP Headquarters | WP/CNN |
| 28-Dec-06 | Unknown | Baghdad | Iraq | Civilian | 10 | 25 | N | Belt bomb | 13 | Gas line near sports stadium | NYT/WP |

| 29-Dec-06 | Unknown | Khalis | Iraq | Religious site* | 9 | 15 | N | Belt bomb | 13 | Shiite Sheik Kadhim Hameed Qassim | CNN/AP |
| 30-Dec-06 | Unknown | Talafar | Iraq | Military^ | 2 | 7 | N | Belt bomb | 13 | Iraqi Army patrol | CNN/REU |
| 30-Dec-06 | Unknown | Talafar | Iraq | Military^ | 2 | 7 | N | Belt bomb | 13 | Iraqi Army patrol | CNN/REU |

\* = Successful assassination

\*\* = Assassination attempt

^ = Multiple, simultaneous or near-simultaneous attacks took place. Due to reporting, it is impossible to disaggregate the casualties from the separate attacks. Total casualties were divided equally among the attacks.

**Campaigns:**

1 = Hezbollah vs. U.S./France (in Lebanon)

2 = Hezbollah/SSNP vs. Israel/SLA (in South Lebanon)

3 = Liberation Tigers of Tamil Eelam vs. Sri Lanka

4 = Hamas/PIJ/PFLP/Fatah vs. Israel (in West Bank/Gaza)

5 = Egyptian Islamic Jihad (EIJ)/al-Gamaah al-Islamiyah and other groups vs. Egypt

6 = Chechen Separatists/RaS vs. Russia

7 = al-Qaeda and associated groups vs. United States and allies (other than Iraq)

8 = Kurdistan Worker's Party (PKK) and Revolutionary People's Liberation Party/Front vs. Turkey

9 = Kashmiri Separatists (LeT/JeM/HM and others) vs. India

10 = Pakistani militant groups vs. Pakistani government and Shia Muslims

12 = Taliban and associated groups vs. United States and allies in Afghanistan

13 = Iraq Insurgents vs. United States and Allies in Iraq

14 = Islamic militants in Uzbekistan vs. Uzbek government

15 = Jamatul Mujahideen Bangladesh (JMB) vs. Government of Bangladesh

16 = Islamic Courts Union (ICU) vs. Transitional National Government (TNG) and allied militias

| Abbreviations for Groups: | Abbreviations used: |
|---|---|
| Abu Hafs = Abu Hafs al-Masri Brigade | ABN = Airborne |
| al-Gamaah = al-Gamaah al-Islamiyah | AR = Armor |
| al-Islambouli = al-Islambouli Brigades of al-Qaeda | AUB = American University Beirut |
| al-Tawid = al-Tawhid wa al-Jihad (Unification and Holy War) | BDE = Brigade |
| Amal = Afwaj al Muqawama al Lubnaniya (AMAL) | BFV = Bradley Fighting Vehicle |
| ARA = Armenian Revolutionary Army | BIAP = Baghdad International Airport |
| Assirat al-M = Assirat Al-Moustaqim and Salafia Jihadia | CMOC = Civil Military Operations Center |
| BKI = Babbar Khalsa International | COL = Colonel |
| Chechen sep = Chechen separatists | COS = Chief-of-Staff |
| DHKP-C = Revolutionary People's Liberation Party/Front | CP = Checkpoint |
| FARC = Revolutionary Armed Forces of Columbia | CRPF = Central Reserve Police Force |
| Fatah = Al-Aqsa Martyrs Brigade | DOD = Department of Defense |
| GAM = Free Aceh Movement | ECP = Entry Control Point |
| GIA = Armed Islamic Group | FATA = Federally Administered Tribal Areas (Pakistan) |
| HAMAS = Harakat al-Muqawammah al-Islammiyya | FOB = Forward operating base |
| Hizbul M = Hizbul Mujahideen | FSB = Federal Security Service of the Russian Federation |
| ICS = Islami Chhatra Shibir | HQ = Headquarters |

| | | | | | | | |
|---|---|---|---|---|---|---|---|
| IAI = Islamic Army in Iraq | | | | HSBC = Hong Kong and Shanghai Banking Corporation | | | |
| IJU = Islamic Jihad of Uzbekistan | | | | IDF = Israeli Defense Force | | | |
| IMU = Islamic Movement of Uzbekistan | | | | ING = Iraqi National Guard | | | |
| Islamic Glory = Islamic Glory Brigades in Land of the Nile | | | | ISAF = International Stability and Assistance Force (Afghanistan) | | | |
| Jamatul = Jamatul Mujahideen Bangladesh | | | | KDP = Kurdish Democratic Party | | | |
| JeM = Jaish-e-Muhammad | | | | KG = Kilogram | | | |
| JI = Jemaah Islamiyah | | | | KIA = Killed in action | | | |
| LeJ = Lashkar-e-Jhangvi | | | | LSA = Logistics Support Area | | | |
| Levant Army = Army of the Levant | | | | LT = Lieutenant | | | |
| LeT = Lashkar-e-Taiba | | | | LTG = Lieutenant General | | | |
| LTTE = Liberation Tigers of Tamil Eelam | | | | MARDIV = Marine Division | | | |
| MSC = Mujahideen MSC | | | | MG = Major General | | | |
| Mujahideen A = Mujahideen Army in Iraq | | | | MNF-I = Multinational Forces-Iraq | | | |
| PFLP = Popular Front for the Liberation of Palestine | | | | MP = Military Police | | | |
| PIJ = Palestinian Islamic Jihad | | | | MV = Merchant Vessel | | | |
| PKK = Kurdistan Worker's Party | | | | NATO = North Atlantic Treaty Organization | | | |
| Prophet's C = Soldiers of the Prophet's Companions | | | | NWFP = Northwest Frontier Province (Pakistan) | | | |
| RaS = Riyadh-as-Saliheen Martyrs' Brigade | | | | PM = Prime Minister | | | |
| Rasul M. = Rasul Makasharipov | | | | PRT = Provincial Reconstruction Team | | | |
| SSNP = Syrian Social National Party | | | | PUK = Patriotic Union of Kurdistan | | | |
| Sunna = Ansar al-Sunna | | | | QRPF = Quick Reaction Police Force | | | |
| Tanzim = Tanzim Al-Jihad fi Bilad al Rafidayn (AZM/AQ related) | | | | RCT = Regimental Combat Team (US Marines) | | | |
| Tawhid = Tawhid and Jihad (Syrian militant group - AQ related) | | | | SCIRI = Supreme Council for the Islamic Revolution in Iraq | | | |
| | | | | SF = Special Forces | | | |
| | | | | SLA = South Lebanon Army | | | |
| | | | | UK = United Kingdom | | | |
| | | | | UN = United Nations | | | |
| | | | | UNP = United National Party | | | |
| | | | | US = United States | | | |
| | | | | VP = Vice President | | | |
| **Sources:** | | | | | | | |
| AA = Al-Arabiyah | | | | | MK = Moskovsky Komsomolets (Moscow, Russia) | | |
| AAIW = Asia Africa Intelligence Wire | | | | | MNFI = Multi-National Forces Iraq | | |
| AAL = Asharq Alawsat (http://aawsat.com/english) | | | | | MOS = Moscow News (http://www.mosnews.com) | | |
| ABC = American Broadcasting Corporation | | | | | MST = Minneapolis Star-Tribune | | |
| ADR = APS Diplomat Recorder | | | | | NAW = Nawaiwaqt Group of Publications Ltd (http://www.nawaiwaqt.com.pk) | | |
| AFP = Agence France Press | | | | | NCTC = National Counter Terrorism Center (U.S.) | | |
| AFT = Air Force Times (U.S.) | | | | | NDC = Newsday (http://www.newsday.com) | | |
| AFX = AFX News | | | | | NH = Northwest Herald (Chicago, IL) | | |
| AIP = Afghan Islamic Press | | | | | NOW = News of the World (London, England) | | |
| AIW = America's Intelligence Wire | | | | | NP = National Post | | |
| AJ = Al-Jazeera (Qatar) | | | | | NPII = New Patterns in the Iraq Insurgency ( Cordesman, 2005, CSIS) | | |
| ALB = Al-Basra (http://www.albasrah.net) | | | | | NTF = News Twenty-four.com ( http://www.news24.com) | | |
| AP = Associated Press | | | | | NTV = National Television Turkey | | |
| AS = Al-Sharqiyah (Baghdad, Iraq) | | | | | NYP = New York Post | | |

| | |
|---|---|
| AST = Anniston Star | NYT = New York Times |
| AT = Albuquerque Tribune | PAC = Pacific Islands Broadcasting Association |
| BG = Boston Globe | PAN = Pajwhok Afghan News |
| BJ = Beacon Journal (Akron, Ohio) | PDO = People's Daily Online (http://english.people.com.cn) |
| BL = Business Line | PPI = Pakistan Press International |
| BLM = Bloomberg (http://www.bloomberg.com) | PRN = PR Newswire |
| BNS = Belleville News-Democrat (St. Louis) | PS = Paducah Sun (Paducah, Kentucky) |
| BP = Birmingham Post (England) | PT = Pakistani Times |
| BT = Belfast Telegraph | PTI = Press Trust of India |
| CAP = Capital Times (Madison, Wisconsin) | PW = Prague Watchdog (http://www.watchdog.cz) |
| CBN = China Business News | QP = Quds Press |
| CDC = Chinadaily.com | REUT = Reuters |
| CDI = Center for Defense Information (http://www.cdi.org/) | RFE = Radio Free Europe/Radio Liberty |
| CG = Charleston Gazette (Charleston, West Virginia) | RG = Register Guardian (Eugene, Oregon) |
| CNN = Cable News Network | RMN = Rocky Mountain News |
| CO = Charlotte Observer | RT = Roanoke Times |
| CSM - Christian Science Monitor | RTE = RTE News (http://www.rte.ie/news) |
| CSS = Intelligence and Terrorism Information Center at the Center for Special Studies (CSS) | SABC = SABC News (http://www.sabcnews.com) |
| CT = Chicago Tribune | SAS = Stars and Stripes |
| CYD = China Youth Daily | SATP = South Asian Terrorism Portal |
| DE = Daily Excelsior (Jammu, Kashmir) | SB = Sunday Business (London, England) |
| DI = Daily Intelligencer | SBC = Suicide Bombing Chronology |
| DM = Daily Mail (London, England) | SBO = Suicide Bombings in OIF (http://www.ausa.org/pdfdocs/lwp_46bunker.pdf ) |
| DMN = Dallas Morning News | SCMP = South China Morning Post |
| DOS = U.S. Department of State | SDU = San Diego Union Tribune |
| DN = Deseret News (Salt Lake City, Utah) | SEA = Seattle Times |
| DR = The Daily Record (Glasgow, Scotland) | SFC = San Francisco Chronicle |
| DS = Daily Star (Bangladesh) | SITE = SITE Institute (http://www.siteinstitute.org) |
| DT = Daily Telegraph (London) | SJMN = San Jose Mercury News |
| DTL = Daily Times (Lahore, Pakistan) | SL = The Star Ledger (Newark, NJ) |
| DVB = Democratic Voice of Burma | SLPD = Saint Louis Post - Dispatch |
| DWS = DAWN Wire Service (Pakistan) | SM = Sunday Mercury (Birmingham, England) |
| EC = Evening Chronicle (Newcastle, England) | SOS = Scotland on Sunday |
| EFE = EFE Spanish news (http://www.efe.com) | SPI = Seattle Post - Intelligencer |
| EIU = Economic Intelligence Unit: Country Newswire | SPPP = St. Paul Pioneer Press |
| EIW = European Intelligence Wire | SPT = Saint Petersburg Times |
| ERRI = Emergency Response and Research Institute | SPUR = Society for Peace, Unity and human Rights in Sri Lanka |
| ET = Evening Times (Glasgow, Scotland) | SSB = Serbia Studio B Television |
| FB = Fresno Bee (Fresno, California) | ST = Suicide Terrorism |
| FOR = Forbes (http://www.forbes.com) | STA = Star Tribune (Minneapolis, Minnesota) |
| FTU = Florida Times Union | STR = Stratfor (http://www.stratfor.com) |
| FWN = FWN Select | SUN = The Sun (London, England) |
| FWST = Fort Wayne Star Telegram | SUNT = Sunday Telegraph (London, England) |
| GMA = Greater Manila Area Network | TA = The Australian |
| GN = Gulf News | TCF = The Century Foundation |

|  |  |
|---|---|
| GNA | German News Agency |
| GOA | Government of Australia |
| GRP | Grand Rapids Press |
| GU | Guardian Unlimited |
| HAA | Ha'aretz |
| HC | Houston Chronicle |
| IC | Iraq Casualties (http://www.icasualties.org/oif) |
| ICG | International Crisis Group (http://www.crisisgroup.org) |
| IHT | International Herald Tribune |
| IMFA | Israeli Ministry of Foreign Affairs (http://www.mfa.gov.il/mfa/terrorism) |
| INDY | http://www.indybay.org |
| INT | Interfax |
| IPSN | Inter Press Service English News Wire |
| ITAR | ITAR/TASS News Agency |
| IPCS | Institute of Peace and Conflict Studies |
| ITV | Israel TV (Channel 1) |
| JA | Johnston's Archives (http://www.johnstonsarchive.net/terrorism/index.html) |
| JAP | Jakarta Post |
| JTIC | Jane's Terrorism and Insurgency Center |
| JU | Jihad Unspun (http://www.jihadunspun.com) |
| KCS | Kansas City Star |
| KHA | Khabat (Irbil, Iraq) |
| KM | Kurdish Media (http://www.kurdmedia.com) |
| KNA | Kuwait News Agency |
| KNT | Knight Ridder/Tribune News Service |
| KST | KurdSat TV |
| KT | Kenya Times |
| KTI | The Khaleej Times (Dubai, UAE) |
| KWN | Kyodo World News Service |
| LAT | Los Angeles Times |
| LE | Liverpool Echo (Liverpool, England) |
| LHL | Lexington Herald Leader |
| LVRJ | Las Vegas Review - Journal |
| MAS | Muslim American Society |
| MB | Manila Bulletin |
| MC | The Morning Call (Allentown, PA) |
| MEO | Middle East Online (http://www.middle-east-online.com/english) |
| MH | Miami Herald |
| MIPT | MIPT Terrorism Knowledge Base |
| TDN | Turkish Daily News |
| TEL | Sunday Telegraph (London) |
| TES | The Evening Standard (London. England) |
| TG | The Guardian (London, England) |
| TH | The Herald (Glasgow, Scotland) |
| THI | The Hindu |
| TI | The Independent (London, England) |
| TIME | Time Magazine (including collaboration with CNN) |
| TJ | The Journal (Newcastle, England) |
| TM | The Mirror (London, England) |
| TN | Tamil Net (http://www.tamilnet.com) |
| TNE | The News (Portsmouth, England) |
| TNL | The News Letter (Belfast, Northern Ireland) |
| TOI | Tribune of India |
| TOL | The Times of London |
| TOO | Times of Oman |
| TP | The People (London, England) |
| TPC | Turkish Press (http://www.turkishpress.com) |
| TR | The Record (Bergen, NJ) |
| TRT | Turkish Radio-Television Corporation |
| TS | The Scotsman (Edinburgh, Scotland) |
| TST | The Statesman (New Delhi, India) |
| TT | Taipei Times |
| UN | United Nations |
| UNB | United News of Bangladesh |
| UPI | United Press International |
| URU | Uruknet (http://www.uruknet.info) |
| USA | USA Today |
| WE | The Wichita Eagle (Kansas) |
| VBPJ | Vero Beach Press Journal (Vero Beach, Florida) |
| VOI | Voice of Israel |
| WN | Wireless News |
| WP | Washington Post |
| WPA | Weekly Petroleum Argus |
| WS | Winston-Salem Journal |
| WSJ | Wall Street Journal |
| WT | Washington Times |
| XNA | Xinhau News Agency |
| YN | Yahoo News |

# BIBLIOGRAPHY

Aaron, David, and Rand Corporation. "Three Years After : Next Steps in the War on Terror." (2005).

Arnold, J. L., P. Halpern, M. C. Tsai, and H. Smithline. "Mass Casualty Terrorist Bombings: A Comparison of Outcomes by Bombing Type." *Annals of Emergency Medicine* 43, no. 2 (Feb 2004): 263-273.

Arnold, J. L., M. C. Tsai, P. Halpern, H. Smithline, E. Stok, and G. Ersoy. "Mass-Casualty, Terrorist Bombings: Epidemiological Outcomes, Resource Utilization, and Time Course of Emergency Needs (Part I)." *Prehospital and Disaster Medicine : The Official Journal of the National Association of EMS Physicians and the World Association for Emergency and Disaster Medicine in Association with the Acute Care Foundation* 18, no. 3 (Jul-Sep 2003): 220-234.

"Genesis and Future of Suicide Terrorism." in Interdisciplines [database online]. Paris, France 2005 [cited 9 September 2006]. Available from http://www.interdisciplines.org/terrorism/papers/1/printable/paper.

Bjørgo, Tore. *Root Causes of Terrorism : Myths, Reality and Ways Forward.* London; New York: Routledge, 2005.

Bloom, Mia. *Dying to Kill : The Allure of Suicide Terror.* New York: Columbia University Press, 2005.

Bunker, Robert J., John P. Sullivan, and Institute of Land Warfare (Association of the United States Army). "Suicide Bombings in Operation Iraqi Freedom." Arlington, Virginia, (2004).

Connor, Robert J. *Defeating the Modern Asymmetric Threat.* Moterey, California: Naval Postgraduate School, 2002.

Crabtree, J. "Terrorist Homicide Bombings: A Primer for Preparation." *Journal of Burn Care & Research : Official Publication of the American Burn Association* 27, no. 5 (Sep-Oct 2006): 576-588.

Cragg, Kenneth. *Faith at Suicide : Lives Forfeit : Violent Religion, Human Despair.* Portland: Sussex Academic Press, 2005.

"Executive Summary Candy & Snacks." in Food Management [database online]. Cleveland, Ohio June 2004 [cited 27 February 2007]. Available from http://www.food-management.com/article/5939.

Forest, James J. F. *The Making of a Terrorist : Recruitment, Training, and Root Causes.* Westport, Conn: Praeger Security International, 2006.

Friedman, Lauri S. *What Motivates Suicide Bombers?* Detroit: Greenhaven Press, 2005.

"Suicide Terrorism: An Overview." in Institute for Counter-Terrorism [database online]. Herzliya, Israel 15 February 2000 [cited 2006]. Available from http://www.ict.org.il/articles/articledet.cfm?articleid=128.

Gil, Itay, and Dan Baron. "The Citizen's Guide to Stopping Suicide Attackers : Secrets of an Israeli Counterterrorist." (2004).

Goold, B. J. *CCTV and Policing : Public Area Surveillance and Police Practices in Britain.* Oxford ; New York: Oxford University Press, 2004.

Great Britain. Parliament. House of Commons. *Return to an Address of the Honorable the House of Commons Dated 11th may 2006 for the Report of the Official Account of the Bombings in London on 7th July 2005.* London: Stationery Office, 2006.

Hafez, Mohammed M. *Manufacturing Human Bombs : The Making of Palestinian Suicide Bombers.* Washington, D.C: United States Institute of Peace Press, 2006.

Hafez, Mohammed M. "Suicide Terrorism in Iraq." *Studies in Conflict & Terrorism* 29 (2006 2006): 595.

Hafez, Mohammed M. *Why Muslims Rebel : Repression and Resistance in the Islamic World.* Boulder, Colo.: Lynne Rienner Publishers, 2003.

Harari, Haim. *A View from the Eye of the Storm : Terror and Reason in the Middle East.* 1st ed. New York, NY: HarperCollins Publishers, Inc, 2005.

Hoffman, Bruce. *Inside Terrorism.* Rev. and expanded ed. New York: Columbia University Press, 2006.

Howard, Russell D., and Reid L. Sawyer. *Defeating Terrorism : Shaping the New Security Environment.* Guilford, Conn: McGraw-Hill Companies, 2004.

"Al-Qaeda Targeting Guidance v1.0." in Intelcenter/Tempest Publishing [database online]. Alexandria, VA 1 April 2004 [cited 1 March, 2007]. Available from http://www.asisonline.org/newsroom/aq.pdf.

International Policy Institute for Counter-Terrorism (Hertseliyah, Israel), B'nai B'rith, Anti-defamation League, and Interdisciplinary Center (Hertseliyah, Israel). "Countering Suicide Terrorism." (2002).

International Policy Institute for Counter-Terrorism (Israel), and Interdisciplinary Center (Hertseliyah, Israel). "Countering Suicide Terrorism : An International Conference : February 20-23, 2000, Herzliya, Israel." (2001).

Israeli Ministry of Defense. *Execution Aspects of the Security Fence.* Israel: The State of Israel, 2005. Database on-line. Available from Ministry of Defense, Israel's Security Fence, .

Kapur, G. B., H. R. Hutson, M. A. Davis, and P. L. Rice. "The United States Twenty-Year Experience with Bombing Incidents: Implications for Terrorism Preparedness and Medical Response." *The Journal of Trauma* 59, no. 6 (Dec 2005): 1436-1444.

Katz, Samuel M. *Jihad in Brooklyn : The NYPD Raid that Stopped America's First Suicide Bombers.* New York: New American Library, 2005.

Katzman, Kenneth. *Iran's Influence in Iraq.* Washington, D.C.: Congressional Researach Service, 2005. RS22323.

Kluger, Y., A. Mayo, D. Soffer, D. Aladgem, and P. Halperin. "Functions and Principles in the Management of Bombing Mass Casualty Incidents: Lessons Learned at the Tel-Aviv Souraski Medical Center." *European Journal of Emergency Medicine : Official Journal of the European Society for Emergency Medicine* 11, no. 6 (Dec 2004): 329-334.

"In the Spotlight: Japanese Red Army (JRA)." in Center for Defense Information [database online]. Washington, D.C. 2003 [cited 9 September 2003]. Available from http://www.cdi.org/friendlyversion/printversion.cfm?documentID=1771.

Kushner, Harvey W. *Essential Readings on Political Terrorism : Analyses of Problems and Prospects for the 21st Century.* 1st ed. New York : Gordian Knot Books ; Lincoln, Neb. : Distributed by the University of Nebraska Press, 2002.

Kushner, Harvey W. *Terrorism in America : A Structured Approach to Understanding the Terrorist Threat.* Springfield, Ill: Charles C. Thomas, 1998.

"The Battle of Okinawa." in Military History Online [database online]. 13 April 2003 [cited 9 September 2006]. Available from http://www.militaryhistoryonline.com/wwii/okinawa/default.aspx/.

Laqueur, Walter. *No End to War : Terrorism in the Twenty-First Century.* New York: Continuum, 2003.

Lim, R. Augustus. *Anti Terrorism and Force Protection Applications in Facilities.* Gainesville, FL: University of Florida, 2003.

Lyon, David. *Surveillance as Social Sorting : Privacy, Risk, and Digital Discrimination.* London ; New York: Routledge, 2003.

Maniscalco, P. M. "Terrorism Hits Home." *Emergency Medical Services* 22, no. 5 (May 1993): 31-2, 34-7, 40-1 passim.

Martin, Gus. *The New Era of Terrorism : Selected Readings.* Thousand Oaks, CA: Sage Publications, 2004.

Mayo, A., and Y. Kluger. "Terrorist Bombing." *World Journal of Emergency Surgery : WJES* 1 (Nov 13 2006): 33.

Moghadam, Assaf. *The Roots of Terrorism.* New York: Chelsea House Publishers, 2006.

National Research Council (U.S.). Committee for Oversight and Assessment of Blast-effects and Related Research. *Protecting People and Buildings from Terrorism : Technology Transfer for Blast-Effects Mitigation.* Washington, D.C.: National Academy Press : Available from Board on Infrastructure and the Constructed Environment, National Research Council, 2001.

Oliver, A. M., and Paul F. Steinberg. *The Road to Martyrs' Square : A Journey into the World of the Suicide Bomber.* New York: Oxford University Press, 2005.

Pape, Robert Anthony. *Dying to Win: The Strategic Logic of Suicide Terrorism.* Random House Trade Paperback ed. New York: Random House Trade Paperbacks, 2006.

Pape, Robert Anthony. "The Strategic Logic of Suicide Terorrism." *American Political Science Review* 97, no. 3 (August 2003 2003): 5.

Parliamentary Office of Science and Technology. *CCTV.* London, England: House of Commons, 2002.

Pedahzur, Ami. *Root Causes of Suicide Terrorism : Globalization of Martyrdom.* New York: Routledge, 2006.

Pedahzur, Ami. *Suicide Terrorism.* Cambridge ; Malden, MA : Polity, 2005.

Philpott, Don. "London Bombings." *Homeland Defense Journal* (2005). Journal on-line. Available from http://www.homelanddefensejournal.com/pdfs/LondonBombing_SpecialReport.pdf, 27 February 2007.

Rabena, William S., and Army War College (U.S.). *An Information Operations Approach to Counter Suicide Bomber Recruiting.* AD-A449 231 ed. Carlisle Barracks, Pa: U.S. Army War College, 2006.

"The War on the Word Jihad." in National Public Radio [database online]. 15 March 2007 [cited 2007]. Available from http://www.npr.org/templates/story/story.php?storyId=6392989.

Reuter, Christoph. *My Life is a Weapon : A Modern History of Suicide Bombing.* Princeton, NJ: Princeton University Press, 2004.

Rising, David, "Iraqis using Kidnap Victims as Bombers," *Washington Post,* 21 September 2006 2006, (World).

Rodoplu, U., J. L. Arnold, R. Tokyay, G. Ersoy, S. Cetiner, and T. Yucel. "Mass-Casualty Terrorist Bombings in Istanbul, Turkey, November 2003: Report of the Events and the Prehospital Emergency Response." *Prehospital and Disaster Medicine : The Official Journal of the National Association of EMS Physicians and the World Association for Emergency and Disaster Medicine in Association with the Acute Care Foundation* 19, no. 2 (Apr-Jun 2004): 133-145.

Rodoplu, U., J. L. Arnold, T. Yucel, R. Tokyay, G. Ersoy, and S. Cetiner. "Impact of the Terrorist Bombings of the Hong Kong Shanghai Bank Corporation Headquarters and the British Consulate on Two Hospitals in Istanbul, Turkey, in November 2003." *The Journal of Trauma* 59, no. 1 (Jul 2005): 195-201.

Schoennauer, Eric M., and Naval Postgraduate School (U.S.). "Suicide Terrorism : How Psychological Operations can make a Difference." (2005).

Schweitzer, Yoram, Merkaz Yafeh, and Sari Goldstein Ferber. *Al-Qaeda and the Internationalization of Suicide Terrorism.* Tel Aviv: Tel Aviv University, Jaffee Center for Strategic Studies, 2005.

Schweitzer, Yoram, ed. *Female Suicide Bombers : Dying for Equality?* Tel Aviv, Israel: Jaffee Center for Strategic Studies, Tel Aviv University, 2006.

Schweitzer, Yoram, and Shaul Shai. *The Globalization of Terror : The Challenge of Al-Qaida and the Response of the International Community.* New Brunswick N.J.: Transaction Publishers, 2003.

Scott, B. A., J. R. Fletcher, M. W. Pulliam, and R. D. Harris. "The Beirut Terrorist Bombing." *Neurosurgery* 18, no. 1 (Jan 1986): 107-110.

Shai, Shaul, Interdisciplinary Center (Hertseliyah, Israel), and International Policy Institute for Counter-Terrorism (Israel). *The Shahids : Islam and Suicide Attacks.* New Brunswick, N.J: Transaction Publishers, 2004.

Skaine, Rosemarie. *Female Suicide Bombers.* Jefferson, N.C: McFarland, 2006.

Smith, Jerry D., and Naval Postgraduate School (U.S.). "Israel's Counter-Terrorism Strategy and its Effectiveness." (2005).

Teague, D. C. "Mass Casualties in the Oklahoma City Bombing." *Clinical Orthopaedics and Related Research* (422), no. 422 (May 2004): 77-81.

United States, Army Training and Doctrine Command, and Office of the Deputy Chief of Staff for Intelligence. *Suicide Bombing in the COE.* Fort Leavenworth, Kansas: US Army Training and Doctrine Command, 2005.

United States, Department of Defense. *Department of Defense Dictionary of Military and Associated Terms.* Washington, DC: Government Reprints Press, 2001.

"The Six Simple Principles of Viral Marketing." in Web Marketing Today [database online]. 1 February 2005 [cited 12 March, 2007]. Available from http://www.wilsonweb.com/wmt5/viral-principles.htm.

Zedalis, Debra D., Army War College (U.S.), and Strategic Studies Institute. "Female Suicide Bombers." (2004).

www.ingramcontent.com/pod-product-compliance
Lightning Source LLC
Chambersburg PA
CBHW081839170426
43199CB00017B/2787